IMAGINING THE
SOUL
A HISTORY

ROSALIE OSMOND

SUTTON PUBLISHING

128.1

First published in 2003 by
Sutton Publishing Limited · Phoenix Mill
Thrupp · Stroud · Gloucestershire · GL5 2BU

British Library Cataloguing in Publication Data
A catalogue record for this book is available from the British Library.

ISBN 0 7509 2961 8

Typeset in 11/14.5 pt Sabon.
Typesetting and origination by
Sutton Publishing Limited.
Printed and bound in England by
J.H. Haynes & Co. Ltd, Sparkford.

Contents

Preface

I have been fortunate during the writing of this book to have been surrounded by friends, colleagues, and family who have been not only sympathetic but actively helpful in many ways. What follows is not complete, but merely an acknowledgement of the most significant contributions.

Cora Portillo spent countless hours translating the two Spanish plays, which do not exist in any other English translation, and I am profoundly grateful. Dr Richard Axton of Christ's College Cambridge helpfully drew my attention to the articles on the appearance of souls on the stage by Meg Twycross. Jeannie Cohen was my constant source of reference for queries about matters classical, and read and commented on the typescript in its entirety. Professor Donald Cross suggested the opening quotation from Browning, and read the complete text with his usual scrupulousness. At an early stage of my research the Revd Charles Pickstone drew my attention to *The Spiritual in Art*, which proved an important resource for the section on modern images of the soul.

As for my family, my three adult children were all interested in the progress of the book (having lived through this at closer quarters before), but special mention must be made of Adrian, who suggested a number of references I would probably not have picked up by myself. Oliver, my husband, seems to have put almost as much work into this book as I have. Indeed, to enumerate everything he has done might lead his colleagues and parishioners to conclude that he must be neglecting his spiritual duties!

I am also indebted to the library staff who have been helpful in my research, particularly the librarians at the British Library, Cambridge University Library, and also Acadia University Library, which was my chief resource for work during the summer.

Finally, I must thank the staff at Sutton and particularly my editor, Christopher Feeney, who has been unfailingly helpful and patient. Above all, he has allowed me to write the book I wanted to write. This leaves me with a huge responsibility, but, as any author knows, it is also a rare privilege.

Upper Kingsburg, Nova Scotia
August 2003

Introduction

> Your business is to paint the souls of men—
> Man's soul, and it's a fire, smoke . . . no, it's not . . .
> It's vapour done up like a new-born babe—
> (In that shape when you die it leaves your mouth)
> It's . . . well, what matters talking, it's the soul!
>   *Robert Browning, 'Fra Lippo Lippi'*

Human beings are imaginative creatures – that is, creators of images. Language and abstract thought may appear to be our unique characteristics, but our impulse for giving concrete form to abstractions, not only in our thoughts but in art and literature, is just as essential. Much of the time we instinctively think in pictures. Nowadays we probably do not envisage Dürer's full-blown allegorical figures when thinking of Melancholy or Hope, but we may well visualize a colour or an associated form or object. Sometimes these will come from very personal experience, sometimes from centuries of use.[1]

So it is with the soul. While it has nearly always been *defined* as spiritual and invisible, it has with equal consistency been *imagined* as visible, a concrete entity. What is fascinating is the variety of imagined forms this soul takes in different periods and contexts. Sometimes it is a beautiful woman (or, more unusually, a man); at others it is a sexless and childlike being. It can take on non-human forms as well – those of bird, butterfly, even grasshopper.

These variations in the portrayal of the soul are not capricious or arbitrary, but evidence of its infinite complexity. Each depiction is intimately connected to the varying role the soul plays, and these portrayals reveal much about its contrasting aspects. In turn these multiple roles and guises that the soul takes on tell us much about our deepest fears and desires. Our fear of death, our hope for some kind of immortality, our need of help and guidance through life – all are exposed in the ways we imagine the soul. To lose the soul has been seen as the ultimate human tragedy. Whether it is Faust (who sells his soul for knowledge) or Bart Simpson (who sells his for money), a 'soulless' being is portrayed as doomed, in this life as in the next. So Faust, once he has made the bargain of giving up his soul for knowledge, does not go on to gain the wisdom he has desired but spends his power in devising cheap, childlike tricks.

Why should this be the case? Why do we need to posit a soul at all? The basic answer probably lies in the visible inadequacies of the body. For people who did not have our modern understanding of the mechanics of the brain and its interaction with the rest of the body, the soul was necessary as a kind of ghost in the machine, an animating principle that gave life to the body. Death was seen as the departure of this animating principle.

The inadequacies of the body, however, extend beyond this. It is visibly changeable and transient. From the moment of birth the human form is in a state of flux; it develops and then decays. As Jaques in *As You Like It* succinctly puts it, 'And so from hour to hour we ripe and ripe | And then from hour to hour we rot and rot.' We have always found this mutability deeply disturbing and have tried to devise ways of countering it. So against this constantly changing body we have set the soul, which we view as changeless.

This changeless soul provides us with a sense of permanent identity that follows us through life, regardless of what accidents may occur to the body. We need to see a person who is paralysed, suffers a debilitating illness or, less dramatically, who loses some of the beauty or physical stamina that defined his or her youth as 'just the same', 'not changed at all, really'. In this sense, the soul is the essential person.

Many religions, especially Christianity, extend this assurance of immutability and consistent identity beyond the present life. The soul is the part of us that not only remains the same here and now, but survives death and guarantees us immortality. Of all human desires this need to believe that there is something beyond our natural human span seems to be the most persistent, evident from the burial practices of the ancient Egyptians to modern attempts to freeze the corpse for some doubtful posterity. Quite simply, while we have difficulty in imagining an eternity, we cannot accept the alternative – an absolute end.

The soul also expresses other human traits. One such trait is our difficulty in experiencing ourselves and our acquaintances as a unity rather than as a series of impressions and emotions, some of which occur simultaneously and are conflicting. I remember well the superb organist who played for me Bach's 'Canonic Variations on "Vom Himmel Hoch"', then immediately turned around on the organ bench and spewed out his vitriolic hatred of the people in the small town where he lived. We are constantly engaged in an internal dialogue with ourselves. Whether we see this in moral terms as a battle between a 'good' soul and a 'bad' body or simply in terms of conflicting desires that pull us in opposing directions, the dualism of body and soul has provided both a dramatic framework and an explanation for this observable characteristic within ourselves.

The soul also provides an explanation for our conviction that at times we need and receive guidance from something other than a bodily source. In this instance the soul that gives guidance may be that of the individual concerned, or it may be the soul of another, alive or dead. Thus in the *Paradiso*, Dante's beloved Beatrice, after her death, serves him as interpreter and guide. In this guise the soul becomes closely associated with other incorporeal beings such as angels, and its imagined appearance changes accordingly.

All of this might appear to argue that the soul is a construct of our own devising, shaped to fulfil our deepest needs. This may be the case. However, it could equally be argued that our deepest needs, persisting over the recorded history of mankind, suggest the reality of the soul, since it is the very thing that most fully satisfies them.

This book is neither a critical examination of philosophical theories concerning the soul, nor is it an argument from a particular ideological point of view for the existence or otherwise of the soul. Rather, it is about different ways we have imagined the soul in art and literature from the Greeks to the present day, and what this tells us about ourselves.

Introduction

To understand the history of our imaginings about the soul it is necessary to have some knowledge of the literature and philosophy that helped form them. The first chapter, therefore, is a discussion of the development of ideas about the soul in Greek, Egyptian, and medieval Christian philosophy and literature, with particular reference to those beliefs that have influenced our visualization of the soul.

After this, the chapters are arranged not according to the chronological development of ideas about the soul but according to differing perceptions of it in life, at the time of death, and after death. The second chapter shows the soul as a beautiful woman – a guide during life on this earth. In the next chapter we look at expressions of conflict and division within the soul and between the soul and the body, also in life. The fourth chapter displays the soul as a character in drama – a genre that necessarily depicts it in a visible and active way. While similes and metaphors for the soul are necessarily scattered throughout the book, Chapter 5 looks at some of these and their significance in a more structured way. In Chapter 6 we move from the soul as we visualize it in life to the soul at the time of death, when it separates from the body and takes on a life of its own. Our conception of what happens is viewed from different historical perspectives, ranging from that of the Middle Ages through to that of the spiritualists of the nineteenth century. Chapter 7 follows the soul through the process of the Last Judgment to its state of immortality – whether blissful or tormented. The final chapter returns to the chronology of the first and looks at modern philosophical and scientific concepts of the soul and its portrayal in the art and literature of the present day.

This is a book about the soul within the Western tradition. While there is occasional reference to other traditions and religions, there is no pretence of universality. If the Middle Ages and early Renaissance figure largely in my discussion, this is because it was during those periods that concerns about the soul were most dominant.

And what of the imagination, that faculty that I claim enables us not just to conceive of a soul but to picture it as well? At its most basic level, the imagination is our capacity to make images (pictures) in our mind. This is the sense in which Aristotle chiefly describes it. These pictures in our minds may be merely copies of the real world recreated from memory, but frequently they are not. Unlike pictures that are transmitted directly from the physical world to our brain, we can change and manipulate them. I am unlikely ever to *see* the head of a man on the hairy body of a goat, or a woman with snakes for hair, but I am quite capable of imagining these things and an infinite variety of others. The ancient Greeks did so. Indeed, one view (not the most prevalent one) argues that in prehistoric times 'soul' referred to the visual image of objects that man could retain in his memory, an ethereal copy of the real world abstracted from sense experience that could be magically manipulated.[2] Things in themselves might not always be under the control of primitive man, but images of them could be. According to this view, the imaginary, the visual, was the essence of man's concept of the soul from the beginning.

As long as imagination was closely linked to the picture-making faculty of man and the senses, it was bound to be judged inferior to reason. For us, however, imagination suggests much more than merely picturing and manipulating the objects sense presents to us. By the late Renaissance, writers such as Francis Bacon and Sir Thomas Browne gave it a much more exalted status. Bacon saw it as the faculty by which we rise above reason to the knowledge that comes through revelation. 'The divine grace uses the motions of the imagination as an instrument of illumination . . . which is the reason why religion ever sought access to the mind by similitudes, types, parables, visions, dreams.'[3] Browne too insists that imagination can go where reason cannot follow.

By the time of the nineteenth-century Romantics, imagination had largely severed its connection with orthodox religion and become the source of poetic inspiration. Coleridge makes a famous distinction between what he calls fancy, the Primary Imagination, and the Secondary Imagination. Fancy can collect and rearrange images and meanings that have been fixed in the mind by the image-making faculty, the Primary Imagination. But Fancy is limited to reassembling these things according to what Coleridge calls 'the law of association'. The Secondary Imagination, in contrast, can creatively re-form the world, giving us poetry, and endowing objects with value – qualities such as love, awe and imagination – which they do not intrinsically possess. This imagination is a god-like faculty, far above reason, creative in itself.[4]

So we imagine the soul. Whether we have also created it is open to speculation.

ONE

The Idea of the Soul:
Classical and Early Christian Images

> What do we say about the soul, then?
>
> *Plato,* Phaedo, *79b*

WHEN we think of the soul it may be as one of two distinct
things – our essential self in this life, made up of our desires,
will and power of reason, or that part of us that survives death and
is immortal. We may not even be conscious of these as quite
different things, because for the last two thousand years we have
thought of them as a single entity, the person, embodied while we
are alive and disembodied after death. But this single entity, both
individual and immortal, was not how the idea of the soul began.

Primitive people could never quite believe that the physical –
either in themselves or in nature – was all there was. Animistic ideas,
that saw everything in nature as possessed of a soul, were common
among our earliest ancestors. But quite what they meant by the
'soul' in nature – or even whether different peoples meant remotely
the same thing – is not at all clear.

The simplest view is that, for primitive people, nature was
'ensouled' in the sense that it was endowed with feeling and purpose
not totally dissimilar to that which human beings feel. Oddly enough,
it seems easier for us to imagine things as endowed with sense and
will than as completely inanimate. We still find this idea in certain
children's stories and fairy tales, where not just animals but trees,
rivers and even rocks may speak to the hero, and help or hinder him
in his quest. The Romantics' feeling of communion with nature has
links to this primitive past, as do certain strands of modern 'green'
philosophy. In these ways we still retain some connection with the

1

'ensouled' primitive world, but our understanding is necessarily impressionistic and incomplete. It is only from the time of written records that we can begin to have a reasonably clear idea of what people meant when they spoke of the soul.

The Egyptians placed tremendous importance on the burial of the dead. The pyramids are a surviving testimony to the need for a grandiose dwelling for the person after death. But did this necessarily indicate a belief in a soul or an afterlife that we would recognize? They conceived not of a single soul but of 'souls' in various guises. One of these was the *ka*-soul. This soul could be either a vital force associated with breath, or a double of the individual. It could also mean one's personality or intelligence. These diverse ideas about soul are all developed in important ways in later Greek thought.

It is the *ba*-soul (or heart soul) of the Egyptians that comes nearest to the concept of the soul that survives death. Significantly, this soul has a clear visual identity. It is pictured as a human-headed bird, thus combining the idea of a surviving human identity with the notion of free flight. Winged creatures – birds, butterflies, bees – are all among the earliest images of the soul. Yet the Egyptian *ba*, though it is winged and leaves the body at the time of death, does not travel far but remains nearby. This shows the extent to which the Egyptian notion of the life after death could never really divorce itself from the physical. In fact, one of the functions of the *ba*-soul was as an agent to reintegrate the dead person into a whole being. It could also mediate between the living and the dead, bringing funerary gifts from the earth's surface down into the deep tomb for the use of the dead.[1] The functions of the *ba*-soul are in essence physical, designed to help preserve the body and person in his/her totality. In this they are perfectly consistent with everything else we know about the Egyptian attitude to death with its emphasis on mummification, the preservation of the body. Life after death would ideally be not that different from the good life before death. Funnels from the surface down to the dead in the tomb facilitated the giving of food and water to the dead and emphasized the physicality of the Egyptians' ideas. There is no indication that they had a concept of the soul as an entity capable of surviving alone after death.

No one is certain of the precise route the image of the *ba*-soul took, but we do know that, as a visual concept, it migrated from Egypt to ancient Greece. Here it took on a new and less physical role in keeping with the general Greek belief that death involved a radical severance of soul and body. Thus, while in its new context the *ba*-soul became one of the pre-Socratic visual images of the soul,[2] that does not mean that the Greeks in general took over Egyptian beliefs concerning the life after death. Quite the contrary! It is the Greeks who have given us the first ideas of a soul that is separable from the body and can survive death independently of the body.

'THE SOUL HAD WINGS IN HOMER'

Memorable images that convey particular ideas of the soul begin in ancient Western literature with Homer, the author to whom the two great epics of the ancient world, the *Iliad* and the *Odyssey*, written in the late eighth century BC, are attributed. The tale of the Trojan War and the subsequent account of the homeward journey of one of its greatest heroes, Odysseus, provide ample descriptions of death, ceremonies for the dead and, in the case of the *Odyssey*, a journey to the Underworld as well. In the story that Homer is telling, of course, we do not find a consistent system of thought, but the hopes and dreams of a people.

The common Greek word that we associate with the soul is *psyche*. Today we connect it with feelings, with our whole interior life as its incorporation into the word 'psychology' shows. But this meaning would have been totally incomprehensible to Homer. In Homer *psyche* means only two possible things. First, it is the life lost at death and then, in Hades, it is a shade or phantom.

Other words are used to express the elements of man that feel and think during life. For the most part, these are words that also signify a part of the body, thereby showing the close connection the Greeks of the eighth century BC perceived between emotions and bodily states. Two such words are *kradie*, and *phrenes*. *Kradie*, which is the anatomical heart, also means courage, or a combination of courage and wrath. *Phrenes*, which is identified with the breast, is the seat of deep emotion.[3]

3

(Later in Greek thought, the location of *phrenes* migrates to the head, which perhaps says something about changing notions concerning where emotion is generated.) It is difficult for us today to be certain whether this identification of body parts with emotion indicates that the early Greeks actually believed that the emotion was produced by the particular part of the anatomy, or whether it was rather another example of the desire to make the abstract concrete – to personify the emotion by linking it to a body part.

Psyche itself was not linked with a specific body part, but it is linked etymologically with the Greek *psychein*, to blow or breathe. This meaning is suggested in Homer when the *psyche* leaves the body in a swoon and returns afterwards:[4]

> The darkness of night misted over the eyes of Andromache.
> She fell backward, and gasped the life breath from her . . .
> And about her stood thronging her husband's sisters and the
>   wives of his brothers
> and these, in her despair for death, held her up among them.
> But she, when she breathed again and the life was gathered back
>   into her,
> lifted her voice among the women of Troy in mourning.
>
> (Iliad, xxii. 466–7; 473–6)[5]

The breathing out of the *psyche* in a swoon or in death is a concept familiar to us, and is, as we shall see, closely associated with pictures of the dying man breathing out his soul as a small body in medieval pictures. But in Homer's time there was another word for breath as well. This was *thumos*, and it was *thumos* that was also frequently described as leaving the body at death. *Thumos*, unlike *psyche*, was also clearly a part of the living body and, like *phrenes* and *kradie* mentioned above, was also associated with emotion – in this case with joy, fear and grief. The *thumos* was the warm, vital element of life that is extinguished by death, and the *psyche* 'the cold evanescent quality of death and extinction itself'.[6] There appears to be a stage (as there is in physiological reality), when the prospect of death cannot be reversed but is inevitable, and this, in

Homer, is pictured by the soul reaching a point of no return on its journey out of the body via the mouth: 'a man's life cannot come back again, it cannot be lifted | nor captured again by force, once it has crossed the teeth's barrier' (*Iliad*, ix. 408–9).

Interestingly, once death has occurred the *thumos* is heard of no longer. It has been essentially a part of the body, and when the body dies it disappears. The same is not true of the *psyche*. As a 'free' soul, it must leave the body, but it does not cease to exist. Rather it becomes the wraith-like surviving part of the individual in the Underworld.

There are two completely identical passages in the *Iliad* describing death, the first the death of Patroclus and the second that of Hektor:

> He spoke, and as he spoke the end of death closed in upon him,
> and the soul fluttering free of his limbs went down into Death's house
> mourning her destiny, leaving youth and manhood behind her.
>
> (*Iliad*, xvi. 855–7 and xxii. 361–3)

The imagery here is very suggestive. The soul (*psyche*) 'flutters' as it frees itself from the limbs of the dying man, implying a flying, bird-like creature. Unlike the warm breath, the *thumos*, it does not disappear but leaves the body to go down into Death's house. Thus we can see the transition from the living soul or life force that controls the body in life (though not endowed with many of the qualities we would attribute to the soul today) to the free soul, existing independently of the body, transformed into a shade in the Underworld.

The other significant thing to note in this passage is that there is no suggestion of joy or happy release in it. The *psyche* that is changed into a shade in Hades is a rather poor creature, 'mourning its destiny', not to be remotely compared with the felicitous souls who will later enjoy the Christian heaven. Nothing good can be expected in the future. The good things, youth and manhood, have been left behind with the end of earthly life. In his famous descent to Hades in the *Odyssey*, Odysseus meets the shade of his mother. It is a disastrous encounter, as he is appalled to find that she will not wait for him so that they may 'throw [their] dear hands | Round each other and take pleasure in cold lamentation' (*Odyssey*, XI. 211–12). To this plaint she replies with sorrow and resignation, indicating that it is not her personal will, or even her personal fate, that dictates the limitations of their meeting:

> But this is the rule for mortals, whenever one dies.
> No longer do the sinews hold the bones and the flesh,
> But the mighty power of burning fire subdues them
> When first the spirit has abandoned the white bones,
> And the soul, flying off like a dream, flutters.
>
> (*Odyssey*, XI. 218–22)[7]

Again, the image of 'fluttering' reinforces the notion of a bird-like entity, but in combination with 'dream' suggests also something wraith-like and insubstantial.

This raises one of the fundamental problems for anyone discussing the soul, which persists down to the present day. As a philosophical concept, it may be immaterial and invisible, but if it is to be pictured in art or visualized in literature, then the abstract must, to some extent, become concrete. Pictures on Greek vases from the fifth century (much later than Homer, but still pre-Socratic) flesh out the suggestive but vague images of Homer. They depict the soul as a tiny winged body, sometimes bearing incense to welcome the dead, congregating in swarms around Charon in the Underworld, or hovering over the head of a body mourning at its grave.

There is yet another way in which the souls of the dead are shown in early Greek art – the image of the *eidolon*. This, while clearly also a picture of the dead, is not usually found in Hades but appears, rather like a ghost, in earthly places that are particularly associated with the dead person on earth. Perhaps because of this closer connection with the dead as they were in life, it is more physical than the winged *psyche* and resembles the dead person in some detail. Between death and burial or cremation, the soul may remain in this form near its body, as various illustrations on Greek vases show.[8] But while these *eidoloi* may resemble the living in general physical characteristics, they are shades, not concrete beings. Even

6

more significantly, they lack the psychological qualities associated with the parts of the living body and its vital qualities. Once the soul has passed into the Underworld, its existence, as the passage spoken above by Odysseus' mother shows, is very limited indeed. Here it cannot even speak without drinking blood, which gives it temporarily some of the powers of a living being. At other times, souls are described as squeaking like bats as they fall away from the rock to which they cling (*Odyssey*, XXIV. 4–9).

There is a suggestion in the speech of Odysseus' mother, quoted above, that the funeral rites, cremation or burial, help the soul on its way to this Underworld. Patroclus appears to Achilles after his death to beg him to bury him for this very reason:

> The souls, the images of dead men, hold me at a distance,
> and will not let me cross the river and mingle among them,
> but I wander as I am by Hades' house of the wide gates.
>
> (*Iliad*, xxiii. 72–4)

Despite the phantom existence that awaits the dead in Hades, it is still better than lingering in the no-man's-land between life and death, and as such is to be desired. But in comparison with life – life of any kind – it is a poor substitute:

> I would rather serve on the land of another man
> Who had no portion and not a great livelihood
> Than to rule over all the shades of those who are dead.
>
> (*Odyssey*, XI. 489–91)

In summary, what we find in Homer is, first of all, a number of 'souls' connected with psychological activity in life that are seen to be closely associated with body parts. This gives them a certain concrete and visual quality. However, these 'souls' that govern feeling and thinking during life are not linked in any precise way with the *psyche* that appears only as it is about to be lost in death and survives as a shade in the Underworld. This *psyche* may retain some of the physical attributes of its body in life, but only in an attenuated and insubstantial form. And it does not possess, as it did not in life, anything of the psychological essence of the person. Even in this most limited state, it is not necessarily immortal. It will only survive as long as the memory of its possessor survives in the minds of the living. This clearly presents the famous with a more optimistic prognosis than those 'who have no memorial'!

There is no real connection between the individual soul in life and the surviving soul in death; consequently, the notion of individual immortality in any meaningful way does not exist. The Homeric soul shows the beginnings of a resistance to annihilation at the time of death, but there is no optimism about the quality of the survival for the individual. All this begins to change in the succeeding centuries.

THE SANCTIFICATION OF THE SOUL

As early as Hesiod's *Works and Days* (early seventh century BC), there is the suggestion of a more optimistic scenario for men after life on earth. In Hesiod the best among the race of Heroes (those who died in the wars at Thebes and Troy) are rewarded not by dying absolutely and being sent to Hades as shades (a view of the afterlife not likely to encourage heroism in battle), but by being translated to the Isles of the Blest where they live 'with no sorrow on their spirit . . . beside the deeply swirling Ocean, prosperous heroes for whom the grain-giving field bears honey-hearted harvest ripening three times a year . . .'.[9] Significantly, these Heroes are not really souls since they have been translated to the Isles of the Blest without dying, and the emphasis on the physical delights of their life reinforces the idea that they are enjoying an eternity not dissimilar to a life they might ideally have hoped to enjoy on earth. The physicality of their state suggests an Egyptian influence, but the precise way in which this may have come to Greece is uncertain.

As well as the favoured heroes who lived in the Isles of the Blest, Hesiod also imagined an enviable eternity for those who had lived in the Golden Age, that morning of the world when life was perfect.[10] These survived after death as *daimones*, souls ruling the earth in the service of the gods. Those who lived in the Silver Age also survived, but they were consigned to rule in the Underworld. Unlike the *daimones* that appeared near their mortal haunts and tombs at the time of Homer, these souls functioned as minor deities, capable of influencing events in their appointed sphere under the direction of the higher gods. This controlling aspect is retained in our modern word 'demon', spirits who act out the will of the devil, though the original *daimones* were not wicked. Still it would be a mistake to equate either the immortal heroes or these *daimones* with anything we (or even Plato) might understand by 'soul'. They were only immortal by special dispensation, not by nature, and they were not necessarily connected with personhood in life.

It is through the influence of the Orphic and Dionysian cults and the consolidation of much of their teaching in the person and teachings of Pythagoras (sixth century BC) that the process of what I shall call the 'sanctification' of the soul begins to take place. Up to this point the soul was essentially a life force that left the body at death, but lacked any unique moral or even psychological qualities. This began to change in the sixth century with the arrival in Greece of various religious cults.

Orpheus was a mythical figure whose cult began in Thrace (now parts of modern Greece and Bulgaria), outside the centre of the Mycenaean world. This northern origin suggests that he may originally have had connections with the shamans of Siberia and the East.[11] A shaman is a kind of magician capable of leaving his body and having remarkable adventures outside it. He can communicate with the gods and also with the spirits of the dead. In the case of Orpheus, his remarkable powers were attributed to his extraordinary musical ability – probably a rationalization of raw magic by Greek civilization. In the late sixth century he was further Hellenized by being made a son of Apollo and a Muse.[12]

For our purposes, the most significant thing about Orpheus is the way in which he is shown as conquering death, emerging immortal from all earthly disaster. Dismembered by a group of Thracian women, his head continued to sing, thus proving his essential survival. When he lost his beloved Eurydice to the Underworld, he courageously went down after her, and again his music had such

9

power that Pluto agreed to allow Eurydice to return to the world with him. The one condition was that he must not look back at her following him. Alas, he did so, and she was lost forever. Nevertheless, he had descended to the Underworld and emerged unscathed. In the Tarentine mysteries (fifth century BC) Orpheus' cithara is able to save every initiate from the horrors of death and help him find paradise.[13] These and many other exploits mark him out as a conqueror of death, one who possesses the secret of immortality. The initiates into his cult believed that through an ascetic lifestyle, denial and abstinence, they too could be purified and attain eternal life.[14]

Just as important as the stories associated with Orpheus himself are the large body of Orphic texts that claim him as their origin, but which are mostly much later than the sixth century. Here we enter murky waters. In the first place, Orpheus is a mythical figure who actually wrote nothing and, in the second, the very large collection of writings attributed to him have no common authorship at all. They are 'Orphic' simply by virtue of their attribution. Much later he is being cited as the authority for various doctrines about the soul, including that of its imprisonment in the body, in the works of Plato and Aristotle.

Some of the most interesting writings attributed to Orpheus are those dating from the late sixth or early fifth century BC to the first century BC known as 'theogonies'. They are primarily accounts of the creation of the world but, significantly, they incorporate a large amount of material about that other god who was the source of a major cult – Dionysus.

The cult of Dionysus is closely associated with that of Orpheus, and as with the Orphic cult there is uncertainty as to whether it derived from shamanism in the north or from Egypt or Crete. Like the Egyptian god Osiris, and like Orpheus, Dionysus died and came back to life again, thus showing that there was some essence that could survive the death of the body.

His story, as told in the theogonies, is that he was born in Crete, the son of the god Zeus and Kore (or Persephone), who was herself the daughter of Zeus by his union with Demeter (a little incest never troubled the Greek gods). The young Dionysus, thus doubly descended from Zeus, spent his first five years on Mount Ida, protected by the dancing Kouretes. When Dionysus was five, Zeus announced that he was the new king of the gods. This roused the Titans, an older generation of gods who had already been displaced by the younger Zeus, to furious jealousy. They whitened their faces with gypsum to disguise themselves, and tricked the young Dionysus away from the protection of the Kouretes with a mirror and other baubles attractive to a child. When they had him to themselves they slashed him into seven pieces, which they boiled, roasted and ate. Only his heart and bones were not destroyed. The bones were interred by Apollo on Mount Parnassus, and Athena took the heart, still palpitating, to Zeus, who from it gave life to a new Dionysus.[15]

Several features of this account are important for our understanding of the changing idea of the soul. The first is the death and resurrection motif, which must imply the existence of an element in the individual that can survive death while remaining essentially the same. Indeed, the adherents of the Dionysian cults went far beyond the mere fact of the survival of a soul or essence of the individual after death. They saw the soul in life as a captive god, which could be released in an orgiastic dance and united with the god Dionysus himself.[16] The kind of abandonment that this worship involved further differentiates the cult of Dionysus from the more ascetic Orphics, however tangled their histories otherwise may be.

What is new and significant about the Dionysian understanding of man is that the soul has moved from being a mere pale survival of earthly life to being an entity with a divine connection. If it can leave the body in a state of 'ecstasy' during life, then perhaps it can hope for such a state eternally once it is freed of the body for good by death. But it still is not 'soul' in the fullest modern or even Platonic sense, because it does not contain those attributes of the individual that make him/her unique. It may be moving towards becoming the immortal soul, but it is not yet personal.

Another aspect of the story of Dionysus comes later to have a significance that it probably did not have in the understanding of those who composed the original theogonies. After Dionysus was

11

killed by the Titans, Zeus vented his rage by destroying them with a thunderbolt. Then, from the ashy residue, he created a new race of mortals, from which present-day man is descended. However, given that the Titans had just consumed the god Dionysus, this ash was composed of both earthly and heavenly elements. Later interpreters (notably the Neoplatonist, Olympiodorus the Elder, who lived in the fifth century AD) used this as an explanation and justification of man's dual nature, which was therefore seen as both earthly and heavenly in its very origins. Thus in Dionysus we see the beginnings both of the idea of an independent and immortal soul and also of the opposition of this soul to an earthly and recalcitrant body.

Both Orphic and Dionysian ideas – and much more besides – come together in the partly real, partly mythical figure and writings of Pythagoras. A great deal is believed about Pythagoras; little is actually known. If Orpheus was a practical musician, bringing about magical results by his lute-playing, Pythagoras was a theoretical one. Music, he discerned, is produced on a stringed instrument by vibrations that vary in speed and hence pitch according to the length of the string producing them, and when different vibrations in the right mathematical proportions are produced simultaneously, we find the result harmonious and pleasing. More generally, this means that musical harmony is related to mathematical proportion. And, if harmony and proportion are the key elements of music, the highest earthly art, may they not also be the key to the soul? In linking this mathematical and musical insight to the soul, Pythagoras indicates that the soul possesses qualities of agreeable proportion and harmony. This is a quite new way of thinking about soul. Suddenly it becomes an entity in its own right, with independent properties, rather than a poor fragment of and substitute for the body it has left. This is clearly related to the Dionysian idea of the soul as a captive god, but the Pythagorean soul is an ideal harmonious substance by virtue of its very own nature.

This combination of what we might call scientific and mathematical observation and mysticism can be explained by Pythagoras' background. From the Dionysian cults he took the idea that the soul is immortal and separable from the body. But Pythagoras grew up in

Ionia, before fleeing to southern Italy in 532 BC, and in Ionia he was influenced by a group of philosophers, collectively known as the Milesians, who took a very different approach to reality from that of the Orphics and Dionysians. These thinkers, among whom Thales and Anaximenes were prominent, were interested in the nature of reality in *this* world – what composed matter, what produced life – rather than exclusively in religious ideas of purification and ecstasy. When they thought of the soul, they considered it too as having some link to physical reality. Anaximenes, for example, saw the soul as embodying self-propelled motion in much the same way as the air that imbues the universe is self-propelled.[17] So along with the more mystical and 'religious' ideas of the Orphics and Dionysians, Pythagoras incorporated the more practical approach of the Milesians.[18] The analogy between the soul and music, according to which it represented divine proportion and harmony, brought together in a satisfying whole both religion and mathematics.

Pythagoras also saw a distinction, which in its later development was to become very significant, between matter (the 'stuff' of the world) and the things that limited and controlled this matter, such as shape and number. This, in embryo, is an idea that develops into the Platonic and Aristotelian distinction between form and matter. And in these later philosophers this division between form and matter becomes a distinction also between soul and body: form is identified with soul and matter with body. Pythagoras also sees a connection between the way in which number limits the limitless chaos of matter and the way in which ethical ideas limit human behaviour. We shall see later how this connection between form and morals, matter and lack of moral responsibility becomes important in thinking about body and soul.[19] It is soul that is believed to impose moral restraints on body. The seeds of a great deal of later philosophy are found in Pythagoras' teaching.

At the same time, some of Pythagoras' ideas concerning the soul are based more exclusively on mysticism and his inheritance from the Orphic and Dionysian cults. The soul has a divine origin. Not only is it independent of the body, but it can exist in various different bodies. In other words, it can transmigrate from one body – human or animal – to another. An Homeric *psyche* is at once so bound up with its identity with an earthly person and at the same time so lacking in psychological qualities either of that owner or independent ones, that we cannot conceive of it moving to inhabit another body. But this is precisely what the Pythagorean soul is alleged to do. As late as the early seventeenth century the imprisoned Malvolio in Shakespeare's *Twelfth Night* knows the correct answer to Feste's question, 'What is the opinion of Pythagoras concerning wildfowl?' and replies, 'That the soul of our grandam might haply inhabit a bird'. Malvolio sees this notion as degrading to the soul, and continues, when asked his view of Pythagoras' doctrine: 'I think nobly of the soul, and no way approve his opinion'. What Malvolio does not realize, but we do, is that in the context of his age Pythagoras' notion of the soul was a huge step forward in its 'ennoblement' rather than the reverse.

The notion of the transmigration of souls was almost certainly encouraged by various contemporary stories of people who left their bodies for a time to wander the universe and enjoy various adventures. Both Pindar and Herodotus tell the story of one Aristeas, who apparently dies, but who subsequently is seen in other locations. Pindar claims he had the gift of prolonged ecstasy (the ability to exist and experience things while out of the body but able to return to it at will), while Herodotus says he died. Either way, his soul was able to leave his body and live a life of its own.[20]

Not only can the soul separate itself from the body in Pythagoras' philosophy; it is desirable that it should do so. We have met this idea already in Orphic and Dionysian thought. The difference in Pythagoras is that man can free his soul from the body and from the cycle of transmigration, which otherwise has no definite terminus, through pure thought. This purification, or *katharsis*, can be brought about through the agency of human reason. Mind itself is the purifier. It is then a short step from this idea, that thought can liberate the soul, to the concept that thought is part of, or belongs to the soul.[21]

Finally, the dualism that we saw implicit in the cult of Dionysus, where the believer, through orgiastic dance, can release his soul temporarily from his body in ecstasy, is reinforced in the philosophy of Pythagoras. Once soul and body are separated in this way, and the soul has the ability to dwell in different bodies, the foundations are laid for the separation of soul and body in religious thinking as well. And the distinction described above between the amorphous matter of the universe and number that Pythagoras believes gives shape and limit to this matter lays the foundation for a dualism in the broader universe as well. In the philosophy of Plato and Aristotle both these dualisms merge into a coherent philosophy.

I must end this discussion of Pythagoras with the kind of health warning attached to products of a slightly dubious nature. Pythagoras undoubtedly existed, but he became a repository or dumping ground for the disparate ideas of the age that seemed to cling to him and that he may or may not actually have held himself. Also, as I have indicated, we know of his ideas chiefly through the accounts of later writers such as Plato and Aristotle, and it is impossible to be sure whether what they recount are his own unadulterated views or the gloss others have put on them one hundred or more years later.

For our purposes, however, this does not matter. What does matter is the way in which the raw ideas of these earlier thinkers provided the material for the concept of the soul that was to follow. By the time of Pythagoras we have a soul that unites the element that gives man emotions and thoughts in life with that which survives death. Immortality is no longer the shadowy, anonymous existence envisaged in the poems of Homer but the endurance of something recognizable and individual.

PLATO AND THE IDEA OF THE SOUL

The first systematic account of the soul in Western thought is found in the writings of Plato. Here we are no longer extrapolating ideas from myth or poetry but dealing with logically reasoned accounts of the nature and function of the soul. Not that this means things suddenly become simple! First of all, in most of the dialogues Plato attributes the arguments to his teacher, Socrates. Secondly, possibly in part at least because the ideas in the earlier dialogues are genuinely those of Socrates while those in the later develop independently according to Plato's own changing philosophy, there is no absolute consistency in the views expressed.

The Immortality of the Soul

About one thing there is complete certainty: the soul is immortal, and the human soul, in its immortality, retains what is essential of the person whose soul it has been in life. The dialogue in which this is most poignantly expressed is the *Phaedo*, the account of the last hours of Socrates' life on earth. With complete equanimity, Socrates talks to his friends, arguing himself and them out of a fear of death because of his certainty that what is truly the self will survive.

Death is the separation of soul and body, but this is by no means a tragedy for the individual. The true philosopher is entirely concerned with the soul and not the body. The senses of the body are inaccurate and hinder the soul; therefore only when it is freed from the body can the soul attain truth. 'So long as we keep to the body and our soul is contaminated with this imperfection, there is no chance of our ever attaining satisfactorily to our object, which we assert to be truth.'[22]

As in all the Socratic dialogues, other speakers (in this case Socrates' friends who have gathered to bid him farewell before he dies) raise objections, thereby testing the truth of Socrates' assertions. Cebes says men fear that when the soul leaves the body it may be 'dissipated like breath or smoke, and vanish away, so that nothing is left of it anywhere' (70 a).[23] But Socrates gently ridicules this notion: 'You are afraid, as children are, that when the soul emerges from the body the wind may really puff it away and scatter it, especially when a person does not die on a calm day but with a gale blowing' (77 e). The soul that Socrates envisages is not this fragile.

The proofs for the immortality of the soul as set forth in Plato's dialogues can be divided into four broad categories. I shall look briefly at three of them.

One argument is based on the theory of recollection. Souls come into this world with knowledge gained from their life in a previous,

16

disembodied state. We first encounter this notion in an earlier Platonic dialogue, the *Meno*, where Socrates elicits certain mathematical proofs from a slave boy, who has never been taught them. From this Socrates concludes that the boy must have prior knowledge of these ideas, which he can therefore be brought to recollect. And from where else can this prior knowledge come, but from the soul having learned them in a pre-existent state? Therefore, the soul exists before it is born in the body, and what exists prior to birth will hardly disappear at death.

Another is found in the fact that the soul above all bears life. Life is the opposite of death, and since essential opposites can never exist in the same thing, the soul can never receive into itself what is the opposite of its essence. Thus the soul cannot admit of death, and therefore is immortal. The soul that follows reason and has in this life beheld the true and divine will not be scattered and blown away by the winds after death. Like the swan, who sings at its death, Socrates can face its prospect with positive joy. And in the *Republic* Plato cites the passage I have already quoted above from Achilles ('I would rather serve on the land of another man | Who had no portion and not a great livelihood | Than to rule over all the shades of those who are dead') with disapproval. Poets must speak well of the other world, and death must not be represented as something to be feared.[24]

A final, highly abstract proof of the soul's immortality is found in a later dialogue, the *Phaedrus*. Here the soul is said to be self-moving – that is, the soul moves itself with no external assistance, unlike the body which cannot move itself but is moved from without – that is by the soul. What is self-moving must always have moved; it cannot have had a beginning. What has no beginning can never have an end. Therefore the soul must be immortal.[25] It is worth noting that the initial premise here, that the soul is self-moving, is not itself proven but is taken to be self-evident. Also, the highly abstract, rhetorical language used in this passage is untypical of these dialogues and more reminiscent of the opening of the Gospel of John. And, indeed, Plato's insistence on the immortality and absolute superiority of the soul provided a somewhat uncomfortable legacy for Christianity, as we shall see.

The Nature of the Soul

The soul in the early dialogues of Plato such as the *Phaedo* appears to be a unity, not divided into parts in any way. Conflict, when it occurs, is between the soul and the body, not between various elements within the soul itself. But by the time of the writing of the *Republic* things are not so simple.

The *Republic* is a work, as its title indicates, that at one level is about society and how it should best be governed. But Plato sees an intimate connection between the classes of people in society at large and how they should be governed and the little kingdom within man and how its elements are to govern themselves. In Chapter IV he speaks of two parts within the soul – a better and a worse. A man is his own master when the better part of the soul has the worse under control (IV. 431a). There must be more than one element in the soul, he argues, because otherwise how could conflict about the right course of action to pursue take place? Yet we know that such conflict is common. It is possible for a man to be thirsty and yet pulled back from drinking. So there must be both a rational element and an irrational appetite within the soul.

This alone does not explain everything, however. Sometimes we will give in to irrational desires even though we know they are not for our ultimate good. At others we follow reason and behave in our own long-term interests. So what makes the difference? To explain this Plato gives the soul a third element – the spirited element or will. It is this will that sides with either the higher soul (reason) or the lower soul (irrational appetite) and decides which will control our actions. Ideally it should always side with reason. 'Does it not belong to the rational part to rule, being wise and exercising forethought in behalf of the entire soul, and to the principle of high spirit to be subject to this and its ally' (IV. 441e). Thus the soul becomes a mini-state, with all the possibilities of both good governance but also of insurrection. The unjust soul is under a tyranny. 'Being always perforce driven and drawn by the gadfly of desire it will be full of confusion and repentance' (IX. 577e).

To illustrate the multiple soul and the perils that may beset it, Plato then presents us with a remarkable picture. Imagine, he says,

18

that the soul is like a fabulous many-formed monster of antiquity. This beast has the heads of tame and wild animals that it can grow out of itself and transform at will. Now suppose that this many-headed beast joins to itself two other creatures – a lion and man, so that all three grow together into one. Finally, transform the outside of this multiple creature into the shape of the man alone, so that to the outside observer the man is all that there is. Now this strange being, unified to appearances, but multiple underneath, will naturally have different needs and desires. And for it wrongdoing will be to feed and strengthen the composite beast and the lion and to starve the man. Similarly, in doing good, the man will be given complete mastery over the whole creature, taking particular care to secure the lion as his ally in this enterprise (IX. 588c–589b). The meaning of this elaborate metaphor is clear. The man is the rational part of the soul, the many-headed creature is the multiple desires of our lower natures, and the lion is the powerful will, which can decide whether desire or reason will rule.

In the *Phaedrus* we have another picture of the soul with a similar meaning. Here the multiple soul is like two horses and a charioteer. But unlike the chariots of the gods, the horses of this chariot are not well matched. One is noble, while the other is ignoble, so they are very difficult to manage. 'He that is on the more honorable side is upright and clean-limbed, carrying his neck high, with something of a hooked nose; in color he is white, with black eyes; a lover of glory, but with temperance and modesty; one that consorts with genuine renown and needs no whip, being driven by the word of command alone. The other is crooked of frame, a massive jumble of a creature, with thick short neck, snub nose, black skin, and gray eyes; hot-blooded, consorting with wantonness and vainglory; shaggy of ear, deaf and hard to control with whip and goad' (253d–e). The significant difference between this description of the soul and that in the *Republic* is that the white horse, or will, seems always to be obedient to the human charioteer, or reason, rather than being susceptible to the temptation of following the dark horse, which is appetite.

The *Timaeus* gives us a still different picture of the multiple soul, which associates the various faculties with different parts of the body. The immortal soul is given by God, and is encased in a mortal physical globe (the head) with the body as a whole for its vehicle. But there is another soul that is encased in the body and is made quite differently by the offspring of God the creator. This soul is 'mortal, subject to terrible and irresistible affections' – pleasure, pain, rashness and fear, anger and hope. 'These they mingled with irrational sense and with all-daring love according to necessary laws, and so framed man.'[26]

These baser elements are housed in the breast and trunk, with the will (the seat of courage, passion and ambition) located between the midriff and neck, and the appetite for food and drink and other natural needs between the midriff and the navel 'contriving in all this region a sort of manger for the food of the body, and there they bound it down like a wild animal which was chained up with man, and must be nourished if man was to exist' (70e). The neck serves as a kind of isthmus and boundary, dividing the head that contains the rational soul from the will and appetite.

These differing images, and Plato's own comprehensive interpretation of them, tell us a number of things of continuing importance in Western thought and imagination. First of all, the human being is a seat of conflict. We want and we do not want at the same time. Secondly, these conflicts have a moral dimension. There are lower and higher desires, desires that spring from appetite, and desires that either come from or can be approved by reason. Will not only exists as a free arbiter of these conflicting desires but in most cases seems to be the deciding factor. There can be no question, however, about the fact that the higher elements of the soul are to rule the lower, and that the soul as a whole is to rule the body: 'He [God] made the soul in origin and excellence prior to and older than the body, to be the ruler and mistress, of whom the body was to be the subject' (34c).

The Platonic Soul in Myth and Vision

For all the rational and philosophical analysis that Plato brings to bear on the soul, his most enduring images and ideas about it are couched in myth and vision. The most notable of these is the Myth of Er, which comes at the very end of the *Republic*.

This myth is presented as the vision of one Er, who is killed (or nearly killed) in battle, but who miraculously recovers as he is about to be laid on his funeral pyre ten days after his supposed demise. During the ten days he has been journeying in the other world, and has come back with a remarkable account of his adventures. (This tale is obviously in the tradition of earlier stories about Orphic and Dionysian figures who left their bodies to gain supernatural knowledge.)

When Er's soul left his body he first travelled to a place where there were two holes in the earth below and two in the sky above. Between the holes sat judges who directed the souls either to the left, to descend below the earth or to the right, to ascend to the sky, depending on whether their lives had been good or evil. From the other two holes, the one earthward and the other heavenward, souls are returning to the meadow from which Er is observing all this. Those who have come down from the sky are bright and rejoicing; those who have come up from the earth weep for sorrow. Er learns that each of these souls is returning from a journey of a thousand years, during which they have either been punished for their evil deeds in their life on earth or rewarded for their good ones. These returning are lucky; some have committed sins so terrible that there is no possibility of return, and they are cast into Tartarus.

After seven days in the meadow, the souls journey on. Four days more, and they reach a place where a shaft of light, like a pillar, stretches from heaven to earth. This shaft of light binds the heavens and the firmament, and from its extremities stretches the Spindle of Necessity, which encompasses the spheres of the Fixed stars, the sun, and the planets. Here also are the Fates, the daughters of Necessity. All the souls are to begin a new round of life on earth that, like the previous one, will end in death. To choose their fate, they must go before Lachesis, the second of the Fates, who apportions life. There they are free to choose their own destiny. The onus is on them to choose well. 'The blame is his who chooses; God is blameless' (X. 617e). The order in which they choose is determined by the Interpreter, who scatters lots in front of them; each picks up the lot that falls nearest. Er is assured, however, that there are more possible lives than individuals, so even the last to choose may still make a good choice.

It would seem that good or bad choice must be calculated by the soul according to its own constitution. The determining factor is whether the choice will lead the particular soul, in its next earthly life, to become more or less just. But in general, Er observes, the souls choose badly. Earthly status is not a good criterion. One who chooses to be a despot discovers that this will entail devouring his own children. Most, despite the thousand years that have elapsed since their previous incarnation, choose according to the habits of their previous life. After the souls have chosen, each is given into the charge of the guardian genius (*daimon*)[27] that he has chosen to escort him through life (X. 620e). Then they drink from the waters of Lethe so that they can no longer remember their previous existence. At midnight there is thunder and lightning, and the souls are carried up to their birth like shooting stars.

This myth presents certain features that are of great interest. The first is the fully developed notion of the judgment of the souls, and even the symbolic significance of right and left in this judgment. We have a three-tier universe, with the good souls ascending and the bad descending – even if they do not remain in these locations for eternity. There is also the notion of free will; the souls choose their fate – although it might be objected that the chance of the lot determines just how wide the choice they are presented with is. Finally, we have the idea of souls with an individual character, since each person ought to choose a fate that is appropriate to him, 'with his eyes fixed on the nature of his soul' (X. 618d). This nature, however, which has presumably been formed in part from experiences in their previous existence, may be further changed 'because the choice of a different life inevitably determine[s] a different character' (X. 618b). Life as it is lived moulds the soul, which then retains this character until it enters into another life, and another modification.

The vision in the *Phaedrus* deals primarily with the experience of pre-existent souls before embodiment. In large part Plato is attempting to explain how something as ideal as the soul could possibly unite itself to a body at all. It does this because the self-moving soul, without beginning or end, is inherently troubled as a result of its mixed nature, which Plato explains in terms of the two horses and charioteer imagery. The 'good' soul (the white horse and the charioteer) longs only to attain a vision of truth and beauty, but the dark horse, depicting passion and appetite, wishes to drag it down to the earth. When the chariot of the soul tries to ascend to the heights of heaven, to attain knowledge of the Good, the evil steed 'pulls down his driver with his weight. . . . And now there awaits the soul the extreme of her toil and struggling' (247b). The immortal soul can apprehend the colourless and formless and intangible essence visible to the mind, but the other lower souls see true being imperfectly. They seek to follow, but are not able, 'sucked down as they travel they trample and tread upon one another, this one striving to outstrip that. Thus confusion ensues, and conflict and grievous sweat. Whereupon, with their charioteers powerless, many are lamed, and many have their wings all broken, and for all their toiling they are balked, every one, of the full vision of being, and departing therefrom, they feed upon the food of semblance' (248b).

Such a soul, who fails to behold the full vision of truth, finds that her feathers fall from her and she drops to earth. In other words, the soul becomes embodied. *How* precisely it becomes embodied, that is, what kind of man it will enter, depends on the degree of truth it has witnessed and attained. Not until ten thousand years have passed can the soul again ascend to the region where it can gain a vision of the truth. In the meantime it appears to alternate between various kinds of embodiment, interspersed by the thousand years of punishment described in the Myth of Er. Only the soul of the philosopher (Plato always looked after his own!) is perpetually rapt in heavenly things to the exclusion of earthly.

This description explains at the philosophical level how souls come into the body with some pre-existent knowledge and why they enter the body at all. In terms of its imagery, however, a great deal more is happening. We begin with the now-familiar image of the soul as two horses and charioteer, but midway we find the soul (now definitely feminine) having her feathers fall from her. A horse with feathers? I think not. Rather the soul has now become a winged creature, familiar to us from earlier iconography, a kind of bird. What Plato does is to change the imagery to fit the point he is illustrating. The horses and chariot explain the diverse nature of the soul, but the image of the winged creature falling to earth is a kind of Icarus, a being designed for and capable of soaring, but also capable of distraction and descent.

Later in the *Phaedrus* Plato uses the imagery of sexual love in language reminiscent of the Song of Songs to describe the torn urges of the soul. In its immortal nature, the soul seeking beauty is like a mad lover seeking her beloved:

> At last she does behold him, and lets the flood pour in upon her, releasing the imprisoned waters; then has she refreshment and respite from her stings and sufferings, and at that moment tastes a pleasure that is sweet beyond compare. . . . Above all others does she esteem her beloved in his beauty; mother, brother, friends, she forgets them all. . . . All the rules of conduct, all the graces of life, of which aforetime she was proud, she now disdains, welcoming a slave's estate and any couch where she may be suffered to lie down close beside her darling, for besides her reverence for the possessor of beauty she has found in him the only physician for her grievous suffering. (251e–252b)

It is worth noting here that the soul is feminine, fervently seeking an ideal of beauty and love that is masculine. This will take on added significance when we look at the myth of Psyche in the next chapter.

Conclusion

The soul in Plato has taken on most of the characteristics that were both to enlighten and trouble Western philosophy and theology for centuries to come. This soul is indisputably immortal, retaining the essential characteristics of the living person after death. It is complex rather than simple, composed of differing elements that can explain psychological struggle and uncertainty. Within this complex structure there is an implicit moral hierarchy, so that notions of control are linked to good and evil. Finally, with the myths of Er and those in the *Phaedrus*, we have a rich storehouse of images that are not to be taken literally but enhance our conception of the soul well beyond that of an abstract life-principle.

ARISTOTLE

What the Platonic soul does not provide for is any real contact with the body and the material world. As we have seen, embodiment is a 'fall', and all true knowledge contained in the soul is as a result of its exposure to the world of the Ideal Forms in a pre-existent life. Aristotle, Plato's pupil and successor, took a quite different view.

In his treatise *De Anima*, Aristotle defines the soul as 'the first grade of actuality of a natural body having life potentially in it'.[28] What on earth does he mean by this? Fundamentally, he means that soul is what makes the living creature become what it is, makes it 'actualize' itself.

Aristotle thinks of everything that has life – plants and animals, as well as human beings – as composed of two essential elements, matter and form. These two elements can also be called body and soul. In every case, the body produces the matter that is able, potentially, to be a lily, or a giraffe, or Aristotle himself. But without the existence of the *form* of the lily, or the giraffe, or Aristotle, the matter will remain what it might be only potentially. It is the addition of form or soul that makes living things what they are in actuality. The form or soul impresses itself on the matter in much the same way as the seal impresses itself on wax.

Several things must follow from this account of soul. The first is that such a soul cannot be exclusively human. Aristotle sees all living things, including plants, as 'ensouled', though not in the same way. Plants have a nutritive and reproductive soul; they are capable of taking in food, of growth and reproduction. Animals have this soul, but they also have a sensitive soul. In addition to the things that plants can do, animals can receive sensations through their five senses, and can process this information in order to make rudimentary choices that will enable them to live. Man has not only the nutritive and

25

sensitive souls of plants and animals, but also a rational soul that enables him to think abstractly and to reason. These souls do not remain separate within animals or man, however; the lower are contained within the higher, so that the soul is one, not many.

It also follows that such a soul cannot exist without a body. If it is the actuality of a body, it can scarcely be thought of outside any relation to such a body. Yet it does not exist *for* the body. On the contrary, it is the body that exists *for* the soul, since it enables the soul to fulfil itself. The creature is what it is by virtue of its soul, not its body. The soul is the essential 'whatness' of a body.

All this is radically different from Plato. While the soul here is very different from the body in its nature and function, there is no suggestion that it would be better off if the body did not exist. Indeed, the implication of Aristotle's ideas as set out above is that the soul would be not merely less well off without the body; it would itself cease to exist. Embodiment is not a punishment. Just as body remains mere potentiality without the addition of soul, so soul's capacity to actualize matter cannot be realized without the existence of that matter.

Aristotle's theory of how we come to know and think also confirms the way in which the higher parts of the soul depend on the lower, and the lower are ultimately dependent on the body. In Plato's philosophy, we saw how the rational soul gained its knowledge in a pre-existent state. Once it was born, this knowledge remained dormant within it and could be elicited by someone who knew how to ask the right questions. Aristotle, here as elsewhere, is much more firmly grounded in the world of sense perception. While he says that thinking is different from perceiving, it is clear that it is based on perceiving in the first instance. Thinking, he says, is in part imagination, and in part judgment (427b, 25).

What does Aristotle mean by imagination? It lies within our own power, and is our ability to conjure up a mental picture. It is different from sense perception because the object we imagine does not need to be present (though presumably at some time we must have seen it), and it is different from reasoned thinking because when we form opinions they can be shown to be either true or false, but imagination can be shown to be neither true nor false. Yet this same imagination forms the very basis of our thinking. To the thinking soul, images serve as if they were the contents of perception. 'That is why the soul never thinks without an image' (431a, 15). However, the mind does not stop here. Because the image is not the thing itself, the mind can manipulate it. Thus it can abstract from various images of the same thing the form of that thing. So, for example, from perceiving many examples of actual triangles, the mind can abstract and picture the essence of triangularity. In this way the mind can arrive at a Platonic form by a wholly different route. In Aristotle our highest flights of abstract thought have as the ground of their being images that come from sense perception and are retained and manipulated in the imagination.

This discussion of imagination might seem peripheral to the soul. But while Aristotle's ideas about the soul as a whole are not ones that will predominate in later chapters, the core notion that one can only think about the soul (and, by extension, about all abstract things) by using the imagination to picture them, is one that is central to this book. Such evidence as we have suggests that primitive man tried to capture the soul in this way. At every point, from Dante to Milton, writers are presented with the fundamental conflict between the demands of philosophy and theology on the one hand, and the limitations of human thought on the other. Aristotle had the honesty to confront the issue squarely. It is images that must try to bridge the gap. We may define in abstractions, but we think and imagine in pictures.

Everything I have said about the Aristotelian soul up to this point, particularly the emphasis on its close relationship to body, might lead one to suppose that Aristotle's soul could not have the essential Platonic qualities of separability from the body and of immortality. And indeed, the lower souls of growth and sense cannot be separated from body. But the rational soul, which Aristotle calls *nous* or mind, can be so separated.

Like the sensitive part of the soul, *nous* has no nature of its own. It is rather a *capacity* for thought. It is potentially whatever is thinkable, but until it has engaged in thought, it is in actuality nothing (429b, 30). In the case of objects that involve no matter, what thinks and what is thought are identical, because speculative knowledge and its object are identical (430a, 5). In this way, mind can know itself. All this may seem (and indeed is) rather abstruse and removed from the direct subject of the imaginable soul. It has to do chiefly with how we know, and how our knowing differs from that of lower forms of life. But following on from this Aristotle makes a remarkable statement about this highest part of the soul, *nous*. He says that 'when mind is set free from its present conditions [that is, when it is free of the body], it appears as just what it is and nothing more: this alone is immortal and eternal . . . and without it nothing thinks' (430a, 25).

So at the last, this pupil of Plato who has been so careful, in contrast to his teacher, to ground the soul and all its powers firmly in the world of the physical and finite, comes up with a statement that seems to undermine all this at least in relation to the highest part of the soul. 'This alone is immortal and eternal . . .' Yet so enigmatic is Aristotle's description of this 'immortal' soul that commentators have disagreed for centuries about precisely what it means. Since *nous* is divided into an active and passive faculty (the passive receives and holds images; the active makes these images intelligible) there is disagreement about whether immortality belongs to both parts of this *nous* or only to the active element. But while the precise meaning of Aristotle's assertion has been a matter of dispute among scholars for centuries, its significance in subsequent thought about the soul cannot be overestimated. It provided the opening for Christian thinkers to adopt Aristotle as their own. The Prime Mover of Aristotle's Metaphysics, a being who was the first cause of motion without Himself being moved, could be identified with the Christian God, the creator of *nous*, which then became the Christian soul, operating within man in much the same way as Aristotle's soul but divine and immortal in ways that would have been quite foreign to Aristotle himself. Nothing in Aristotle's account leads to the idea of the survival of a human soul with an individual personality, but this difficulty was largely ignored or glossed over by later Christian commentators.[29]

What Aristotle has given us, then, is a soul that is much more explicable in its workings during life than any accounts we have found hitherto, but that, perhaps because it is so closely defined in terms of its function, is not really an 'imaginable' entity. At the same time Aristotle's theory of knowledge and perception emphasizes the importance of images (pictures) in the process of thinking, and thus gives a psychological basis for the fact that we do, almost inevitably, picture the soul when we think of it. By asserting the separability and immortality of at least part of the soul, he enables his philosophy to be taken over and used by Christian thinkers. Aristotle's rather practical description of the soul and its relationship to the body combines in later theology with the more theoretical and imaginative description of Plato in many different permutations in Christian thought. Where Plato saw the body as a hindrance to the soul, a necessary but unfortunate encumbrance in this life, Aristotle asserted that their interdependence was a necessary good. These dual attitudes are still present in much of our thinking about the soul.

STOICS AND EPICUREANS

Aristotle's inclination to a more physical and practical approach than that of Plato was taken much further by two other philosophical schools that grew up in Athens in the latter part of his lifetime. Both were essentially materialist philosophies, and both were designed to give peace of mind in an age of increasing political and military instability.

To the Stoics, God is the Primal Fire (itself material, though in a very refined way), and out of this Primal Fire he creates the universe. This is then diversified through the other elements of earth, air and water, thus creating the world. But the whole process is cyclical, and eventually God draws the universe back into Himself as fire once more, and the whole process begins again.

There are no transcendental forms in this universe, and indeed the Stoics denied their existence. The soul of man, nobler than that of plants, is part of the divine fire that comes from God, and which descended to men at their creation. But since even this divine fire is essentially material, it can be passed on by generation. And, at the final conflagration, it is drawn back into God, along with everything else, thus making personal immortality impossible.

God ordains everything for the best, and if seen in the light of eternity this would be clear to all men. Things on earth are controlled by God or fate, and man has only a very limited free will which allows him to change his perception of or attitude to events – remarkably close to the kind of freedom offered by the modern psychoanalyst, it seems! Therefore sin, or conflict between body and soul, is scarcely a possibility.[30]

Even more materialist than the Stoics were the Epicureans. They took over the atomist system of Democritus, in which everything is made up of varying kinds of atoms that are neither created nor destroyed – they merely combine and break down again into their constituent entities. (These atoms, of course, should not be understood as identical with the atom in modern science.)

The soul as well is composed of atoms, though of a particularly fine nature. Man possesses a rational soul that is diffused throughout the body, though still material. At death the atoms of the soul are separated, and there can be no more perception. Death is therefore not to be feared, since it is mere extinction. In contrast to the Stoics, the Epicureans decided there was no controlling God or fate in human affairs; everything that happens does so because of material causes. In this materialist universe, the highest happiness is pleasure itself, though this is not to be understood in a hedonistic way. In fact, both the Stoics' and Epicureans' emphasis on control and restraint in living one's life fed into the Christian tradition of asceticism.

The Stoics and Epicureans provided a radical contrast to the more idealistic Greek philosophy that had gone before. Within the context of Western Christian thought they never gained the same influence as Plato and Aristotle. But their insistence on the physicality of the soul and, in the case of the Stoics, its physical transmission through the parents, would provide a tempting solution to theological problems, such as the transmission of original sin, faced by some early Christian thinkers. It also provided a philosophical justification for making the soul physical, visible, 'imaginable'.

PLOTINUS

A much greater influence on the idea of the soul in Western thought than the Stoics and Epicureans was the thought of Plotinus.

Chronologically Plotinus, who lived from AD 204 to 274, belongs with the Church Fathers and other early Christian writers. But as a non-Christian and devoted follower of Plato, I have placed him here at the end of one tradition (the classical) before I consider the Hebrew and Christian strands of thought and the confluence of the two.

From Plotinus we receive the idea of a soul that begins pure in the heavens, but as it gives of itself in order to fill the universe it gradually mingles more and more with matter or body, and so loses its original purity. Because there is no single dividing point between soul and matter, but a series of shaded gradations, there is at one level less opposition between the two than in Plato or even Aristotle. All creation exists within an overarching monism, descending from Pure Spirit at the top to pure matter at the bottom. But beside this Plotinus insists on the fundamental difference between soul and matter, which places a sharp dualism against the larger structure of monism.

The process by which God (The One or The Good), who is prior to all that exists, gives of Himself and descends to the multiplicity of created things is a necessity. The higher must give to the lower, continually unfolding itself. 'To this power we cannot impute any halt, any limit of jealous grudging; it must move for ever outward until the universe stands accomplished to the ultimate possibility.'[31] From God or The One comes *Nous*, which is divisible, but still eternal and beyond time. From *Nous* descends the All-Soul, and from All-Soul individual souls. Last of all, formless matter, the lowest gradation of creation, emerges from soul. This matter is not so much *actively* evil as in a state of privation, lacking good. Insofar as soul is linked to this matter, it too can be called 'evil'.

The contradictions between the monistic and dualistic elements in Plotinus' thought are reflected in his vacillating pronouncements about the value of body. He wrote a treatise *Against the Gnostics* (a sect that saw matter or body as the evil principle in the universe) castigating them for their hatred of the body, and asserting 'As long as we have bodies we must inhabit the dwellings prepared for us by our good sister soul in her vast power of labourless creation' (II.9.18, p. 151). But embodiment is nevertheless a fall for the soul, as it is in Plato, and man must not give in to the temptations of the flesh. Thus he can say, 'Life in the body is of itself an evil but the Soul enters its Good through Virtue, not living the life of the Couplement but holding itself apart, even here' (I.7.3, p. 66). Elsewhere he seems to say that the union of soul to body is doomed to unhappiness, rather like a bad marriage, not because of the innate evil of one or other partner, but because of their utter incompatibility. 'But when two distinct things become one in an artificial unity, there is a probable source of pain to them in the mere fact that they were inapt to partnership' (IV.4.18, p. 301). These ideas contribute to later Christian notions about moral conflict either within the soul or between the soul and the body.

The soul desires above all else to leave its embodied state and return to its origins. A divine being, it has entered body under stress of its tendency to bring order to the lower realm. 'If it turns back quickly, all is well' (IV.8.5, p. 362). When it does return, although it becomes part of the All-Soul, it does not thereby lose any of its individuality. Even in a disembodied state, souls retain their identical being (IV.3.5, p. 264).

Plotinus never became a Christian, though he must have been familiar with their beliefs. His views on soul, however, satisfied many of the Christian criteria. It was immortal, derived from The One (God), and it retained its individual personality after its separation from the body. The idea of emanations, proceeding in a creative way from a Supreme Being was easily adapted to the concept of the Son and Holy Ghost proceeding from God the Father, although Christians had to make certain that the ever-diminishing value of the emanations in Plotinus' thought was not applied to the co-equal Trinity. But his negative view of matter and generally ascetic lifestyle encouraged that brand of Christianity that wished to eschew the world and the body. This, as we shall see, was by no means the stance of the religion out of which Christianity chiefly sprang.

HEBREW AND EARLY CHRISTIAN VIEWS OF THE SOUL

The Hebraic view of the soul was more similar to that of Homer than to that of Plato and Aristotle.[32] The very beginning of the Old

Testament asserted that God created the soul (Genesis 2:7: 'And the
Lord God formed man of the dust of the ground, and breathed into
his nostrils the breath of life; and man became a living soul'), but
what this meant to the ancient Hebrews was not what it came to
mean much later to Christians. The words could be interpreted as an
account of man's creation from two distinct elements, the emphasis
in Hebraic thought was always on the whole man as a living entity.
In contrast to the Platonic and later Christian emphasis on death as
a release from the body to a better life after death, the whole thrust
of the Old Testament is on the good to be found in life on this earth.
The supreme favour God granted those who feared and served him
was a long and prosperous earthly life. And those who, like Elijah,
deserved never to die, He took up bodily into the heavens.

Nephesh and *ruach* were the two words used to describe soul. Of
these, *nephesh* was similar to the life force, or *thumos* of the Greeks.
As in Greek physiology, it could be identified with parts of the body
– in this case, with throat, neck or stomach. It really stood for the
whole person, not for some spirit that could survive disembodied
after death.

Ruach, on the other hand, which meant primarily breath or spirit,
was associated with the breath of God and the spirit of God that
gives life to man. When God withdraws this spirit, the individual
ceases to live. But this *ruach* must not be confused with a Platonic
soul; it is not an individual entity that survives death but a creative
energy produced by God and flowing from him to the individual
creature.[33] Also, unlike the Platonic soul, it is placed into the
individual by a personal and purposive God.

In contrast to life in this world, the afterlife, particularly as portrayed in Ecclesiastes, is pale and dull, reminiscent of the Homeric
Underworld. 'Death for the Hebrews was the virtual end of personal
existence – a passing into the land of forgetfulness, the place of
oblivion which is cut off even from God.'[34] The dead were called
rephaim, shades, not souls, and they went to a place called Sheol,
which in some contexts means simply the grave, but in others is
understood more literally as 'The Pit', a place under the earth far
from the heavens, cut off from the light. Here the shades live out a

dim existence; to what extent they are conscious and active is unclear.[35] They may occasionally appear to the living, still in recognizable form, as Samuel does to Saul when he is conjured up before battle (1 Samuel 28) but it is with a sense of grievance and reluctance at being thus disturbed.[36] There is some suggestion that the dead will awaken again, and that this will be linked to judgment (Daniel 12:2: 'And many of them that sleep in the dust of the death shall awake, some to everlasting life, and some to shame and everlasting contempt'), but it remains just that – a fleeting suggestion.

By the time of Christ, Judaism contained a wide range of views about the soul and the afterlife, ranging from the beliefs of the Sadducees, who denied both the existence of soul or spirit as well as the Resurrection, to the Pharisees who believed in all these things (Acts 23:8).[37] But the chief impulse to dualism in Christian thought came, almost certainly, not from within Judaism but through the potent influence of the Greek world. Here Philo of Alexandria (25 BC –AD 40) is a key figure. Alexandria was a meeting point for the Jewish religion and Greek philosophy, and Philo was the chief catalyst in effecting a union of the two. Philo, who was both a Jew and an ambassador of the Alexandrian Jews to Rome, saw that by interpreting the Jewish scriptures allegorically they could be made to agree with many aspects of Greek Platonic thought. God, who was often spoken of in scripture anthropomorphically, as a concession to the understanding of ordinary people, was in fact incorporeal, Pure Being. He saw that this elevation of God made it necessary to devise other intermediate beings to bridge the gap between the Divine and man. The highest of these beings he called the *Logos*, or *Nous*. The extent to which these ideas penetrated Christianity is eloquently shown in the opening of St John's Gospel where we find the magnificent passage describing the procession of the Divine Logos from the Father to earthly creation:

In the beginning was the Word, and the Word was with God, and the Word was God. The same was in the beginning with God. All things were made by him; and without him was not any thing made that was made . . . . And the Word was made flesh, and dwelt among us, (and we beheld his glory, the glory as of the only begotten of the Father,) full of grace and truth. (John 1:1–3, 14)

Despite his insistence on 'bridging' elements between God and the created world, the realms of spirit and matter, Philo remained a dualist at heart. Body is necessary, but it is not equal to soul, and man must seek to free himself from sensual influences.[38] He accepts the *Phaedrus* myth's account of the 'fall' of the soul into the body, interprets the 'coats of skins' in Genesis (3:21) as bodies, and states that the soul lives in the body as in a prison.

St Paul, the most influential teacher and writer of the New Testament, was undoubtedly influenced by this dualism incorporated from Greek thought.[39] It is true that many of the passages in St Paul's writings depicting the flesh fighting against the spirit (as, for example, Galatians 5:17: 'For the flesh lusteth against the Spirit and the Spirit against the flesh: and these are contrary the one to the other') are almost certainly intended to be taken figuratively. But since flesh indicates a life away from God and spirit one devoted to him, they quite naturally become associated with the literal soul and body. What this means is that within Christianity, from a very early stage, there is a moral difference and implicitly a difference in value set up between body and soul. We are all too familiar with this already; we found it at the very heart of Plato's philosophy.

Mitigating, to some extent, this negative view of body in relation to soul was the Christian emphasis on the Incarnation of Christ in a human body, and his Resurrection in that same body. Indeed, the resurrection of the faithful was consistently perceived as a resurrection of the body, which would then be joined to its soul. What happened to the soul in the intervening time between death and the final resurrection was less certain. Did it immediately receive some intimation of the reward or punishment it would receive fully at the last day, or did it enter a state of unconsciousness, waiting for its final salvation or damnation? We shall find these questions still alive to trouble medieval theologians and writers.

EARLY CHRISTIAN THINKERS

The early Church sought to systematize a body of writing and thinking (the Gospels and the writings of the Apostles) that was anything but systematic. It was initially a fluid situation in which contradictory ideas floated disconnected in a general ether of religiosity.

Two major heresies relating to soul and body, Gnosticism and Manicheism, dominated the thought of the second to fourth centuries. For our purposes, the notable feature of both these heresies was that they perceived matter (and by extension body) as inherently evil. Thus there were two principles in the universe – the spiritual and the material – and the battle between them was fought out in the life of every man. One must deny the flesh and strive to cultivate the spiritual in oneself. This was, of course, quite contrary to the Christian emphasis on the Incarnation, but it did fit in well with the ascetic practices of certain Christian sects and with the reality of persecution by hostile forces that early Christians experienced. Neither of these sects was ever accepted as orthodox within the Church, but even those who wrote against them, such as Irenaeus, Tertullian, and later Saint Augustine, were not wholly immune from their influence.

The other notable feature of the early Church Fathers is their need to think of the soul as something picturable, if not actually physical and concrete. Unlike Aristotle and Plotinus, they are not adept at abstract thought. Some of this doubtless came from the influence of the Stoics, but it also derived from a tendency to take the Bible literally, and to use their imagination liberally as they sought to give pictorial expression to the profound reality of the soul as the form of the body. The story of Dives and Lazarus, in which Dives, in torment after his death, begs Lazarus, who is in paradise, to give him some water was taken as evidence that souls were corporeal. Irenaeus (*c.* 130–*c.* 200) believed that souls and spirits always had an ethereal body attached to them as an inseparable envelope. Moreover, this ethereal body had the appearance (*figura*) of the physical body. When the soul entered a body it adapted itself to the body like water to a vase. The soul then kept the imprint of the body it had, remembering it even when separated after death.[40]

Tertullian (*c.* 160–*c.* 220) believed with Irenaeus that while the soul is immortal it is also corporeal and developed an elaborate theory about how it came to be this way through the manner of its propagation. In general, he had little time for Greek philosophy, particularly for the abstract theories of Socrates and Plato, but he does quote Zeno, the father of the Stoic school, to support his argument that the soul is corporeal, though his chief proofs come from his rather literal interpretation of Scripture. When God breathed into man the breath of life, so Tertullian asserts, it congealed and formed the human soul:

> Likewise, as regards the figure of the human soul from your own conception, you can well imagine that it is none other than the human form. . . . For only carefully consider, after God hath breathed upon the face of man the breath of life, and man had consequently become a living soul, surely that breath must have passed through the face at once into the interior structure, and have spread itself throughout all the spaces of the body; and as soon as by the divine inspiration it had become condensed, it must have impressed itself on each internal feature, which the condensation had filled in, and so have been, as it were, congealed in shape. . . . This is the inner man, different from the outer, but yet one in the twofold condition. . . . Thus it happens that the rich man in hell has a tongue, and poor [Lazarus] a finger, and Abraham a bosom.[41]

Here, in this remarkable passage from the late second or early third century, we have the germ that will produce recognizable images of the souls of individuals as they leave the body at death and pass to eternal joy or torment.

Moreover, Tertullian believes that souls are passed on from parent to child by a process he calls 'traducianism'. Since souls are material, the germ of the soul can be passed on in the father's sperm just as the body is. Further, the soul, like the body, has a sex, and receives it simultaneously with the body in the womb: 'The soul, being sown in the womb at the same time as the body, receives likewise along with it its sex; and this indeed so simultaneously, that neither of the two substances can be alone regarded as the cause of the sex' (*De Anima*, xxxvi, II, 497). The theory of traducianism also neatly deals with the transmission of original sin (the sin that Christians believed all people shared as a result of Adam's 'original' sin in the Garden of Eden); the sins of the fathers are visited on the children in the most literal fashion.

The problem with Tertullian's theory is that, while it provides an admirable explanation for the weakness and temptation the soul finds in this life, it is difficult to reconcile with the immortality of the soul. Tertullian *says* that the soul is immortal, but the emphasis on its corporeality makes this difficult to sustain.

In contrast, Origen (*c.* 185–*c.* 254) has a much more Platonic view of the soul's nature and origin. But some of his ideas take him well outside the bounds of Christian orthodoxy. His God, in a very Neoplatonic fashion, has created the world from eternity and out of necessity. The Logos or Word is the intermediary, proceeding from God, which actually fashions all created things.[42] Souls pre-exist as spirits, equal to the spirits of the angels, and their descent into the body is explained by evil deeds in a previous life. (This sounds very much like a reworking of the ideas we have found in the *Phaedrus* or the Myth of Er at the end of the *Republic*.) Thus embodiment is a fall, and the body a prison from which the soul longs to be released. Like Philo, and in contrast to Tertullian, he believes that the 'coats of skins' given to Adam and Eve were bodies. Now bodily appetites form the raw material of sinful impulses, though in themselves they are morally neutral. Eventually all souls, even demons, will, through the purification that comes from suffering, arrive at union with God – a view which, while comfortingly optimistic, denies the orthodox view of hell and eternal punishment.

Despite Origen's emphasis on the spirituality of the soul, pre-existent and created pure, he still attaches to it what he calls an 'ethereal body'. Thus the soul remains in some way visible, and imaginable, though there is still a vast difference between this and the soul as Tertullian conceives it. Origen's soul *has* an ethereal body, yet remains quite distinct from it; Tertullian's soul is so bound up with body, so dependent on it for its origins, that his assertions about its spirituality ring rather hollow. In both cases, however, we see the fundamental need to visualize at work. The abstract and conceptual must be clothed in visible garments.

THE SYRIAC HYMN OF THE SOUL

A literary example of early Christian (or in this case Gnostic) ideas concerning the soul is found in an ancient hymn written in Syriac (probably second to fourth century, though the manuscript in which it is to be found is tenth century), and interpolated into 'The Acts of Judas Thomas the Apostle'.[43] The sentiments are scarcely orthodox, but they represent an important strand of thought that exalted the soul at the expense of the body. Here the soul, a little child, is stripped of his bright robe and his purple toga (the celestial body), and prepared for a journey to Egypt to find one pearl guarded by a serpent in the midst of the sea. (The choice of Egypt as the country to which the soul is sent has Old Testament overtones of slavery and bondage.) Two messengers accompany the soul, because the way is dangerous. When the soul reaches Egypt, his companions leave him, and he goes to stay near the dwelling of the serpent to accomplish his mission. But then, 'single and alone', he encounters a youth, 'fair and well-favoured', who becomes his intimate. After this he puts on the garments of the Egyptians (an earthly body), and forgets about the reason for which he has descended.

> I forgot that I was a son of kings,
> And I served their king;
> And I forgot the pearl,
> For which my parents had sent me.[44]

His parents grieve, and call all the nobles of their kingdom together to write him a letter, urging him to remember the bright robe and glorious toga he used to wear and to gain the pearl so that he can return.

The letter achieves its purpose.

And according to what was traced on my heart
Were the words of my letter written.
I remembered that I was a son of kings,
And my free soul longed for its natural state.
I remembered the pearl,
For which I had been sent to Egypt.[45]

The soul hushes the serpent into sleep and snatches away the pearls. He returns to his father's house, putting off the 'filthy and unclean garb' of the Egyptians, and returns to heaven where his bright robe and toga are waiting. This garment seems to him 'like a mirror of myself':

For we were two in distinction
And yet one in one likeness.

(78a, b, p. 27)

Similarly, all the gold and jewels with which the robe is decorated recall him to his true nature. 'Again I saw that all over it [the garment] | The motions of knowledge were stirring' (88a, b, p. 29),

And I stretched forth and received it,
With the beauty of its colours I adorned myself.

(96a, b, p. 29)

Then he is received by his father, the King of kings, because he had fulfilled his mission and brought back the pearl.

This allegory of the soul's sojourn on earth ties in with the doctrine of the pre-existence of the soul and the idea of reminiscence present in Origen and earlier in Plato. The soul is perfect and glorious when it descends to earth, though it must cast aside its heavenly body in order to do so. (The idea of the glorious, spiritual body is also present in Origen.) The sojourn on earth is for a defined task, a difficult test that will prove what it is worth. It begins to falter in its quest when it puts on the earthly body, here described as the garb of the Egyptians, the people among whom it has come to dwell. But then it remembers what it was, its heavenly origin and divine mission (surely the letter is simply an objectification of its own divinely inspired memory), and it is recalled, in the most literal sense, to its original purpose. On its return to heaven, it again *remembers* its former glory, and its sense of identity is bound up with the recovery of the glorious robe, the heavenly body. The soul's time on earth is a brief probation surrounded by two periods – the second supposedly eternal – of heavenly bliss.

The other point worth noting, in the light of the premise of the next chapter, is that the soul here is masculine, not feminine: 'I remembered that I was a son of kings' (56a). The important point that appears to lead to this sexual identity is that he is the heir, the child whose success and survival is most to be desired.

SAINT AUGUSTINE

Like many of his Christian predecessors, Augustine (354–430) was torn between the seductions of classical philosophy, in his case Platonism, and the orthodoxies of Christianity. He has little to say about the appearance of the soul, but much to say about its nature and therefore the role it will play in the drama of human life and death.

First he affirms the spirituality of the human soul and its creation directly by God out of nothing. Like the universe itself, it is created by God's free act, not out of necessity as Plotinus and his followers claim. This soul is immaterial and substantial. It is one, not divided into two or three parts as the Aristotelians claim. Neither is it linked to the body as the shaping form is to matter. It is immortal (he uses the argument of the *Phaedo* that since the soul is the principle of life and two contraries, such as life and death, cannot exist in the same substance, it must be immortal), though he is careful to avoid making it wholly independent of God, a self-existent principle. Its immortality is, in the end, dependent on God. Man is not in his entirety a rational animal, but a rational soul using a body. The body is a prison for it.

Against these Platonic notions asserting the superiority of the soul to the body there is another strain in Augustine's writings, inspired by Christian doctrine and specifically by his desire to refute the heresy of the Manichaeans, who believed matter was a separate evil

41

principle, and to whose sect he at one time belonged. Speaking in this vein, Augustine says the soul has a natural inclination to live in a body. Body is not a stranger to man; it is the man himself. If creation is the work of God and God made the body as well as the soul, how can the body be an instrument of punishment for man?[46] The answer to this is that when Adam and Eve sinned they not only became vulnerable to further actual sin themselves, but infected all their descendants with the propensity to sin. It is therefore from the time of this Fall that body became corruptible and warred against the spirit. Yet it is not the body that is responsible for the Fall, as the Platonists held. Since the soul is indivisible, and the will and passions all belong to it, the first sin must have come from the soul, not the body. 'The corruptible flesh made not the soul to sin, but the sinning soul made the flesh corruptible.'[47]

Still questions remain. How does the soul come to sin? Why is it put in a body at all? Since the soul is immaterial, Augustine cannot accept the literal traducianism of Tertullian, which states that it is generated in a physical way with the body. He also rejects Origen's notion of the soul's sinning in a pre-existent state. What he arrives at in the end is an ingenious form of spiritual traducianism. The immaterial soul is still passed from the soul of the parent to the child through the act of generation. And since the souls of the parents are already corrupted by original and actual sin this sin, in a spiritual way, is transmitted through the generations.

This stand on the transmission of sin was open to misinterpretation. The sexual act by which sin was transmitted came, by association, to be seen as sinful in itself. Passages from Augustine's writings seemed to confirm this idea. He refers to 'lust' as being commonly understood as 'the unclean motion of the generative parts. For this holds sway in the whole body . . . with such a mixture of mental emotion and carnal appetite that . . . it overwhelms almost all the light and power of cogitation. . . . The motion will be sometimes importunate against the will.'[48] This last implies a moral struggle within man in which body and soul are pitted against one another. It is easy to see how Augustine, despite his many protestations to the contrary, came to be seen as 'against the body', and in

42

particular against sexual lust. In fact this is a caricature of his position, which was actually much more balanced. But it is a caricature that had its effect on later ideas about and images of the soul and its relationship to the body.

SAINT THOMAS AQUINAS

If Saint Augustine was temperamentally a Platonist, Saint Thomas (*c.* 1225–74) was an Aristotelian and took Aristotle's philosophy as the starting point for his own thought. Again, there is little here to engage us imaginatively, but the theology is behind many later imaginary conceptions of the soul.

Soul is the form of the body; indeed, it is soul that makes a body a body. A corpse is not a body. He is thoroughly against the stance of those like Origen who would see the body as created to imprison the soul. Union with a body is essential to the soul and characteristic of its nature. Matter is good and created by God. Also, in contrast to Plato, he claims the lower faculties such as feeling do not belong to the soul alone but to soul and body together. Therefore man is not just a soul making use of a body as an instrument, he is genuinely a composite of body and soul.

It might seem that Aquinas, by following Aristotle's emphasis on the whole man rather than on one element of it, had established a position much more compatible with orthodox Christianity than the dualism of Augustine. But there were pitfalls in Aquinas' position as well. By wedding soul so closely to body, how could he assert that it was separable from body and immortal? It is here that Aristotle's distinction between soul and *nous* comes to his rescue. Whatever Aristotle meant by *nous*, it is unlikely that he had in mind anything like the Christian soul. But the very vagueness and brevity of his discussion of it ('this alone is immortal') meant that it could be adapted to the uses of Christian theologians. Aquinas takes over the immortality of the *nous* from Aristotle, and adds to it the idea of individuality that is by no means certainly present in Aristotle.

This individual soul, during life, is a unity, but it is not just the immortal *nous*. Again as in Aristotle, it contains the different faculties of the sensitive and appetitive souls, the will as well as the intellect. Among these faculties there should be a proper sense of hierarchy and government. The intellect moves the will and the will moves the lower parts of the soul. Thus the lower parts of the soul (the appetitive) are subject to intellect and reason – or at least in an ideal scenario they are. But Aquinas acknowledges that the sensitive appetite within the soul 'has something of its own, by virtue whereof it can resist the commands of reason'. The sensitive appetite is moved not only by intellect but also by the imagination and sense. In this way we can 'feel or imagine something pleasant, which reason forbids, or unpleasant, which reason commands'.[49] But while external things can move us to sin, they can never be the sufficient cause. Only will, because it is what makes an act voluntary, can be that.[50] And our will is fallible, because although it necessarily seeks happiness, it may not perceive clearly what this is. Thus we can make bad choices through ignorance or misunderstanding. (This, of course, is very close to Aristotle's own explanation for bad conduct.) Even reason may be swayed by passion to judge in a particular instance against the knowledge it has in general.[51] In all this we have the stage set for the dramatic conflict within the soul and between soul and body that produced dialogues, debates and dramas of later ages.

All this is the result of original sin. Before the Fall man's passions were firmly under the control of reason, and his understanding was unclouded. So how does Aquinas account for the transmission of this sin to all of Adam's descendants? To say that embodiment contaminated the soul, as Origen did, would go against his view that embodiment was natural to the soul and his assertion that both were created together on the sixth day. The traducianism of Tertullian that had the soul conceived and born with the body was much too crude and literal. Aquinas' view is that Adam is a kind of first mover, who inclines all his descendants to sin. But, interestingly, this inclination to sin is passed on from the father only. This notion derives from the Aristotelian view that it is the father who provides the active principle of generation, that is the soul, while the mother contributes only matter, or the body. Therefore, Aquinas asserts, if Eve alone and not Adam had sinned their children would not have contracted original sin![52] This eccentric theology bears fruit in the analogies between husband and wife, soul and body, where it is always the man who is portrayed as the active soul and the wife the passive body.

Finally, Aquinas follows Aristotle in claiming that in this life the soul cannot understand without a phantasm – that is, a picture, real or imaginary. We cannot form a judgment while our senses are suspended, because it is through our senses that things are known by us. The embodied soul gains knowledge of material things by abstracting from the information given it by the senses. As for immaterial things, these cannot really be known in our present state, though after death, when the soul is separated from the body, this is possible.[53] So, while he certainly did not believe the soul to be in any way corporeal, and spoke scornfully of 'the philosophers of old' who believed only bodies were real and therefore the soul must be something corporeal, it seems likely that Aquinas would have defended, for the purposes of our limited perception in this life, the idea of the imaginable soul.

SUMMARY

In this outline history of the idea of the soul we have passed through several great cultures over two millennia. What I have tried to show is where and how some of the ideas we shall find in the literature and pictures discussed in later chapters came to exist. We have moved from the flitting, anonymous souls of the dead in Homer, through the separable and immortal souls of the Dionysian and Orphic cults, to the personal soul of Plato and Aristotle. In Plato we meet quite sophisticated concerns about the soul – how and why it is joined to a body, whether it is simple or composed of various parts, how it comes to know, and what happens to it after death. Aristotle looks at many of the same questions, but from a very different perspective. Chiefly he wants to know how the soul operates in life, how it organizes experience. But by separating the intellectual soul, *nous*, from the lower faculties, he provides a system that can, with some ingenious adaptation, be taken over by Christian philosophers.

Christianity, despite its roots in the physicality of Judaism, absorbed many of the Greek ideas concerning the soul such as its incorporeality and immortality. But for Christian philosophers there are additional questions, chiefly moral ones. Even in Plato we found a concern as to why the soul did not always act according to its highest principles. This, in Christianity, translated into questions about both actual sin and original sin. How is the latter passed on through the generations? Indeed, how does the soul itself come to be in the body at all? Is the union of the two a good thing, or is it a result of original sin and the cause of actual sin?

In all these thinkers and their various ways of reflecting on the soul, one thing is fairly constant: however much they assert the immateriality of the soul as a philosophical principle, they continue to refer to it in images. Sometimes these are fairly literal, as when it resembles the body of the deceased; at others they seize on one aspect of it, such as its ability to fly far above the body, when it may be seen as a bird or a butterfly. At still other times they think of it in relation to something else such as the body, and then the image is controlled by the relationship, as when it is seen as a hand using an instrument or the captain of a ship. The remainder of this book will look at these varying images of the soul, and attempt to understand not only what they tell us about the soul, but what they tell us about ourselves.

TWO

The Soul as a Beautiful Woman

O most beautiful soul, how blessed is he who beholds you.
Dante to Beatrice, in the Vita Nuova

When the soul comes to men, it most usually appears in the guise of a beautiful woman. The word 'soul' itself is feminine in Greek, Latin and all romance languages, German, and even Arabic. It is impossible to be certain which came first, the picture or the gendered word, whether the language influenced the image or the image the language. What is certain is that in the end the two reinforced one another, and the image of the soul on its own became predominantly feminine. This feminine soul may reveal herself as a rather remote figure, awe-inspiring in her beauty and purity. Or she may retain elements of the earthly feminine, seductive and approachable, but still refined beyond the merely sexual. She comes in multiple roles – to inspire, advise, reproach, condemn.

I should make it clear that I am not using the word 'men' in the inclusive sense; the feminine soul comes to *men*. They painted the pictures and wrote the texts. And they did this long before Jung attempted to explain *why* they did it – though that does not mean Jung does not have some insight into why the soul should be conceived of as feminine.

Jung would probably see the feminine figure of the soul as pre-dating language altogether. He claims that the soul or *anima* is a universal archetype, embedded within the unconscious of every human being, the internal element of an individual that is the counterpart of the *persona*, which is the external, role-playing part. Three factors, according to him, go to make up the image of the feminine soul in man. The first is that woman (mother and wife) is the most immediate environmental influence on man. She has, so he

47

asserts, a psychology that is very different from that of man and as such she 'can be his inspiration'.[1] Secondly, there is within the man himself an element of the feminine, the *anima*, the inner self that contrasts with the outer, public self, which is the *persona*. If the *persona* is masculine, then the *anima* will be its opposite, that is, feminine. 'Whenever she appears, in dreams, visions, and fantasies, she takes on a personified form, thus demonstrating that the factor she embodies possesses all the outstanding characteristics of a feminine being. She is not an invention of the conscious, but a spontaneous product of the unconscious.'[2] Thirdly, this soul or *anima* is a universal archetype, embedded within the unconscious of every human being. This third factor is the most important; it is not the influence of the mother and wife that makes the image of the feminine so powerful, but the archetype of the *anima* that gives power to the mother and wife. 'An inherited collective image of woman exists in a man's unconscious, with the help of which he apprehends the nature of woman.'[3] And in an essay on marriage, he again declares, 'Every man carries within him the eternal image of woman; not the image of this or that particular woman, but a definitive feminine image.'[4] Needless to say, the woman, according to Jung, is endowed with an *animus*, the male counterpart of her femininity, but this is not explored in the same detail. So why is the soul portrayed as feminine? Because men wrote the books; men painted the pictures.

Still this is not the whole story. Quite independently of Jung's theories, there are very ancient reasons why the female became associated with soul. In primitive societies, before men quite understood the role they performed in conception, women were frequently seen as soul-bearers, the source of new life, and also the recipients of the souls of the dead, from which new life would, in turn, spring. 'This concept of woman is the first concrete human representation of the soul or supreme totem that receives the dead and animates the children with their spirit. Her role as the first human totem representative . . . explains her importance in matriarchal social structure, later expressed in the mother-goddess cult.'[5] Thus the feminine is at the very heart of the mysteries of life and death, a figure standing between the human and the divine. This feminine soul, which appears first in myth and legend, comes persistently to dominate our idea of the soul in art and literature.

PSYCHE

In the previous chapter the word *psyche* was used to refer to the soul in general. But Psyche was also a particular mythological being in Greek culture with her own character and her own story.

The notion of a beautiful girl with wings as a visual image of the soul has a long history. We have already seen that the soul (or elements of the soul) is portrayed as winged in Plato's *Phaedrus*. While the initial image there is of two horses driving a chariot, later in the dialogue we find the soul that strives towards heavenly beauty described as both winged and feminine. A gold earring from this period, now in the Boston Museum, shows a chariot being drawn upwards by a winged female figure, and it has been argued that this is none other than Psyche.[6] In this image she has bird wings, but later, by the third century BC, she commonly has butterfly wings. This is not surprising, since some of the earliest Greek images of the soul in Hades that we have encountered were of flitting creatures with insect-like wings.

Later the butterfly specifically becomes a symbol of the soul. In Roman times, for example, we find a butterfly held in the hand of a skeleton and inscribed *psyche* in relief on a silver cup excavated from Boscoreale at the foot of Mount Vesuvius.[7] And much later still, in the sixteenth century, a painting by Dosso Dossi shows Jupiter, accompanied by Mercury and Virtus, creating souls as butterflies by painting them! (The idea that one can create reality through artistry is almost certainly a Renaissance idea, taken over and magnified later still by the Romantics.)

The mythological Psyche we know today is the one whose story is recounted by Apuleius, and dates not from early Greek times but from the second century AD. This is the Psyche whose fate is indissolubly linked with that of Eros, the god of Love. But while the details of the story come to us through Apuleius, there is good evidence that the intimate relationship between Psyche and Eros long predates that time. As early as the late fifth or early fourth century BC (roughly contemporary with Plato), we find a terracotta relief showing Eros with his arms around Psyche drawing a *biga* (small chariot) holding Aphrodite.[8] From this time onwards there are numerous bronze reliefs and statues of the pair, most commonly embracing. Love and the soul form a pair, united.

Apuleius' story of Psyche and Eros is found as a separate tale within his work *The Golden Ass*, where it is used to entertain a young bride who has been taken captive by bandits. Psyche here is a mortal, but one endowed with supernatural beauty. She is the youngest of three sisters, and far outshines the two elder. Initially, this seems to be a curse rather than a blessing. Her sisters marry well, but no one wishes to marry the beautiful Psyche. So great is her beauty that people stop worshipping at the shrine of Aphrodite, and transfer their affection to Psyche instead. Naturally, this makes the jealous Aphrodite furious.

In despair, her father decides to consult the oracle of Apollo, where his worst fears are confirmed. He is told that Psyche is to be taken, dressed as for a funeral, to the top of a mountain and left there where her husband, a serpent, will claim her. It is of course Aphrodite, jealous of her earthly rival, who has decreed this terrible fate, so there is no appeal.

The funereal wedding takes place, but afterwards, as she is left alone on the cliff edge, instead of a serpent, a friendly wind carries her from the mountain top to a rich valley. There in a wood is a royal palace. There is food and wine and heavenly music as well – all for her.

At night, when she has gone to bed, a mysterious lover joins her. She cannot see him in the dark, and he leaves her before sunrise, refusing to reveal his identity. These visits continue for some time as Psyche continues to live in the beautiful palace. Eventually her sisters wish to come and visit her. The lover warns her not to see them, but Psyche longs for human company and persuades him to allow them to come. The one condition he insists upon is that she must reveal nothing about her lover. If she tells them about him or seeks to see him she will lose him forever. Also, their child, with whom she is now pregnant, will be mortal instead of a god.

The sisters visit three times, and on the last visit, having surmised that Psyche has never seen the person who comes to her in the night, they suggest that he really is the serpent or beast to whom Apollo prophesied she would be given. Terrified, Psyche resolves to disobey and look upon her love. That night when he is asleep she lights a lamp and sees, to her delight and horror, that he is the beautiful god Eros. When she accidentally drops some of the hot oil from the lamp on his shoulder, he awakens and knows her treachery. He tells her that he disobeyed his mother, Aphrodite, by taking her as his own instead of making her love someone worthless. Now she will lose him forever.

When Eros flies away, Psyche, in despair, attempts to drown herself in a river, but the river will not allow this and washes her ashore. She then plots the deaths of her sisters by telling each in turn that Eros now loves her. When the sisters attempt to repeat Psyche's feat by giving themselves to the wind from the top of the cliff they fall and are killed. But this does not help Psyche, who is now brought before Aphrodite for punishment. Aphrodite assigns her four seemingly impossible tasks, the last of which is to descend to Hades to obtain Persephone's beauty ointment. Miraculously, and with assistance from various natural objects and animals, Psyche fulfils all the tasks. But on the way back from Hades with the ointment, she again disobeys instructions and decides to look in the jar. Having done this, she falls into a deep sleep. Eros finds and saves her, and she is finally able to satisfy Aphrodite by giving her the ointment and completing all the tasks. With great pomp and ceremony, Eros and Psyche are married among the gods, to whose number Psyche is exalted. The child born to them is also a god, called Voluptas, or Joy.

This is a rich and complex myth. Many things can be read into it, and most have. It is a story about a mortal who aspires to look on a god; it is about disobedience; it is about a mother-in-law's jealousy; it is about sibling rivalry; it is about having to pass a series of impossible tests before attaining happiness; it is about (according to one prominent modern commentator)[9] the development of the feminine, the insistence of loving a known person rather than an anonymous being. It is about all these things and many more.[10]

What has this Psyche, this exceptionally beautiful girl who is beloved of Eros and after many trials becomes a god, to do with the 'psyche' or soul that her name proclaims her to be?

The oldest allegorical account of the Psyche myth is alleged to come from Saint Fulgentius, who was bishop of Ruspe in what is now Tunisia in the early sixth century, but the attribution is uncertain. Whoever he was, the sixth-century commentator's work is an ingenious but not wholly successful attempt to make the entire story symbolic. The parents of Psyche are God and matter, and the three daughters are the flesh, free will, and soul or spirit. Psyche, soul, is the youngest, because soul is added to the human being after the flesh is formed. She is also the most beautiful, because soul is superior to flesh and will. Aphrodite (or Venus) is lust, and Eros (or Cupid) is desire whom she sends to destroy Psyche. But Eros falls in love with Psyche instead, because desire or greed can be attracted to good and evil alike. Eros does not wish Psyche to learn the pleasure of desire, but her sisters, flesh and will, urge her to look on and recognize it. When she does so, the hot oil that burns Eros signifies the inflaming power of lust. Once Psyche has given in to this temptation, she is no longer pure and must be punished.

At this point Fulgentius breaks off, saying, 'If anyone reads this story in Apuleius he will find other details of my explanation which I have not gone into.'[11] And indeed they may! This is an interpretation that in the end would unite the soul with Greed or Cupidity, with Lust for a mother-in-law. How, from this union, could come the child Joy? Despite its manifold defects, this allegorization of the Psyche myth enjoyed an amazingly long and wide currency, such that Mr Lockman, who translated La Fontaine's French versification of the myth in 1744, knew and comments on it: 'This seems ingenious. 'Tis well known that the Ancients wrote frequently in Allegories; but the Explication sometimes given of them seem no less whimsical, than those of the Vulgar, with regard to the strange Figures perceiv'd by them (as they imagine) in an *Aurora Borealis*.'[12]

A much later, and more Platonic, interpretation comes from the nineteenth-century German scholar Hildebrand who edited *The Golden Ass*. According to his interpretation, Psyche is pure soul as it comes down from heaven, Eros is heavenly love, and Aphrodite is fate 'who sends base desires and envy in the form of Psyche's sisters to remove Psyche from her . . . high place'.[13] Tempted, Psyche falls, but her whole desire remains to be united to heavenly love, and this at length she attains. This interpretation fits with the feminine soul in the *Phaedrus* that strives constantly to look on divine love. 'At last she does behold him, and lets the flood pour in upon her, releasing the imprisoned waters; then has she refreshment and respite from her stings and sufferings, and at that moment tastes a pleasure that is sweet beyond compare. . . . Above all others does she esteem her beloved in his beauty; mother, brother, friends, she forgets them all.'[14]

This striving of the soul to be united to heavenly love is surely the chief significance of the ubiquitous pictures and statues of Psyche and Eros embracing. However, images of the two in an embrace go back at least to the fourth century BC, long predating the tale of Apuleius, and the best evidence is that their symbolic significance as well is therefore rooted in classical antiquity. When images of the two appear on the lids of tombs, the symbolism of Psyche as soul surviving death becomes even more explicit. The lid of a garland sarcophagus found in Tarsus shows two scenes of Eros and Psyche: in one Eros is aiming his bow at Psyche, who is prostrate before him, and in another the couple are in the familiar embrace. 'Two different senses of Eros thus appear: first the daemon, Love, releases the soul from the miseries of earthly life; then the union of Psyche with Eros is used as an emblem of salvation, of the joining of the soul to God.'[15] Just as Psyche represents the soul on tombs, so she also features in creation scenes on two sarcophagi, one in Naples and one in the Vatican. In these scenes, however, she is shown making a gesture of reluctance; the soul at creation is not eager to enter the body.[16]

The relationship between Psyche and Love, and Psyche's reluctance to be embodied, connect perfectly with what we have learned of the Platonic and Neoplatonic ideas about the soul. 'The soul in its nature loves God and longs to be at one with Him in the noble love of a daughter for a noble father, but coming to human birth and lured by the courtships of this sphere, she takes up with another love, a mortal, leaves her father, and falls.'[17] Plotinus also specifically links the Psyche and Eros story to the love that is innate in the soul. 'That our good is There [in God, the fount of Good] is shown by the very love inborn with the soul; hence the constant linking of the Love-God with the Psyches in story and picture; the soul, other than God but sprung out of Him, must needs love.'[18]

While these concepts originated in the pagan world, they were sufficiently compatible with the Christian view of the soul and its relationship to heavenly love that they could be readily taken over by the new faith. As early as the second century AD we find a painting of a beautiful female with her arms outstretched on the ceiling of the crypt of Lucina. Such figures also appear on the tombs of both men and women, dispelling any notion that they are idealized portraits of the person in the tomb. Rather this *orante*, the female figure in the attitude of prayer, is the soul itself, freed from its body.[19] At about the same time, pictures of Psyche and Eros appear on Christian sarcophagi in combination with specifically Christian motifs, such as that of the Good Shepherd. Thus, the visual image of the soul as a beautiful woman quickly moves into the mainstream of the Christian imagination.

THE ASCETIC FEMALE SOUL

The Psyche of the Apuleius myth is not by any means the only representation of the soul as a beautiful woman. There is something at once touching and vulnerable about Psyche, something quite human, that speaks perhaps of her classical origins. Medieval Christianity tended to see women not in this ambiguous way but in terms of extremes – either angel or temptress, Mary or Eve. At the heart of woman there was something fundamentally unknowable. This essential 'unknowability' is played out in the many stories in which women are 'unmasked' and shown to be quite different from their outward appearance. In *Sir Gawain and the Green Knight*, Sir Gawain, meeting two contrasting women, denigrates the older and uglier of the two, who is later revealed to be his aunt, Morgan le Fay.[20] And it was, perhaps, this unknowability that resulted in woman's simplification into two opposing types: beautiful or ugly, good or evil. Thus when the

I 'The City of the Soul' (see pp. 59, 61). Illustration from a medieval manuscript in Musée Condé, Chantilly, France, MS 137/1687, fol. 182v. (*The Bridgeman Art Library*)

II Boethius and Philosophia with the Muses (see pp. 57–9). From Harleian MS 4339 fol. 2. *(British Library)*

III 'Sybilla Palmifera', by Dante Gabriel Rossetti (note the butterflies above her left shoulder). *(Lady Lever Art Gallery, Port Sunlight, Merseyside/The Bridgeman Art Library)*

IV *I Lock my Door upon Myself*, by Fernand Khnopff (see p. 79). *(Munich, Neue Pinakothek/ Artothek)*

V *The Lady of Shallot*, by William Holman Hunt (see pp. 79–80). *(Manchester Art Gallery/ The Bridgeman Art Library)*

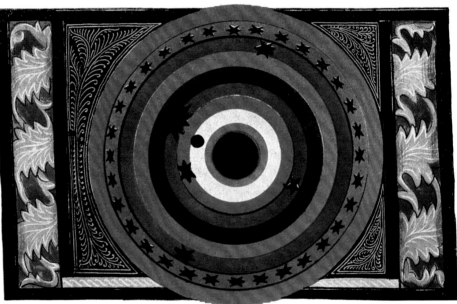

VI An illustration showing the seven planetary spheres, the sphere of the fixed stars, and the outer sphere, the *primum mobile*; above a soul is weighed in the balance (see pp. 96–8, 150). From Guillaume de Deguileville's *Pylgremage of the Sowle*. *(Cambridge University Library)*

VII *The Annunciation*, by Fra Angelico; rays of light, emanating from a dove, stream towards Mary's ear (see p. 138). *(Museo del Prado, Madrid/Art Resource)*

VIII Separation of the soul and body (see pp. 160–1). From the *Rohan Book of Hours*,
MS Latin 9471, fol. 159. *(Bibliothèque Nationale de France)*

IX Crucifixion scene, Christ between the two thieves. An angel takes the soul of the good thief, while that of the evil thief is seized by a devil. From the *Rohan Book of Hours*, MS Latin 9471, fol. 29. *(Bibliothèque Nationale de France)*

X The Resurrection of the Dead. From the *Rohan Book of Hours*, MS Latin 9471, fol. 194.
Cf. *The Resurrection, Cookham*, Plate 43. *(Bibliothèque Nationale de France/The Bridgeman Art Library)*

XI *The Death of Federigo da Montefeltro, Duke of Urbino*, by Gabriele Smargiassi (1798–1882) (see pp. 161–2). *(Galleria d'Arte Moderna, Florence/The Bridgeman Art Library)*

XII Souls traverse a narrow and perilous bridge on their journey to bliss or torment (see pp. 174–5). *(Art Resource)*

XIII *The Last Judgment*, by Fra Angelico (see pp. 185–6). *(San Marco/Scala)*

XIV *The Garden of Earthly Delights*, by Hieronymous Bosch (see pp. 188–90). *(Museo del Prado, Madrid/The Bridgeman Art Library)*

XV Golden rays of the sun illuminate a crowd of naked bodies newly risen from their tombs (see p. 192). From Paolo di Giovanni's illustrations to Dante's *La Divina Commedia*, *c*. 1450. British Library MS Yates Thompson 36, fol. 183. *(British Library)*

XVI Sparks of light, represented as playful souls, swimming and diving in the river of light in Paradise (see p. 192). From Paolo di Giovanni's illustrations to Dante's *La Divina Commedia*, *c*. 1450. British Library MS Yates Thompson 36, fol. 154. *(British Library)*

XVII Hellmouth. British Museum MS Cotton Nero C.IV, fol. 39r. *(British Museum)*

soul appeared to men in the guise of inspirer or guide, it was as an infallible, perfect creation that she manifested herself.

The Soul of Hildebert of Lavardin

Hildebert of Lavardin (1056–1133), Archbishop of Tours, records a remarkable encounter – whether real or imaginary it is difficult to determine – with just such a soul in 'De Querimonia et Conflictu Carnis et Spiritus seu Animae' ('Of the Complaint and Conflict of the Flesh and Spirit or Soul'). At the beginning of the piece (which runs to fifteen columns of tightly packed Latin in Migne's *Patrologia Latina*), Hildebert begins by telling us that his house was destroyed by fire and he became totally occupied rebuilding it. (Again whether this is literally his house or a metaphor for his concern with bodily things is uncertain.) What *is* certain is that his preoccupation with worldly affairs has caused him to neglect his priestly duties.

Suddenly a female figure wearing mourning clothes appears before him. He claims that this figure is paradoxically both impossible to describe, of unknown size, and yet amazingly life-like. She has a great facility for changing expression, and looks down on the earth with sadness and up to the heavens, for which she seems to yearn, with joy. She is whiter than the first snow, decked out with royal accoutrements. But then she changes, and he sees her in mourning garments that need to be cleansed. In her hands is a book, which contains the words: 'Whether you rejoice or grieve, desire or fear, what is the difference?'

Hildebert is understandably perplexed, 'stupefied'. The words in the strange lady's book challenge Hildebert's preoccupation with the things of this world, assert that happiness here should be a matter of indifference. The figure goes on to chastise him, saying: 'I am amazed that you have so forgotten me, and are so forgetful of our long comradeship that you have provided no lodging for me, have not recognized me to be a guest, and have forgotten what I taught you in the words of the apostle: "Here we have no abiding city."' While Hildebert has been building his house, *her* house (which is, of course, Hildebert's body, though he does not know this yet) has been letting her down badly, deceiving her and seducing her with the pleasures of the flesh.

Like any man faced with a troublesome and hysterical woman, Hildebert tries to ignore her and get on with his affairs. But after a while he becomes more curious about this peculiar guest, and puts off his other visitors to talk to her. At first he suffers more berating – why has he not paid attention to her, and prepared a proper guest's lodging for her? To live without her is to live the life of a beast. 'I know your thoughts,' she tells him, 'and the inmost secrets of your heart. If you write, I move the instruments. If you speak, I open your mouth.' At last Hildebert recognizes that it is his own soul who is addressing him.

The chief burden of the Soul's message is that Hildebert has allowed the body or flesh to dominate his life and actions, and has ignored the desires of herself, the Soul. This is not a fault peculiar to him, but is one innate in man since Adam and Eve first sinned. Once pleasure has triumphed over a man, though experience counsels him to do otherwise, his appetite will grow unbridled. The only cure lies within himself. 'If you close your eyes to the poison of pleasure, and control your faults, you will be saved,' she tells him.[21]

The Soul then, in poetry, describes the functions of the human soul in general. Its first activity is existence itself; then comes feeling; thirdly, art; fourth, correction or regulation of life; fifth, virtue; sixth, contemplation; and seventh and highest of all, peace or union with God, an experience beyond sense and understanding. The lower faculties (here the soul becomes an Aristotelian) are shared with the animal kingdom, but the higher belong to man alone. The flesh loves the lower stages of the life of the soul, but it is the duty of man to resist this if he is to attain the highest stage, union with God. The piece ends with the Soul still warning of the dangers of giving in to the desires of the body. The dramatic framework at the beginning in which the Soul appears is not closed at the end by her departure.

Several things strike the reader about this piece. Firstly, there is the extreme asceticism of its tone. Worldly pleasures are not merely to be made subordinate to spiritual, but to be shunned altogether. This connects it with a particular strain of medieval Christianity that emphasized mortification of the body and abstinence in all things – not just sexual.

Secondly, there is the identification of body with flesh, and soul with spirit that runs throughout the soul's complaint. The very title makes this clear: it is the 'conflict of the flesh and spirit *or* soul', so that spirit and soul are apparently in apposition. Flesh and spirit are used commonly in the New Testament in a figurative sense, to indicate two different ways of life, the worldly and the godly – hence the passage in Galatians 5:17, quoted by Hildebert, in which St Paul speaks of the flesh fighting against the spirit and the spirit against the flesh. What happens here is that body becomes identified with 'flesh', and consequently seen as opposed to spirit. Thus the desires of the physical body, which might be seen as morally neutral, become tainted with the desires of the 'flesh', used in a figurative sense to stand for evil. We shall see the effects of this identification in greater detail in the next chapter.

Thirdly, the beautiful woman who appears to Hildebert *seems* on one level to be an external agent, but is actually a part of himself, his own soul. So what we have here is the externalization of an essentially internal conflict.

Finally, the narrative exists on a plane somewhere between realism and revelation. We begin with the practical details of Hildebert's preoccupation with the rebuilding of his house, and the sudden appearance of the woman, though unusual, initially seems to fit into this realistic landscape. But once she is recognized as the soul, her coming takes on some of the elements of a supernatural revelation. Hildebert accepts without question her authority and the fact that she is divinely sent. This aspect of the story links it to later appearances of the soul that are set unambiguously in a dream or vision – a setting that enhances both their plausibility and their authority.

Boethius and Philosophia

There is a prototype for Hildebert's soul. More than five hundred years earlier a Roman Christian, Boethius (AD 480–524/5), had written a book, *The Consolation of Philosophy*, in which Philosophia, also a beautiful woman, plays much the same role as the soul in 'De Querimonia et Conflictu Carnis et Spiritus Seu Animae'.

Boethius' early life was marked by great success. Born of a noble Roman family, he was distinguished both intellectually and politically, and became consul when only thirty. But the Roman state was then ruled by Theodoric, King of the Ostrogoths, who was an Arian (one who did not believe in the fully human and divine nature of Christ), and in the troubled political and religious climate, Boethius found himself, in AD 523, accused of treason, for which he was later executed. The *Consolation* grew out of his attempt to come to terms with this appalling reversal of fortune.

The *Consolation* begins with a complaint. Poetry (in which this section is written) remains his only pleasure, and the Muses inspire him with the elegiac verses he must write. Not for anything would he give up their company. But his situation is still miserable. Old age has come too early. Fortune, who once smiled on him, has proved deceitful.

As he ponders these things there appears standing above him 'a woman of majestic countenance whose flashing eyes seemed wise beyond the ordinary wisdom of men'. Like Hildebert's Soul, her attributes are somewhat contradictory and can change according to the beholder's perception. Her colour is bright, suggesting youth and vigour, 'yet she seemed so old that she could not be thought of as belonging to our age'.[22] Her stature varies; at times she seems of ordinary human height, at other times she seems to touch the top of the heavens, or even to penetrate heaven itself, beyond human eyes. Her clothes are of delicate cloth and consummate workmanship. But now they are darkened by neglect and age and have been torn as well by the hands of violent men. In her right hand she holds various books, and in her left a sceptre.

This imposing figure glares at the Muses of poetry and asks, 'Who let these whores from the theatre come to the bedside of this sick man?' The Muses (who, as always, are also portrayed as women) cannot nourish or cure a sick man; they offer 'sweet poison' for medicine; they kill reason with passion. She ends by ejecting them: 'Get out, you Sirens; your sweetness leads to death.' In place of them she offers her own Muses.

Boethius, his eyes filled with tears, cannot see who she is, but she sits down at the foot of his bed and begins to administer her comfort. She tells him he is only suffering from lethargy, the common illness of deceived minds, and promises to wipe the dark cloud of mortal things from his eyes. Then he recognizes her as Lady Philosophy, who promises to help him as she has always helped those who love and serve her. The sources of his trouble are within himself, and therefore within her power to help.

Gradually, she convinces him that his plight is not as bad as he believes. He has relied on Fortune, and has been favoured by her, but Fortune is a fickle mistress by her very nature. She shows him the vanity of relying on earthly goods or fame or power for happiness. Such things always engender anxiety because they may be lost at any time. The highest happiness and the supreme good are found in God and *are* God. 'Men become happy by acquiring divinity.' Thus Boethius is removed from despair by attaining an indifference to outward circumstances and an internalization of the Good within himself. Much of this is pure Platonism, though in its indifference to the things of the world there is more than a hint of Stoicism as well. God is assumed to be the Christian God, but nothing in the text makes this explicit.

The similarities between Philosophia and her five-hundred-years younger granddaughter, the Soul of Hildebert, are too obvious to need labouring. In addition to the changing, contradictory aspect, the beautiful but soiled clothes, the complaints about ill-treatment, we have the absolute certainty of their message, and the haughty demeanour of the pure and unapproachable beauty. They come to reproach, guide and comfort all at once. They are both internal and external, and their male visitants respond to them with the respect and reverence they demand.

A manuscript from the late fourteenth century pictures this soul as a medieval lady, pale and remote against her castle door, leaning back and touching her stomach in a typical female pose of the age. The illumination is called 'The City of the Soul', and the lady is surrounded by the pink and beige castle towers which, in their turn, are surrounded by a moat. Enclosed and complete, she stands in meditation or judgment – who can know which?

James Howell's The Vision

One final example of the austere, ascetic soul comes from as late as the seventeenth century. James Howell, who became Royal Historiographer after the Restoration in England in 1661, produced a body and soul dialogue, *The Vision*, ten years earlier when his circumstances were somewhat less happy. At this time, during Cromwell's Commonwealth, he was a royalist prisoner in the Fleet. In this dialogue the framework is that of a vision that comes while the author is lying in bed one night at the time of the summer solstice. At first he sees 'a little airie, or rather an athereal kind of spark [that] did hover up and down about my bodie; It seemed to have a shape yet it had none but a kind of reflexion, it was, me thought, within me, and it was not, but at such a distance, and in that posture, as if it lay Centinel. At last, I found it was my Soul which useth to make sollices in time of sleep, and fetch vagaries abroad, to practise how she can live apart after the dissolution, when she is separated from the bodie and becomes a spirit.'[23] Unlike Hildebert and Boethius, Howell recognizes the 'phantasm' for what it is quite quickly; but only after a time does it take on a distinguishable shape. And that shape is, predictably, feminine. 'Afterwards the fantasma varying, she took a shape, and the nearest resemblance I could make of it, was to a veild Nunn with a flaming cross on the left side of her breast . . . .'

Here is a female soul who is not only pure and chaste but actually a nun – and a rather Catholic one at that, with a flaming cross on her breast! Like her predecessors, she offers advice and counsel, though in a less peremptory way. Like them, she appears at a low point in the author's life. The content of this dialogue, which is long and diffuse, will be discussed briefly in a later chapter. But it is interesting to note that Howell does conclude the dialogue in a more decisive way than either Boethius or Hildebert. At the end, the nun vanishes into him, and diffuses 'Her self through all the cells of my brain, and through the whole mass of blood among the spirits. . . . And now 'twas high time for me to awake, which I did.'[24]

This description of the soul 'diffusing' itself throughout the body is new, and doubtless owes much to both the interest in physiology that was prevalent in the seventeenth century, as well as to the philosophy of Descartes, who sought to explain the interaction of soul and body in a physical and mechanical way. But the essentials remain: the soul is at once internal and external; it is visualized as a pure and authoritative figure; it is feminine.

There was another strain of feminine soul, however, that drew its inspiration from real women and for this reason retained a slight but discernible trace of the erotic.

SPIRITUAL AND EROTIC COMBINED IN THE FEMALE SOUL

Whatever allegorical gloss we put on the Psyche myth, at one level it is about love that is at once spiritual and erotic. 'In this myth we recognize the ensoulment or spiritualising of sex, which began in antiquity, only to be interrupted by the church's separation of these two spheres.'[25]

The erotic and the spiritual came together again in the Middle Ages. Looking back at the picture of the medieval soul in 'The City of the Soul' it is possible to see signs of the erotic as well as the unearthly. Why is she standing in what in most medieval paintings would be seen as a provocative pose? The hand on the stomach normally indicates fertility. Can this be so here? The more one looks at the painting the more ambivalent its message seems. There are clear indications that the lady soul is sister to the women caught up in that most ambivalent of medieval concepts – the idea of courtly love.

It would be difficult to think of any convention of human relationships more curious than those that defined courtly love. At one level it could be seen as simple incitement to adultery. At another it was the worship of beauty in human form that led to worship of the divine in a Platonic manner. The first aspect (the adulterous) was signified by the fact that the female object of the man's adoration was never his own wife but the wife of another man. And the ultimate object of the man's passion (if not the woman's) was the consummation of this love. 'Love is a certain inborn suffering derived from the sight of and excessive meditation upon the beauty of the opposite sex, which causes each one to wish above all things the embraces of the other and by common desire to carry out all of love's precepts in the other's embrace.'[26] At the same time, the erotic was carefully sublimated in both the actions and language of the couple. The woman was not just an object of desire; she was, in a Neoplatonic sense, an idea, a pure intelligence, an angelic abstraction. At the same time she did not cease to be an earthly woman.[27] The man bound himself in loyalty and fealty to his lady, in a reflection of the feudal system that bound the knight in fealty to his lord. She ruled him; he obeyed her wishes. Sometimes he might complain of her cruelty to him, her arbitrariness, but over-all the myth of her perfect beauty and goodness must be preserved – or to what end was all his devotion?

The songs of the troubadours first celebrated and spread this cult of courtly love. It was encoded in the work of Andreas Capellanus, written (*c.* 1182) at the court of Marie de Champagne, daughter of Eleanor of Aquitaine. Yet perhaps the most enduring monument of courtly love is a work that ostensibly eschews the secular entirely, while still remaining imbued with many of its values: Dante's *Divine Comedy*.

Beatrice, the Beautiful Soul

In *The Divine Comedy* the dead Beatrice, now enjoying Paradise, is the *deus ex machina* who sends Dante on his miraculous journey through hell, purgatory and paradise. At the beginning of this great poem, Dante finds himself 'in the middle of life', lost in a dark wood, with no prospect of rescue. But Beatrice appears to Virgil, the great Roman poet of the *Aeneid*, who is suffering with his pagan friends in Limbo, and asks him to be Dante's guide through the mysteries of the soul's existence after death. She urges Virgil,

> Fly to him and with your high counsel, pity,
> and with whatever need be for his good
> and soul's salvation, help him, and solace me.

> It is I, Beatrice, who send you to him.[28]

Beatrice did not originate in Dante's work as a heavenly figure. In an earlier book, *La Vita Nuova*, she is very much a human figure. Dante sees her for the first time walking in the streets of Florence when she is nine years old and he himself is a boy. Her dress is crimson, a noble colour, and is 'tied with a girdle and trimmed in a manner suited to her tender age'.[29] From this time, Dante asserts, 'Love ruled over my soul.' This love is both sensual and spiritual. 'The spirit of the senses which dwells on high . . . was filled with amazement. . . . Whereupon the natural spirit, which dwells where our nourishment is digested, began to weep, and weeping said: "Woe is me! for I shall often be impeded from now on."'[30] What Dante appears to recognize here is the paradox that perplexes the courtly lover: insofar as his beloved is an object of pure beauty and wonder, she is a source of delight; but insofar as she is an object of unattainable physical desire, she is a torment.

Nine years later, in this rather gradual love affair, Beatrice speaks to him in greeting. This is followed by a frankly sensual dream in which Dante sees the naked Beatrice, sleeping in the arms of a lordly figure, wrapped lightly in a crimson cloth. The lordly figure then wakens her, and urges her to eat a heart that he carries in his hand. Reluctantly she does so. The heart, of course, is Dante's own. At the same time, Beatrice is an object of the purest reverence. Dante quotes others who say of her as she passes, 'This is no woman; this is one of the fairest angels of Heaven'.[31]

Dante has a dream in which he sees Beatrice dead, and shortly after this Beatrice does die in reality. The way he recounts her death is significant: 'The Lord of justice called this most gracious lady to partake of glory under the banner of the blessed Queen, the Virgin Mary, whose name was always uttered in prayers of the utmost reverence by this blessed Beatrice.'[32] From this point on it is the Beatrice who is associated with the Virgin Mary, not the earthly beauty, who dominates Dante's imagination.

It is towards the end of the *Purgatorio* that Dante meets for the first time the heavenly Beatrice. She appears in Canto XXX, rising out of the chariot in the midst of a heavenly pageant, and showered with a cloud of flowers. She is veiled, and wears an olive crown and a cloak of green on which 'the colours of live flame' (reminiscent of the original crimson gown) play. Dante is 'stupefied by the power of holy awe'.³³ But Beatrice's first words are not conciliatory:

> Look at me well. I am she. I am Beatrice.
>> How dared you make your way to this high mountain?
>> Did you not know that here man lives in bliss?
>>>> (*Purgatorio*, XXX, 73–5)

Despite the pleading of the angel choir for mercy, she chastises Dante for wasting his poetic gifts, and, interestingly, for having ignored her influence once she was dead:

> When I rose from the flesh into the spirit,
>> to greater beauty and to greater virtue,
>> he found less pleasure in me and less merit.
>>>> (*Purgatorio*, XXX, 127–9)

She went to 'the portals of the dead' to obtain Virgil's aid to save Dante; he must now repent of his misdeeds before he is allowed fully into paradise. Her death ought to have shown him that if such earthly perfection as hers could decay, he ought not to trust in any other worldly thing. But instead he still treasured mortal things. Dante stands as a child before this Beatrice, a stern, reprimanding mother, and at the same time a reflection of the courtly lady who expects absolute loyalty from her vassal knight.³⁴ He swoons in sorrow and repentance. After this, and his purification in the waters of Lethe, Beatrice appears in yet another role. Now she is divine love, receiving the purified soul, and, echoing the *Salve Regina* ('Turn, turn, Most Gracious Advocate, thine eyes of mercy towards us') the spirits sing, 'Turn Beatrice, oh turn the eyes of grace . . . upon your faithful one who comes so far to look upon your face' (XXXI, 133–5).

In the *Paradiso* Beatrice is Dante's divine guide. Virgil, who represented human reason, has been left behind, and Dante proceeds by the power of divine illumination that is found in Beatrice. She is able to discern his very thoughts and resolve his perplexities before he voices them. Under her tutelage he learns such things as why the resurrection of the flesh is certain, and the sanctity of the vow and its relation to free will. There is still, however, a strong element of the mother/child in their relationship. Beatrice is 'like a mother, ever prompt to calm | her pale and breathless son with kindly words'.[35] Later she herself acknowledges this role, saying to Dante: 'You have become as mindless as an infant | who screams with hunger, yet pushes away his nurse.'[36]

Guide, educator, nurturer, Beatrice returns at the end of *Paradiso* to her role of 'lady', but a lady purged of any carnal associations, as she leaves Dante and resumes her seat in heaven 'upon the throne her merit has assigned her'.

> O lady in whom my hope shall ever soar
>   and who for my salvation suffered even
>   to set your feet upon Hell's broken floor;
>
> through your power and your excellence alone
>   have I recognized the goodness and the grace
>   inherent in the things I have been shown.
>   (*Paradiso*, XXXI, 79–84)

Beatrice has moved in significance well beyond the 'lady' of courtly love. She is not merely endowed with great physical beauty, which increases in radiance as she and Dante ascend through the spheres of paradise –

> The beauty I saw there transcends all measure
>   of mortal minds. I think only her Maker
>   can wholly comprehend so great a treasure
>   (*Paradiso*, XXX, 19–21)

– but with moral and spiritual beauty as well. Unlike the ladies who appear to Hildebert of Lavardin and James Howell, she is the soul of her own earthly being, not of Dante. As such, she resembles herself, only glorified. (A more general examination of Dante's portrayal of souls after death belongs to a later chapter.) Yet in her

65

relationship to Dante she is mentor, advisor, spiritual guide, just as the female figures that appear to Hildebert, Howell, and Boethius are. The soul of Beatrice in the *Divine Comedy* shows us the perfection of the human soul, immortal, retaining identity, and beautiful beyond all earthly conceiving. Courtly lady, glorified soul, type of Mary – all these combine (probably largely unconsciously) in *The Divine Comedy* to create the ideal soul that is Beatrice.

The other woman who is customarily linked with Beatrice is Laura and her celebrator, Petrarch. Like Beatrice, Laura was a real woman. Also like Beatrice, her relationship with Petrarch was not an intimate one, and she also died young. In Sonnet clix he describes her as formed from an Idea, a Platonic First Form; divine beauty can be found nowhere as perfectly as in her eyes. More significantly, in Sonnet cclxi, written after Laura's death, Petrarch extravagantly claims that the only way for others to attain this divine beauty is through the earthly beauty of Laura's eyes:

> How we can acquire honour and love God,
> How honesty is joined to loveliness,
> Shall be learned there [in her eyes], and the right road and rod
> To climb the sky that awaits her to bless.[37]

But Laura never attains the wholly spiritual quality of Beatrice. She remains first and foremost a woman who, even when she is exalted in heaven, is missed primarily in her earthly perfection.

The notion that earthly beauty (and particularly the beauty of women) provided a means of ascent to spiritual beauty is essentially Platonic. The world of matter, as we saw in Chapter 1, is at the bottom of a ladder of ascent to the world of pure Forms or Ideas. Wisdom and the other Ideas are unable to be seen. Beauty alone, Plato/Socrates asserts in the *Phaedrus*, is 'manifest to sense' and points the way for the soul to mount, 'furnished with wings'.[38] These ideas had a wide currency throughout the Western world, and nowhere more obviously than in the works of the English Renaissance poet, Edmund Spenser. In a sonnet to his betrothed, Elizabeth Boyle, published in 1595, he begins by extolling her physical beauty:

> Men call you fayre, and you doe credit it,
> For that your selfe ye dayly such do see.
>
> (ll. 1–2)[39]

But he then goes on to argue that her physical beauty is not remotely of the same value as her virtuous mind. This is what is the 'true fair'.

> For all the rest, how ever fayre it be,
> Shall turne to naught and loose that glorious hew:
>
> (ll. 5–6)

Only what is free from the corruption of 'frail flesh' is true beauty:

> that doth argue you
> To be divine and borne of heavenly seed:
> Derived from that fayre Spirit, from whom al true
> And perfect beauty did at first proceed.
>
> (ll. 9–12)

He ends with the ringing assertion:

> He onely fayre, and what he fayre hath made,
> All other fayre lyke flowres untymely fade.
>
> (ll. 13–14)

But for the fact that the 'He' of the second last line is the Christian God, the sentiment might well have been expressed by Plato.

Spenser is making a clear distinction between the physical beauty of woman and her moral or spiritual beauty, and asserting that it is the latter that is chiefly important because, unlike physical beauty, it is immortal. One can lead to the other, as John Donne, a younger contemporary, asserted of his wife:

> Here the admyring her my mind did whett
> To seeke thee God.[40]

But this is obviously different from claiming that physical beauty and moral beauty are inextricably linked. It was left to the philosophers and thinkers of the eighteenth century to argue this much more audacious claim.

The Beautiful Soul

In 1755 Joseph Lavater, a Swiss pastor wrote, 'The beauty and the ugliness of a face has a correct and exact relationship to the beauty and ugliness of the moral constitution of a person . . . . The better one is morally, the more beautiful one is; the worse one is morally, the uglier.'[41] This is a statement astonishing in both its content and the conviction of its expression. Yet it was only a few degrees farther along on the scale of a belief shared by much of northern Europe at this time. Physical beauty had come to be seen not just as a means of ascent to moral beauty but as absolutely identified with it – the external manifestation of the internal. There is, of course, a contrary view that is just as extreme, and was frequently enunciated by my mother in my childhood as a protection against incipient feminine vanity: 'Beauty is only skin deep, and the devil is usually underneath'.[42] Clearly my mother had never read Lavater, who asserted that 'like a glove that first shows its true shape when worn on a hand, the human body . . . echoes in perceptible guise the very contours of the soul'.[43] One could only *possess* moral beauty, but according to this doctrine one could *be* a beautiful soul.[44] So how did such an extreme view gain wide and popular currency?

While Lavater's theory is by no means restricted to the female form, in literature and art it was customarily a woman who personified this beautiful soul. And the idea of the beautiful and good female form has a very ancient history, as we have seen. The Church has been described as the 'Bride of Christ' from earliest times. We have followed the persistence of the concept of the spiritual and sensual beauty through the Middle Ages and the Renaissance. St Bernard of Clairvaux wrote about 'the necessity of making one's soul "beautiful" to resemble the example of God so that he would willingly receive his spiritual bride'.[45] And literature in the Middle Ages interpreting the Song of Songs (which, for obvious reasons, had to be allegorized) focused on the beauty of the soul that was united with Christ.

The revival of a passionate interest in Greek culture in the mid-eighteenth century also led to a new focus on the 'beautiful soul'. The Greek language even had a compound word for good-beautiful, *kalogathia*, though the actual term 'beautiful soul' was coined by Plotinus.[46] The characterization of the soul here is primarily in moral terms, but the implicit identification between this virtue and beauty itself within the works of Plotinus and his Greek predecessors was sufficient to allow eighteenth-century philosophers, artists, and writers to seize on it to produce a concrete representation of a 'beautiful soul'.

The rise of the novel at precisely this time was convenient in that it gave the 'beautiful soul' a home outside the confines of philosophy. She could become a character in a story! Romantic love could take over where courtly love ended and idealize the female object of desire both physically and morally. And, with a few notable exceptions such as *Moll Flanders*, this is precisely what the novel does. Samuel Richardson's Clarissa and Pamela are both good and beautiful. Indeed, it is their excessive beauty that provides the grounds for testing their equally excessive virtue. Pursued relentlessly by immoral and devious suitors, they appeal constantly for divine aid and manage to preserve their purity in intent – though in the case of Clarissa not in actuality. Fielding's Sophie (*Tom Jones*), from the moment she rescues the child Tom's bird, is a paragon of virtue and long-suffering fortitude. These fictitious women all undeniably unite the qualities of goodness and beauty.

Two continental novels, both cited by Norton, also use the imagery of the beautiful soul. These are *Agathon* by C.M. Wieland and *Julie, or the New Heloise* by Rousseau. The first of these, *Agathon*, is set, significantly, in the ancient world of Greece, where the hero, Agathon, is at first lost in a wood in a manner reminiscent of Dante. Agathon's rescue comes about in a rather circuitous way. He is introduced to Danae, a beautiful courtesan, who initiates him into the joys of sensual love. Eventually she reforms, redeeming herself through penitence, so that when in the third book of the novel Agathon again meets her at an isolated estate, she is described as a 'beautiful soul'. But is this a quality she has attained, or is the beautiful soul an intrinsic quality that can be tarnished but not lost? The moral seems to be that a surfeit of sensual delight in the end weans us from it. But this is by no means the only possible interpretation.

Julie, the heroine of Rousseau's novel, does not begin life as an ideal either. She begins by having an illicit love affair, and only after penitence does she become a 'beautiful soul', leading a supposedly perfect life at Clarens, her husband's country estate.

It could also be argued that even Clarissa does not begin as a paragon of virtue but as a rebellious young woman. Forced by her family to promise to marry a man she loathes, she finally agrees to run away with the charming but unscrupulous Lovelace, who as a representation of sheer sexuality both attracts and frightens her. After she is in his power, she resists bravely, but is no match for his trickery and force. In the end, physically violated but spiritually inviolate, she dies 'beautifully', forgiving everyone.

As Norton points out, there is something intrinsically suspicious at the heart of the beautiful soul once it is cast in the novel. Virtue is not consistent in real life, and we should not expect its consistency in a literature that was beginning to attempt to portray 'real life'. Furthermore, the tricky novel may undermine the author's intent in ways he had not anticipated – and possibly does not even recognize. The supposedly ideal estate of Clarens where Julie lives is based on autocracy with control established through endemic eavesdropping. Its garden, a self-enclosed space, is arranged with plants and bushes to make it appear the beginning of a wood. All that pretends to be ideal is in fact based on hypocrisy and deception.

The truth is that the beautiful soul became essentially a static concept. In its eighteenth-century beginnings, beauty and moral goodness were seen by a philosopher such as Shaftesbury as something that could be worked at. Good taste, the appreciation of the beautiful, could refine and purify the mind so that it became good, and in the rational eighteenth century there was little distinction between the refined mind and the good soul. But the identification of the beautiful exterior of a face or figure with internal goodness left no room for development. One was or was not a 'beautiful soul'. Consequently, when such a being appeared in the novel one of two things happened. Either she *was* static, as in Richardson's *Pamela*, where external incident provides the main tension, or she was *not* static, as in *Agathon* or *Julie*, and the ambiguities of her complex and changing nature conflicted with the ideal she was supposedly portraying.

After the end of the eighteenth century, the 'beautiful soul' largely disappeared as a philosophical concept, but, despite the difficulties I have outlined above, it continued to have a history of representation in art and literature.[47] Indeed, it merged with and informed the work of Romantic writers and artists, among whom one of the first and foremost was William Blake.

WILLIAM BLAKE

Blake's vision – both poetic and artistic – was so unique that it is difficult to speak of him in terms of influence and tradition. He would have been aware of the cult of the beautiful soul, and many of the souls in his drawings are indeed beautiful women, often clothed in diaphanous, long garments, but it is their vitality and activity rather than their physical perfection that move the observer. The soul in Blake is not a passive, fixed entity, but active, fleeing death, seeking out knowledge hidden from the body, exulting in reunion with its body.

The largest collection of Blake's 'soul' drawings is to be found in his illustrations of 1808 to Robert Blair's poem 'The Grave'. (The original drawings were by Blake, though the engravings, to Blake's chagrin, were done by Schiavonetti, who received immensely more money for this than Blake did for his share in the project.) One drawing not included among the final twelve selected for the volume presents a powerful image of the plight of the soul in this world. A white female figure, her hair cascading down, hangs precariously from the last step of what appears to be the side of a bridge. Her hands are outstretched, either in appeal or to break her fall if she slips over the edge. Behind her, one hand reaching out to capture her, the other holding a torch that lights the scene, comes the spike-winged monster Death. The arch of the cavern from which he is emerging repeats the arch of the bridge from which the soul is falling. One way or another, she is trapped. There is a suggestion here of another aspect of femininity that the soul may reflect: the helpless, frail being, the fallen woman, overcome by life and circumstance. One is reminded not just of Clarissa but of other later literary characters of the nineteenth century such as Dickens' 'Little Em'ly' in *David Copperfield*.

As a counterpart to this, we have the joy of 'The Soul at Heaven's Gate'. Here we see the soul, again clothed in a flowing gown, holding out her hands not in fear and despair but in wonder at the radiance of light before her. Two other figures (angels or other redeemed souls?), both also apparently female, stand facing her in greeting.

The most dramatic of these illustrations is undoubtedly that of the soul greeting the body as they are reunited at the last day, which is, quite simply, passionate. As the body (a young man) rises from a grave surrounded by flames, raising his arms in supplication for deliverance, the soul, bare feet escaping from her diaphanous robes, flies down and clasps him about the neck. Their lips touch. It is a reunion of lovers.

One of the most original conceptions in the series of illustrations for 'The Grave' is 'The Soul Exploring the Recesses of the Grave'. This is the soul as repository of superior wisdom, knowing things hidden from human eyes. A female soul, her hair coiled behind her head rather than flowing as in previous illustrations, is walking into a tomb with a taper. She appears composed and unafraid. In contrast, a muscular young man stands above the cavern of the tomb attempting to look down to see what the soul sees, but from his angle of vision this is impossible. What we and the soul see is that within the tomb a corpse lies, engulfed in flames. Are they flames of destruction or purification? The episode does not occur in Blair's poem, but a later publication of the illustration attaches to it lines from the poem that indicate that the soul has warned the young man of his death and therefore he fears and longs to see what the soul's 'sickly taper' illuminates. But this is only revealed to the prescient soul.[48]

An interesting feature of these souls is that all are clothed. Indeed, most of the souls we have encountered, from Hildebert to James Howell, have been clothed in some fashion. In the case of Hildebert, the clothes are emblematic of the paradoxical poverty and riches of the soul; in the case of Howell, they betoken the soul's status – that of a pure nun. Beatrice is clothed according to her beatified state. But these souls of Blake are clad in diaphanous robes that seem, like the flowing gowns of angels, not to conceal the naked truth beneath but to enhance it. Of no particular time or period, they convey the timeless and universal.

One further female soul in this collection of illustrations, 'The Soul Hovering Over the Body Reluctantly Parting with Life', presents interesting problems of interpretation. Firstly, as we shall see in the chapter on the soul at the time of death, the soul that separates from the body, if it is of any discernible sex at all, is usually the sex of the body that is dying. Here this is not the case. A young man, clad like the soul in flowing clothes, and laid out in the pose of an effigy, lies dead and unresponsive while a female soul floats over him, holding up her hands in a gesture of sorrow and gazing down lovingly at him. This picture has a somewhat confused history since an earlier version of the drawing contains emblems suggesting a life of 'intemperate pleasure'.[49] These have disappeared in the final version. But the gaze that the soul casts upon the young man appears to be that of a lover, reluctantly leaving the pleasures of the body behind. Bound still to a love of the body, she floats hesitatingly, uncertain of her role and fate.

The truth is that there is a fundamental ambiguity at the heart of the female form in art and literature, just as there is a fundamental ambiguity at the heart of our understanding of women. The *anima* is not always seen in a positive light, as one might conclude from the opening pages of this chapter. Commenting on Jung, C.A. Meier examines the various guises in which the *anima* may appear – and among them lists the prostitute.[50]

Jung himself emphasizes the human desire for the wholeness or *syzygy*, first examined by Plato in the *Symposium*. According to this doctrine, male and female were originally one, and since their separation they long for nothing more than to be reunited so as to gain their original totality.[51] Could this last be an additional explanation for the reluctance of the parting in this picture and the peculiar distress of the soul? Or does it simply indicate a soul that is less than perfect, too bound to the things of this earth?

Final evidence of Blake's diverse use of the female form comes in his drawing of 'The Fall of Man'. Here, seated at the right hand of Death at the bottom of the picture, is Sin – and she is indisputably a woman.[52]

THE PRE-RAPHAELITES

By the time of the Pre-Raphaelites, the philosophical arguments for the linking of beauty and goodness, at least in any directly physiognomic way, had largely been rejected. But the looser Platonic tradition linking the two continued in their works. Their concerns were above all with pure beauty, which they saw embodied not in the art of their period but in art as it had existed before Raphael – that is, a more 'genuine' art, stripped of preoccupations with light, shadow and other artificial rules based on an inordinate admiration for the great Renaissance painter. Above all, the subjects of the paintings must be significant, and for the Pre-Raphaelites this often meant they must be medieval, the period in which, as we have seen, the union of the feminine as ideal and as erotic object flourished.

The best-known poem of the Pre-Raphaelites is surely Dante Gabriel Rossetti's 'The Blessed Damozel'. How many adolescents have thrilled to the musical description of this perfectly good, perfectly beautiful, soul-woman?

> The blessed damozel leaned out
> 　From the gold bar of Heaven;
> Her eyes were deeper than the depth
> 　Of waters stilled at even;
> She had three lilies in her hand,
> 　And the stars in her hair were seven.[53]

Here we find the mix of purity and eroticism – indeed, eroticism enhanced by purity – that preoccupied Dante and his followers. In some respects she seems a nineteenth-century Beatrice: she has concern for her lover, who is still on earth, and waits for him in heaven. But the emphasis is on *her* needs and longings, rather than those of the divine scheme of things. In the end, she does not really want heaven at all. When her beloved arrives she will ask Christ the Lord

> Thus much for him and me:—
> Only to live as once on earth
> With Love, – only to be,
> As then awhile, for ever now
> Together, I and he.

(p. 15)

The beautiful female soul here is pure, but not ethereal; she is still subject to the desires and passions of earth.

In contrast, the soul in the poem 'Who Shall Deliver Me?' (the title is from St Paul's Epistle to the Romans: 'O wretched man that I am! who shall deliver me from the body of this death?') by Dante Gabriel Rossetti's sister, Christina, longs to escape from the body, which is perceived as

> Myself, arch-traitor to myself;
> My hollowest friend, my deadliest foe,
> My clog whatever road I go.[54]

This potential conflict between soul and body, or the world of ideas and the world of concrete reality, was already a concern in the works of the eighteenth-century philosophers writing about the 'beautiful soul'. At one level, the idea of the 'beautiful soul' seemed to be 'an elegant bridge over the chasm separating mind and body, spanning a gulf that had troubled thinkers from Plato to Descartes'.[55] But the bridge was always threatening to break under the pressure of the tension between the physical and the abstract. Was beauty a Platonic concept, standing above and apart from the world, or could it only be apprehended through the senses, in the physical world?

We saw how, when the beautiful soul became a character in a novel, it was either inconsistent in its portrayal of virtue or static as a character. It might also reject the physical altogether. Clarissa comes perilously near to doing this in her long flight from Lovelace. And in the sixth book of Goethe's *Wilhelm Meister*, called 'The Confessions of a Beautiful Soul', the 'Beautiful Soul', based on the character of a woman who was at one time Goethe's spiritual mentor, retreats from the world and its realities, prefers solitude to company, and becomes increasingly self-absorbed, intent only on self-improvement. She is not even at home in her own body; during sleepless nights she looks on her body as foreign to herself, 'the way one views, say, a dress'.[56] Like Christina Rossetti in 'Who Shall Deliver Me?' the body (and, by extension, the physical world) are no longer parts of the self, and this undermines the concept of the physical as the external manifestation of the soul.

The uncertainty about where beauty truly resides and how it can be conveyed to others is at the heart of a remarkable short story by Rossetti called 'Hand and Soul'.[57] Chiaro dell'Erma is a young man from Arezzo who strives from boyhood 'towards the imitation of any objects offered in nature'. He has an extreme longing 'after a visible embodiment of his thoughts'. He seeks out a famous painter in Pisa with whom he wishes to study, but when he meets the man and sees his work he knows this famous artist has nothing to teach him.

He begins to work on his own, but there are distractions – women love him, and he 'partakes of life'. Then he hears of another young talented painter in Lucca and, motivated by jealousy of him, begins to work arduously, living alone in Pisa. At the end of three years he is known throughout Tuscany. At this time he has a dream reminiscent of Dante's in which a girl he has loved, 'his mistress, his mystical lady', who is still not nine years old, has died, and other spirits worship her. After this dream, he realizes that much of the reverence that he had mistaken for religious faith was in fact a worship of beauty.

From this time on he 'puts a watch on his soul', and resolves to do no works other than those that have as their end the portrayal of moral greatness. For this he does not choose the medium of action and the passion of human life, but cold symbolism and abstract impersonation. He loses his popularity as an artist; people say his works are cold, and probably they are.

One feast day his model goes out to join in the celebration, and Chiaro, unable to work, sits at his window and watches a throng of people coming out of the Church of San Rocco. Among them are members of two feuding houses. After a simple provocation, they begin to fight with swords. Inside the church porch, and forming the background to the battle, Chiaro sees scenes he has painted on the walls depicting peace. He is in despair, thinking that fame and faith have both failed him.

Then a woman appears in his room, 'clad to the hands and feet with a green and grey garment, fashioned to that time . . . . Though her hands were joined, her face was not lifted, but set forward; and though the gaze was austere, yet her mouth was supreme in gentleness.'[58] Chiaro is aware that although she does not move closer to him, she is as much with him as his breath. Then she says, 'I am an image, Chiaro, of thine own soul within thee. See me, and know me as I am. Thou sayest that fame has failed thee, and faith failed thee; but because at least thou hast not laid thy life unto riches, therefore, though thus late, I am suffered to come into thy knowledge.'[59] She tells him to look into his own conscience – not his mind's conscience, but his heart's, 'and all shall approve and suffice'. Chiaro looks into her eyes and weeps. She chastises him for divorcing love and faith. What was wrong with his previous offerings that he thought were only of the earth? She continues, 'How is it that thou, a man, wouldst say coldly to the mind what God hath said to the heart warmly. . . . Know that there is but this means whereby thou may'st serve God with man:— Set thine hand and thy soul to serve man with God.'[60] Then she asks him to paint her, just as she is. 'So shall thy soul stand before thee always, and perplex thee no more.' Chiaro does so, and as he paints, 'his face [grows] solemn with knowledge'.

The appearance of this soul has certain things in common with that of Hildebert of Lavardin. Chiaro's soul is not said specifically to be wearing mourning garments, but the green and grey suggest mourning as well as the possibility of growth. Her gaze is austere, and she comes to chastise, encourage and give advice. But the burden of this soul's message is quite different from that of Hildebert's. It is full of the Pre-Raphaelite preoccupation with morality and beauty and the relationship between them. And the soul's advice, to abandon the abstract and purely symbolic to return to find beauty in the world of human beings and nature, is the conclusion of most of the artists of that time. The soul is displayed as a beautiful woman, and it is as he paints this physical likeness that knowledge and understanding come to Chiaro. Salvation comes through the image.

This idea extended well beyond the circle of the Pre-Raphaelites. It is the theme of Tennyson's 'The Palace of Art',[61] where the soul, again portrayed as a beautiful woman, is housed by the poet in a beautiful mansion, 'royal rich and wide', built for her alone. But the isolation and self-preoccupation of this soul are self-destructive, and reflect that of Goethe's 'beautiful soul' in *Wilhelm Meister*. After three years alone, she falls. Despair grips her. 'A spot of dull stagnation, without light | Or power of movement, seem'd my soul.' At the end of the fourth year, she throws away her royal robes and begs for a cottage where she 'may mourn and pray'. Tennyson himself was quite specific about the meaning of this poem. In 1890 he wrote: '"The Palace of Art" is the embodiment of my own belief that the Godlike life is with man and for man'.[62]

The Pre-Raphaelites' arguments about the dangers of withdrawal from life inherent in artistic pursuits may stem from their awareness of the ease with which their own painting could become guilty of this defect. These paintings show women – admittedly usually modelled on the real women they knew and loved – nearly always alone, surrounded by symbolic props, in poses of isolated contemplation. Rossetti's *Sibylla Palmifera*, is one such work. The accompanying sonnet is titled 'Soul's Beauty', and the meditative soul/sibyll (Alexa Wilding) seated in front of an elaborate frieze that incorporates two poppy wreaths, gazes out composedly at the viewer. She holds a palm branch, a sign of victory (over death?) and is accompanied by two butterflies (symbols of Psyche) and a burning lamp. There is little that is humanly engaging in the work, though it undoubtedly holds the viewer with a compelling, almost super-natural power.

Far stranger (and considerably later) is the painting by the symbolist painter and Rosicrucian, Fernand Khnopff. Titled *I Lock my Door upon Myself*, it is inspired by a line in the poem 'Who Shall deliver Me?' by Christina Rossetti, discussed above. Here the red-haired soul-woman has an unearthly quality shown in the pale, upcast eyes and the melancholy pose. Surrounded by lilies, her head is supported by the hands that rest under her chin, her elbows spread wide on the dark blue table top that forms the foreground. She gazes at the viewer but does not appear to see him, wrapped in her own particular misery.

The Lady of Shallot, a favourite subject of Pre-Raphaelite painters, was also seen by them as a soul-figure and a symbol of the artist. Holman Hunt, whose numerous paintings of the subject show a certain obsession with the lady, wrote:

> The parable, as interpreted in this painting, illustrates the failure of a human Soul towards its accepted responsibility. The lady typifying the Soul is bound to represent faithfully the workings of the high purpose of King Arthur's rule. She is to weave her record, not as one who, mixing in the world, is tempted by egoistic weakness, but as a being 'sitting alone'; in her isolation she is charged to see life with a mind supreme and elevated in judgement. In executing her design on the tapestry she records not the external incidents of common lives, but the present condition of King Arthur's Court, with its opposing influences of good and evil.[63]

This is a view manifestly contrary to that Rossetti expresses in 'Hand and Soul'. Here the soul-artist must remain in isolation, observing and recording. The Lady of Shallot tires of her isolation and of seeing the world only through the mirror. She turns to the external world, thus breaking the compact and the mirror, and dies.

SUMMARY

The female soul is determined by the gender of language, and the predisposition of men to see woman as guide and nurturer. It is impossible to be sure which was the prior influence, but once each had come into being, it could not help but reinforce the other. From the Psyche figure of Greek mythology to nineteenth-century art and literature, this soul comes to men to advise, chastise and inspire. She is both good and beautiful. Sometimes this beauty is pure and austere; at other times there are strong overtones of the erotic in her appearance and demeanour. In either case, her image, whether in literature or art, is itself instructive. Her influence lies not just in what she says or does, but in her very appearance.

In the nineteenth century, this figure of the feminine soul becomes entangled with questions about how one achieves moral beauty – whether by a contemplative withdrawal from the world, or by an immersion in real life. The essential conflict this reveals is but one aspect of the many ways in which we experience uncertainty and conflict in our psychological and moral lives. In other guises, the soul features in our externalization, our playing out of these conflicts, and it is this aspect of the soul that is the subject of the next chapter.

THREE

The Soul in Conflict

þe saule and þe lycome
Selde be beaþ isome.
(The soul and the body
Are seldom in agreement.)
From 'Death' in An Old English Miscellany

We all know what it is to be torn between alternative choices and courses of action. At one level we see ourselves as a single person, 'the self', but at another we know that often we are made up of conflicting desires and impulses and pulled in different directions. We say we 'can't make up our mind', and the very idiomatic way we express this shows that only a decision will restore the mind to wholeness, 'make it up'. Sometimes the choices we are torn between are more or less neutral alternatives – should I spend the evening watching television or going out to a party? – but often they are real moral choices – should I try to bed that pretty girl or should I remain faithful to my wife? Those who cannot 'make up their mind' remain in a constant state of tension and difficulty. At the extreme end of the spectrum of conflict the very personhood of the individual seems torn in two: one thinks of Jekyll and Hyde, or those psychiatric patients who claim to suffer from a 'split personality', to be several people inhabiting one body.

Naturally, we want to explain this conflict within ourselves. It is both troubling and, if we think deeply about it, mysterious. Are we not a unity? One possible explanation is to insist that we *are* a unity, and that one element in the conflict we experience is outside us. The tempting devil is such an externalization. Another possibility is to acknowledge that the conflict is essentially within ourselves, but to dramatize and externalize it to make it more understandable.

81

It is this latter solution that is at the heart of the next incarnation of the soul we shall look at. Here the moral conflict that we see within ourselves is imagined as taking place within different faculties of the soul (the sensitive and appetitive, the will, and the reason). In this drama the different elements of the soul become personae in their own right. Alternatively, and more commonly, the conflict takes place not among the different faculties of the soul, but between the soul as a united whole and the body. This, of course, provides even greater opportunities for visual and dramatic scenarios.

If Jung was the psychoanalyst who explained the female soul to the modern age, then it was Freud who provided the model for the divided, conflicted soul. Freud divided the 'mental apparatus' of the individual (he would scarcely have used the word 'soul') into three parts. There is the *id*, which contains our inborn primitive and instinctual impulses; the *super-ego*, which is the source of conscience and morality and seeks to inhibit instinct, and between these two extremes the *ego*, which negotiates between them and, in the well-adjusted individual, presents a coherent persona to others and to society at large.[1] There is much scope for conflict here, and it may be irresolvable. A great deal of our unhappiness, according to Freud, comes from the inhibiting power of the *super-ego* on both the *ego* (our public self, which relates to the world and others) and the *id* (our hidden, deepest desires). 'The super-ego is the vehicle of the ego ideal by which the ego measures itself, which it emulates, and whose demand for ever greater perfection it strives to fulfil.'[2] We may present a 'whole' self to society, but inside we are probably fragmented.

Freud was by no means the first to observe this element of conflict within man. In the first century, Saint Paul wrote, 'The good that I would I do not: but the evil which I would not, that I do.' And four centuries before that, Plato was explaining and dramatizing this conflict in terms of the different elements he discerned within the soul.[3] He saw the struggle chiefly as one between reason and desire, with the spirited element, will, as the ultimate decider of the conflict. It is easy to think of ordinary examples of conflict that can be viewed in this way. Indeed, Plato's own example of being thirsty and yet pulled back from drinking can be fleshed out by imagining that you are lost at sea with no drinking water. Your reason tells you that drinking sea water will only make matters worse – probably fatally worse – but you have, nevertheless, an overwhelming desire to drink anything that looks like water.

To explain and make concrete the idea of struggle between abstract elements in the person, Plato in his dialogues summons up different images. The composite made up of monster, lion and man in the *Republic*, the head, heart and stomach of man in the *Timaeus*, and the two horses and charioteer in the *Phaedrus* are all examples of this attempt to make the conflict within the individual both visible and dramatic.

Unlike Plato, who sets the division of the soul within a moral framework, Freud would not have been so ready to give the *super-ego* free rein. In contrast, he was quick to defend the claims of the *id*, which might be suppressed for a time, but only at enormous cost to the whole person. Freud was not a moralist. Plato was, and had no qualms about insisting that the individual should be governed by reason, not base desires, just as the state should be ruled by a philosopher-king, not by a rabble.

Freud, of course, is a very late addition to the history of human thought. Throughout early Christianity, the Middle Ages and the Renaissance, the notion of the conflicted individual, based chiefly on Plato's division of the soul, but imbued with Christian moral teaching that provided a kind of superstructure to the Platonic inheritance, dominated Western thought. In the process, it gave rise to one of the most curious literary forms ever to grace European writing: the body and soul dialogue.

BODY AND SOUL DIALOGUES

The body and soul dialogue is not based on the division of faculties within the soul. Rather the conflict here is between the soul and the body – an idea that is at once philosophically simpler but better dramatically. Here the body plays the role of the irrational part of the soul, and the soul is equivalent to the rational element. Even in classical Greece, there was uncertainty as to whether man's internal conflicts took place entirely within the soul, or between the soul and the body. The *Phaedrus* and the *Republic* come down on the side of conflict within the soul, but we also saw that in the *Phaedo*, a relatively early dialogue, Socrates claimed the body was the culpable element in man's makeup and did not distinguish between different faculties of the soul. In most respects, however, these debates are far removed from the world of classical philosophy.

The first 'given' that is essential to them is the perception of both body and soul as visible, imaginable entities. In order to debate, both must be endowed with speech and some kind of physical being. Thus we are involved in contradictions from the very beginning: the body must take on some of the characteristics of the soul – it must be possessed of enough intelligence to argue its case; similarly, the soul must become a concrete, recognizably human entity, with the faculties of speech, sight and smell. None of this seemed to trouble the medieval mind, but it would have been anathema to Plato or Aristotle. For Plato, the body was merely passive matter, and for Aristotle, the two were a composite. To be fair to the Middle Ages, St Thomas Aquinas, following Aristotle, could not have endorsed the assumptions of the debate tradition either. But its dissemination throughout Europe from the twelfth to the fifteenth centuries in both Latin and the vernacular – there is even a Norwegian version – gives firm evidence of its popularity.

The conflict that is played out in the body and soul dialogue, while based on classical ideas of the division within man, is nevertheless thoroughly Christian in content. It is really a debate about which of the two, body or soul, bears the greater responsibility for sin. For the most part, the debate takes place after death, and the result determines not just whether the person lived a good and profitable life, but whether he is damned or saved at the last day. Not merely temporal but eternal issues are at stake here.

The details of the debates vary, but the essentials are much the same. One of the most popular was the fourteenth-century *Vision of Saint Bernard* – though there is not a shred of evidence to link any of the versions to him personally. This, as its title suggests, is presented as the vision of one Bernard, a saint (or in some cases of a hermit,

Philibert or Fulbert) and, like most dreams, reveals some of the deepest fears of its creator. In the silence of a winter's night, as he is lying in bed, he sees a soul and a body arguing with one another. They are the soul and body of someone who has died recently and who has been damned, and they are arguing about which of them has been most responsible for this sorry state of affairs. The wonderful illustrations accompanying this dialogue in a manuscript version in the Cambridge University Library show a skeleton lying in a coffin, and a soul depicted as a rather plump, sexless body with wiry sprigs of hair sticking out of its round head.

The soul speaks first. It is very distressed, wailing and crying. Created in the image of God, it is now 'fouler than a Toad'. It berates the body for having loved worldly things, 'turrets gay of costly masonry', and palaces, which it has now been forced to change for a little tomb. It taunts the body, in language borrowed from the medieval *ubi sunt* tradition:

> Where thy rich beds, | thy sumptuous Tapestry,
> Thy change of rayment, | many coloured vesture?
> Thy dainty Spices | (baites of luxury)
> Plate, Tables, Carpets, | and rich furniture?[4]

The roof of the house where the body now dwells is level with his nose; his friends have vanished; his heirs will not mourn long because they have inherited his fields and vineyards; even his wife and children would not exchange one penny of what they now own to have him back. The soul then reminds the body that, although it suffers no torments in the grave, at the last day it will be reunited with it, and both of them will be punished eternally. 'To this, I trow, | answer thou knowest none,' the soul asserts with confidence.

In this the soul is wrong; the 'ghastly corpse' raises itself up and prepares a spirited defence. The body (here referred to as 'flesh', with its overtones of Galatians 5:17: 'For the flesh lusteth against the Spirit and the Spirit against the flesh: and these two are contrary the one to the other') admits that it has often led the soul astray, but claims that if this can happen the fault is really the soul's. It was the soul's responsibility to rule the body; it has reason and ought to tame the flesh with 'abstinence, and stripes'. Everything the body does derives from the soul, therefore the responsibility and guilt must lie with it.

> The body of it selfe | none ill hath knowne,
> All that it knows | proceedeth from thy head:
> If I doe what thou bidst | the fault's thine owne,
> For without thee | the body resteth dead.

The point the body is making is that it is only the instrument of the soul. Indeed, whether the debate about relative responsibility for sin is between the soul and the body or among different faculties of the soul depends on where one draws the dividing line between soul and body. If the sensitive soul (in Aristotelian terms) or the 'irrational soul' (according to Plato) belongs to the body, then the body can tempt the soul and be deemed, in part at least, responsible for sin. But if the body, as it implies, is merely passive matter, the instrument of the soul, then it can hardly be held guilty. The secondary point that the body is making is that, even if it can tempt the soul, the latter, as the superior part of man, endowed with reason, ought to govern conduct and be master (or mistress) of the body. (The astute reader will note that these two arguments are mutually exclusive, since the first implies a passive body, while the second concedes the body's ability to tempt the soul, thereby implying that sensation and base desire belong to the body – but comprehensiveness was more important than consistency to the average medieval mind.)

In the soul's reply, it admits it should have restrained the 'sensuall appetites' of the body, but insists that the body deceived it 'with so faire a glasse, | That thy offence | the greater ought remaine'. Here we find echoes of the beliefs of Aristotle and Aquinas that man cannot deliberately choose evil over good; rather, to do evil he must be mistaken about the very nature of evil and good.

The body now begins to weep, thinking on its end, and gives a humble reply in which it admits it never thought of the grave when it was alive. Both of them will stand guilty before God. Yet, not wholly cowed, it returns to the argument that the greater responsibility still lies with the soul, which should have restrained it.

Giving in to despair, the soul howls with a 'hollow fearfull voice', lamenting its very nature, and the fact that it was ever put into a body at all. Animals are happy, because when they die there is nothing more; they simply cease to exist. When the body tentatively asks the soul what hell is like and whether there is provision or any hope of redemption for kings or the rich by giving land or money, the soul scorns the shallowness of the question. Once one is dead, there is no hope of changing one's estate by bribery.

The dialogue then moves back into the voice of the author, who watches as two fiends 'more blacke then pitch' with 'sharpe steely prickes' and snakes crawling out of their nostrils come and bind the soul and drag it howling to hell. The dialogue ends not with a resolution of the conflict, but with the violence of the devils. Saint Bernard awakens, suitably frightened, and resolves to lead a holy life henceforth.

One might dismiss these dialogues as just another aberration of the medieval mind, along with self-flagellation, but this does not explain their strange resurgence in the early seventeenth century. William Crashaw (1572–1626), the father of Richard, the poet, translated the *Vision of St Bernard* or *Visio Philiberti*, as the manuscript from which he was working styled the debate, and indeed it is his translation that I have used for the passages quoted above. Nor did he translate it merely as an exercise in bringing to life an obscure literary form. In his introduction he assures the Christian reader that it is a 'help to holinesse', and 'stuft with godly truthes, and wholesome instructions. . . .'[5] The elder Crashaw, unlike his son who famously converted to Roman Catholicism, was a devout Puritan, who took seriously the wickedness of the age and the need to reform it.

But the appeal of the body and soul debate was far wider than the circle of the Puritan devout. We have already encountered the nun-like soul that features in James Howell's body and soul dialogue called *The Vision*.[6] Much of this dialogue is, in fact, not taken up with the traditional subject matter, but with speculation about the

Imagining the Soul

nature of the soul, whether or not it is indivisible, how it is connected to the body, and other matters of a pseudo-scientific nature that are seventeenth-century, not medieval, concerns. There are even discussions of topical religious issues about which the soul instructs the body. All this is preceded by the familiar medieval disputes: the soul complains the body has contaminated it; the body replies that it is merely an unwieldy lump of earth that can do nothing. The Platonic horse and rider analogy makes another appearance, with the dark horse again identified with body rather than being a faculty of the soul.

Even greater evidence of the debate's hold on the imagination is found in *The Roxborough Ballads*, where three versions of body and soul dialogues, almost certainly based on Crashaw's translation of the medieval debate, are to be found – from 1640, 1683 and 1730. In addition there is an anonymous version that survives in a collection of Irish tracts, and is probably early nineteenth century.[7] The earliest of the ballads in the Roxborough collection specifies that it is to be sung to the tune 'Fortune My Foe', a popular melody of the period that can be found in a keyboard version by William Byrd in the *Fitzwilliam Virginal Book*, should any modern reader wish to try the effect!

Settings of Body and Soul Dialogues

The medieval dialogues not only have descendants in the seventeenth century and later, they are already part of a long literary tradition, stretching back to the fourth century. It is to these sources that we must look for answers to questions about their origin and real nature. What disparate elements originally came together to produce the literary form? When exactly do the debates take place and why? How can there be such uncertainty about the dividing line between body and soul?

The body and soul dialogue almost certainly had its origins in two fourth-century sources: 'The Homily of Macarius' and the 'Visio Pauli'. In the 'Homily of Macarius',[8] which is Egyptian in origin, Macarius is walking in the desert with two angels (as one did in the fourth century), when they come upon a stinking corpse. This might be deemed a purely naturalistic touch, but not so. It is the soul and its sins, the angels assert, that have caused the corpse to stink. They then describe the separation of the soul and the body and also the tour of the universe, which it was assumed souls undertook between death and judgment, so that they could see the joys of the blessed and the torments of the damned and rejoice or tremble, depending on their own particular status. A much later manuscript of this legend, from the eleventh or twelfth century, incorporates an address of a good soul and also of an evil soul to their respective bodies at the time of separation.

The 'Visio Pauli', based on the slender evidence of 2 Cor.12:2–4 ('I knew a man in Christ . . . such an one caught up to the third heaven. And I knew such a man, (whether in the body, or out of the body, I cannot tell: God knoweth;) How that he was caught up into paradise, and heard unspeakable words, which it is not lawful for a man to utter.'), contains many of the same elements as the Macarius homily – a separation scene of soul and body and a tour of the universe. But here these elements are put in a vision setting, and the tour of the universe takes place during life. Also, when visiting hell, Paul makes a plea for the weekly release of the souls there, from a Saturday evening until Sunday night.

In these two sources we find some clues as to the settings of the body and soul debates. They do not, by any means, all take place at the same time. The 'Vision of Saint Bernard', whose contents I have summarized above, takes place some time after the person has died. A French dialogue, written about one hundred years earlier, and with considerable similarities in content, suggests a more specific time frame. It begins, 'Un samedi par nuit' ('One Saturday night'), and thus precisely establishes the time and setting of the encounter between its body and soul. The soul has been released, as Saint Paul petitioned in the 'Visio', to come back from torment to the world on a Saturday night. And it uses this time to berate its body, whom it blames for its present uncomfortable situation. A tenth-century address of the soul to its body also takes place at this time. 'The soul must come crying out with sorrow; always on every seventh night, the soul must seek out the body, which it formerly wore for a long time.'[9] It seems probable that the 'Vision of Saint Bernard' belongs in this Saturday night setting as well.

Where is the soul residing at this time? The Last Judgment has not yet taken place, because the soul's final threat to the body is that it will be raised to join it at the last day. Yet it clearly comes from a place of torment. It would seem that the implicit belief behind this apparent anomaly is that there are *two* judgments of the soul – one immediately after death, which sends it to hell or purgatory, and a final judgment at the last day when, as it threatens, it will be reunited with its body. This reunion with the body is necessary not just so that the body may share in the punishment, but so that the punishment may be made more acute – without the body the soul cannot feel pain or pleasure with the same intensity. This again implies a body that either contains the senses or through which the senses are filtered.

There are also addresses and dialogues that manifestly do not take place on a weekly return basis, or after death at all. Addresses of the soul to the body, which predate the dialogues by several centuries, nearly all take place at the time of death itself. It seems natural that, as it leaves its life-partner, the soul should say some words of farewell. Also, this setting ties in with the origin of the dialogue in Coptic separation scenes, as recounted in the 'Homily of Macarius'. Frequently these addresses come in pairs: first there is an address of a wicked soul to its body, and then this is followed by an address of a good soul to its body. Predictably, the evil soul is abusive and blames the body for all its ills, while the good soul thanks its body for having served it and being supportive during life.

Also predictably, it was the address of the evil soul to its body that was the more interesting and hence had a literary future. The address of the good soul to its body simply disappeared. As for the address of the evil soul, it continued to flourish and transform itself; once the body began to reply, the address became a debate. When this happened, the moment of death was no longer appropriate or plausible; the body could scarcely be expected to engage in complex argument in this extremity. The setting therefore changed to after the time of death, and the already common belief in the weekly return of the soul to its body provided a convenient framework.

The vision setting of the dialogue, derived from the 'Visio Pauli', also remained popular. This had the ability to combine the *frisson* of an after-death setting and bitter recriminations with an in-life lesson for the observer of the vision.

Issues in the Debates

The content of the debate, like its setting, is made up of disparate and sometimes contradictory elements. Its ostensible purpose is to act as a moral lesson to the living by showing the unhappy fate of a wicked soul and body. The actual subject matter is the relative responsibility of body and soul for sin. Who has the better of the argument depends, as stated above, on where we draw the dividing line between body and soul, whether body is simply passive matter controlled wholly by the soul and its faculty of will, or whether the senses, that certainly need the physical organs in order to operate, are in fact wholly located in the body, so that it feels, desires and hence tempts. The philosophical arguments are for the body as passive matter, but the commonsense feeling of most people is that the senses are in the body. Within the context of the debates, the issue is further blurred by the need to give both body and soul the composite characteristics they need in order to function as dramatic actors in a dialogue.

Augustine made his position quite clear in the fifth century. The first sin came from the soul, not the body. 'The corruptible flesh made not the soul to sin, but the sinning soul made the flesh corruptible.'[10] The argument about relative responsibility for action long predates Augustine, however, and is by no means limited to Christianity. A fragment by the early second-century classical writer Plutarch summarizes the views of Democritus and Theophrastus, two Greek philosophers, on the subject. Democritus insists that the guilt is the soul's. It is the controlling principle, and the body is merely its instrument. But Theophrastus places the guilt entirely on the body, precisely because the passions – anger, desire, jealousy – are all in the body, and it is these that persuade the soul to action.

The preferred solution of Christianity is that body and soul are mutually responsible. This solution links the dialogues to other ancient debates such as that in the Talmud between the blind man and the lame. A prince places a blind man and a lame man in charge of his garden, to guard the precious fruits that grow there. These guardians, it seems, cannot steal the fruit themselves, because the blind man cannot see it, and the lame man cannot climb up to pick it. But the blind man lifts the lame man up on his back, and together they enjoy the spoils. Thus it is with the body and the soul. Each, alone, claims it is pure before God. But God puts the soul back into the body and says, 'See, you have recovered; now be accountable'.[11]

A second important element in the understanding of how sin occurs is the role of the will. The will is indisputably a faculty of the soul and ought to ally itself with that other faculty of the soul, reason. Turning back once more to the *Phaedrus*, we recall that there were two horses, a black and a white. The white horse represented will and the black horse the passions. When the white horse obeyed the rider in the chariot (reason), the direction in which they moved was likely to be correct and good. If it obeyed the black horse, both horses and rider would plunge down to earth.

This same analogy of the horse and rider reappears in a Middle English body and soul dialogue, 'Als I Lay in a Winteris Nyt':

> To teche ʒwere thou me bi-tauʒt, ac ʒwan thouʒ thoʒ test of the
>   qued,
> With thi teth the bridel thouʒ lauʒt, thouʒ dist al that I the forbed.
> (You were assigned to obey me, And when you thought of testing
>   the evil one
> With your teeth you seized the bridle. You did everything that I
>   forbade you.)[12]

But here again, as with most of the other medieval debates, the conflict that the Platonic image depicts has moved from being between different faculties of the soul, to being between soul and body.

Dante, on the other hand, presents the conflict in rather more sophisticated terms borrowed from Aristotle and Aquinas, and places it entirely within the soul. This soul is created with the instinct to love (or desire), and is naturally drawn to what pleases it. From the 'real' world, it abstracts a form or essence that pleases it. The soul is naturally drawn to this abstracted form, and aspires towards it. But no one can be certain that the object of his love is actually a good. The innate counsel of his reason ought to inform him, and his will then should act to obey this reason. 'All love . . . springs from necessity; I but you still have the power to check its sway.'[13]

Lest we imagine that this interest in the role of the will in sin was a peculiar obsession of the classical period and the Middle Ages, here is a passage from Descartes, the seventeenth-century philosopher who first attempted to explain in scientific terms how body and soul interacted: 'And it is only in the repugnance which exists between the movements which the body by its animal spirits, and the soul by its will, tend to excite in the [pineal] gland at the same time, that all the strife which we are in the habit of conceiving to exist between the inferior part of the soul, which we call the sensuous, and the superior which is rational, or as we may say, between the natural appetites and the will, consists.'[14]

The freedom of the will is never questioned, because to do so would remove the grounds for holding man responsible for sin at all. Despite the Aristotelian conviction that if the soul or reason truly knew what was good, it could not possibly choose a lesser good or evil, Christianity, influenced by notions of original sin and innate depravity, insisted (as we have seen above in Dante) that as long as the good presented by reason was not wholly, unambiguously good, 'still there is place left for the Will to take or leave'.[15] In the final chapter we shall consider what happens to the soul when, as in our modern society, the complete freedom of the will *is* questioned.

A third key element in the conflict between the soul and the body is the matter of proper subordination – that is, which of them should rule the other. (The notion of equal partnership was not really something that would have occurred to anyone in the hierarchical society of the Middle Ages.) On this point there was no real contention; the soul as the higher element should be in charge. But who is most responsible when the body rebels? The rebellious body itself, or the soul that should have kept a firmer grip on its control? The analogy with parents and children might seem appropriate to us, but the most common analogy in the Middle Ages was in fact that of the relationship between husband and wife. And this could occur in surprising contexts.

In the previous chapter we found the soul in Hildebert of Lavardin's 'De Querimonia et Conflictu Carnis et Spiritus seu Animae' portrayed as indisputably feminine, when she appears to Hildebert to chastise him for his preoccupation with worldly things. Hildebert first casts himself into the role of body and argues against her, his soul, in the manner of the body in other dialogues we have examined – it was really her fault that he went astray; she should have held him in check. Hildebert claims that she seems to be arguing that proximity to the flesh destroyed her, just as Hercules' life was destroyed by the poisoned shirt his mother-in-law sent him. But Hercules did not poison the garment that killed him as the soul has poisoned the body by using it in the purposes it now finds hateful. At this point, Hildebert is still identified with the physical and his feminine visitor with the soul. But then something quite peculiar and apparently inconsistent happens: the man becomes equated with the soul and spirit and the woman with the body or flesh.

The soul replies that sin originated when Eve (flesh) tempted the spirit of Adam to agree to taste the apple in the Garden of Eden. This was the beginning of all subsequent sin. Adam succumbed to Eve's temptation, and she thus gained mastery over him.

> By these enemies [the serpent and the apple] fragile nature was
> tempted and sex was too weak to resist. For our flesh was
> tempted; woman was tempted, and in her person was wrought a
> state that either yielded through hunger or was deceived by
> simplicity. . . . And so flesh was delighted and roused by new
> counsels and took on a new daring. By the same means that it
> had been provoked to eat, it provoked the spirit to consent.
> Universal authority testifies to the fact that the first offence was
> born as a result of the flesh dominating and the spirit being
> subjugated, as a husband by his wife.[16]

94

The soul is masculine here not so much as a concrete visual image as through its abstract function: it is to rule the body just as a husband is to rule his wife. If wife or body gets out of hand, at least part of the responsibility must be that of the husband or soul. As in earlier dialogues, this defence of the soul depends on the body possessing the faculty of sense, rather than being just passive matter. This sensual body *can* tempt the soul just as Eve tempted Adam.

If soul and body in conflict are seen as similar to husband and wife, it should come as no surprise that husbands and wives arguing about who has done what often bear a remarkable similarity to medieval bodies and souls. The most notable example is to be found in Milton's *Paradise Lost*. The sin of Adam and Eve in this poem, as in Hildebert's dialogue, is seen as one of improper subordination: understanding no longer rules, and will does not choose to hear its wisdom. Both fall under the subjection of sensual appetite that claims superior sway.[17] Eve takes on certain qualities of body as she is seduced by the serpent's appeal to her vanity, and the look and taste of the apple. And Adam makes weak resistance when she offers it to him. Once they have each eaten of the apple, and the Fall has occurred, they begin to accuse one another in terms remarkably similar to those of a body and soul in the debates. Eve accuses Adam of not having forbidden her to leave him; he permitted her to be tempted and sin, she argues. Adam, furious, replies that he warned her and therefore cannot be held responsible. This dispute about whether the rebellious subordinate or the controlling superior is chiefly responsible for sin is by now very familiar. The final lines of Book IX might be the conclusion of any medieval or seventeenth-century debate:

> Thus they in mutual accusation spent
> The fruitless hours, but neither self-condemning,
> And of thir vain contest appeer'd no end.
>
> (IX. ll. 1187–9)

The General Incompatibility of Soul with Body

The passage just quoted from *Paradise Lost* portrays an unending struggle in which neither side can win. It is, indeed, like a bad marriage. Body and soul cannot live in this life without one another, but neither can they live with one another in harmony. The issue is not so much one of guilt as of incompatibility. As the quotation at the beginning of this chapter states, 'The soul and the body are seldom in agreement'. Medieval Christianity, for its own purposes, needed to assign guilt, but earlier and later writers did not see this as the only scenario. Plato saw the union of the soul with the body as a 'fall' for the soul, a union that was likely to cause it difficulties, but it was Plotinus who emphasized the inevitable instability of this union. Here is a fuller version of the quotation cited in Chapter 1:

A unity is independent: thus body alone, a lifeless thing, can suffer no hurt . . . and soul in similar isolation cannot even suffer dissolution, and by its very nature is immune from evil. But when two distinct things become one in an artificial unity, there is a probable source of pain to them in the mere fact that they were inapt to partnership. This does not of course, refer to two bodies; that is a question of one nature, and I am speaking of two natures. When one distinct nature seeks to associate itself with another, a different order of being . . . then the essential duality becomes also a unity but a unity standing midway between what the lower was and what it cannot absorb, and therefore a troubled unity.[18]

What this passage expresses very eloquently is the sense of inevitable struggle and opposition between soul and body that runs throughout Western literature.

The instinctive sense of the incompatibility of soul with the body pervades Guillaume de Deguileville's *The Pilgrimage of the Life of Man*, which was translated by John Lydgate in 1426. Much of the content of this lengthy poem is conventional – the discussion of original sin, the need for proper subordination of soul to body, and their mutual guilt. But around line twelve thousand (yes, it really *is* a long poem) we come upon an analogy that moves the conflict outside the narrow moral framework of the body and soul debates. The soul and the body, says Deguileville, are like two wheels turning within one another, similar to those Ezekiel saw (Ezekiel 10:9–14).

Deguileville's two wheels are one within the other and move in opposite directions, one eastward and one westward. The westward movement represents sensuality, or the body, while eastward movement represents the soul. There is constant conflict between these two contrary motions:

> Thys sayde whel (who kan espye)
> That I off spak, doth sygnefye
> Lust off the body, in hys mevyng,
> Wych clerkys calle (in ther wrytying
> And name yt) Sensualyte;
> The wych wyl nat brydled be,
> But ffroward euere in hys entent,
> Mevyng toward the occydent,
> Evere in on, bothe day & nyht,
> Wyth swych a swegh & swych a myght
> That, wher the spyryt gruchche or mourne,
> He maketh hym offtë to retourne
> Wyth hym ageyn by vyolence,
> Mawgre al hys résystence,
> Al-thogh the spyryt (in hys entent)
> Meueth toward the oryent,
> Wych thenys kam.[19]

[This wheel (whoever can see it) that I spoke of, signifies lust of the body in its moving, which clerks in their writing call sensuality. This will not be bridled but moves ever forward in intention towards the west, both day and night, with such a momentum that, when the spirit complains or mourns, it [the body] often makes the spirit return with him by violence, despite all its resistance, even though the spirit in intention moves towards the east, from which it came.]

Deguileville is borrowing his image here not primarily from Ezekiel, as he might like us to believe, but from the ancient movement of the spheres codified by the early thirteenth-century priest Sacrobosco.

According to this system, the outer sphere or *primum mobile* moves westward, and in its movement attempts to drag with it the inner spheres of the sun and planets. These, however, resist and try collectively to move in the opposite direction towards the east. The result of this is that the overall movement remains that of the *primum mobile*, but this is significantly retarded by the movement of the inner spheres in the opposite direction.

A further difficulty, from the symbolic point of view, is that the outer movement, which Sacrobosco calls 'rational', is westward, and the inner movement, 'irrational', is eastwards. This, derived from the classical Ptolemaic system of the spheres, does not accord with the Christian view that to move westwards is to move away from God, while eastward movement is towards God. John Donne, using the same analogy in the seventeenth century, is obviously troubled by this and, in 'Goodfriday, 1613. Riding Westward', makes the inner sphere, which moves towards the east, symbolic of his soul's good desires, which strive towards the scene of Christ's crucifixion, while the westward movement of the *primum mobile* represents both the physical movement of his body riding westward and the evil desires of the soul towards pleasure or business.

> Hence is't, that I am carried towards the West
> This day, when my Soules forme bends toward the East.[20]

Not only does Donne change the significance of the outer and inner spheres to make their motion more compatible with Christian symbolism; he moves the whole conflict from one between soul and body to one that is entirely within the soul, between its different faculties.[21] This is not original to him but is a return to the version of the conflict as envisaged in the later dialogues of Plato. In many ways it is more compatible with sophisticated Christian thinking, since it does not denigrate the body that has been sanctified by the Creation and Incarnation.

Whatever the precise working out of the symbolism, the contrary spheres, fighting against each other even as they move, are a potent sign of the impossibility of man functioning as a harmonious unity.

It is this incompatibility, this recognition that the union itself is detrimental to both soul and body, that is the basis of a short dialogue by the enigmatic A.W. (does it stand for Anonymous Writer?). Here the soul and body are not arguing about their specific sins or plight; neither are they focused on what will happen after death but rather on lamenting their mutual incompatibility in this life.

[*Soule*]	Ay me, poore Soule, whom bound in sinful chaines
	This wretched body keepes against my will!
Body	Aye mee, poore Body, whom for all my paines,
	This froward soule causlesse condemneth stil.
Soule	Causles? whenas thou striv'st to sin each day?
Body	Causles: whenas I strive thee to obay.
Soule	Thou art the meanes, by which I fall to sin,
Body	Thou art the cause that set'st this means awork.
Soule	No part of thee that hath not faultie bin:
Body	I shew the poyson that in thee doth lurke.
Soule	I shall be pure when so I part from thee:
	So were I now, but that thou stainest mee.[22]

The prison image predominates from the opening couplet, but as the poem progresses it is not at all clear who is the jailer and who the prisoner. The soul begins by chastising the body for keeping it in chains against its will, but the body insists that the soul's condemnation is unfair. It does not try to rebel and sin but obeys the soul. In the second stanza, however, the argument becomes more complicated, and it seems that the body's obedience to the soul may indeed have been their mutual downfall. The soul accuses the body of being the 'means' by which it falls to sin – that is, the agent through which its sin can be carried out in the world. But the body, which displays quite a level of sophistry for a being that on other occasions can plead its innocence as passive matter, accuses the soul of being the *cause* which moves desire to evil action. The planning of the evil is the soul's. The body merely 'shows' or manifests this evil by acting it out.

There is a remarkable parallel to this in the thirteenth-century Old French 'Un samedi par nuit', in which the body says to the soul: 'You were my lady. When you spurred me, I ran. You whipped me so that I could never rest.'[23] And in a subsequent passage the dominant role of the soul is stated with even more emphasis: 'I was tricked by you. You plotted the evil and then announced it to me. You thought it and I did it.'[24] This dialogue, from a much earlier period, is still imbued with concerns about sin and moral indignation. A.W.'s dialogue, which takes place during life, ends with the simple assertion on the part of the soul that it will be pure when it is separated from the body – an assertion that could just as well come from classical Greece as from Christian England in the early seventeenth century.

Even farther removed from religious and moral concerns is the seventeenth-century body and soul dialogue by Andrew Marvell – probably the best known of all these dialogues.[25] There are four stanzas, two each by soul and body. The Soul speaks first, bewailing its imprisonment within the body in very specific, physical terms:

> O who shall, from this Dungeon, raise
> A Soul inslav'd so many wayes?
> With bolts of Bones, that fetter'd stands
> In Feet; and manacled in Hands.
> Here blinded with an Eye; and there
> Deaf with the drumming of an Ear.
> A Soul hung up, as 'twere, in Chains
> Of Nerves, and Arteries, and Veins.
> Tortur'd, besides each other part,
> In a vain Head, and double Heart.

The soul's complaint is fundamentally paradoxical. Those parts of the body that ought to serve it for good are described as functioning in ways precisely opposite to that. Thus it is 'deaf' with the drumming of an ear, blinded with an eye, manacled in hands, and 'hung' or suspended in nerves, arteries and veins. Imprisonment is the essence of its misery, but the way this is described reminds the reader of the two ways in which man can acquire knowledge – through the senses, or directly and intuitively from a higher power. When the soul says it is deafened by an ear or blinded by an eye it does not mean that these bodily senses cannot perform their duty, but rather that the kind of information they provide is *only* physical, and therefore not what the soul really desires.

But the body insists its plight is just as dreadful:

> O who shall me deliver whole,
> From bonds of this Tyrannic Soul?
> Which, stretcht upright, impales me so,
> That mine own Precipice I go;
> And warms and moves this needless Frame:
> (A Fever could but do the same.)
> And, wanting where its spight to try,
> Has made me live to let me dye.
> A Body that could never rest,
> Since this ill Spirit it possest.

The soul is a tyrant to the body. The very properties of motion, heat and action all depend on it, and these are not necessarily desirable from body's point of view. Upright, able to act, the body finds itself in a precarious state, its 'own Precipice', as it carries out the bidding of the soul. At the end of 'Saint Bernard's Vision' we found the soul wishing it had never been put into a body. Here the body wishes it had never been united to a soul. Robbed of rest and tormented by emotion, it does not even have the promise of staying alive forever. The soul has endowed it with life only that it may eventually experience the horrors of death.

The soul can complain of unreasonable punishment as well:

> What Magick could me thus confine
> Within anothers Grief to pine?
> Where whatsoever it complain,
> I feel, that cannot feel, the pain.
> And all my Care its self employes,

> That to preserve, which me destroys:
> Constrain'd not only to indure
> Diseases, but, whats worse, the Cure:
> And ready oft the Port to gain,
> Am Shipwrackt into Health again.

The initial image of the soul confined by magic within the grief of another (the body) calls to mind the scene in *The Tempest* where Prospero threatens to confine Ariel inside an oak tree if he will not do his bidding. After this opening, the soul piles paradox upon paradox. Life in the body means it feels, through the body, the pain it could not feel in isolation from it. The soul must care for the body, but this care, which lengthens the time of their union, destroys the soul. Diseases might be welcome if they led to death and hence release, but the cure of these bodily diseases prevents such a release. The image of the soul as a boat about to make a safe landing (through death, presumably), and then being 'shipwrackt' into health highlights the way in which our normal expectations and perceptions are turned on their heads.

Unusually in these dialogues, it is the body that has the last word:

> But Physick yet could never reach
> The Maladies Thou me dost teach;
> Whom first the cramp of Hope does Tear:
> And then the Palsie Shakes of Fear.
> The Pestilence of Love does heat:
> Or Hatred's hidden Ulcer eat.
> Joy's cheerful Madness does perplex:
> Or Sorrow's other Madness vex.
> Which Knowledge forces me to know;
> And Memory will not foregoe.

Here the body goes through a whole catalogue of painful emotions it suffers as a result of its union with the soul. Despite the soul's talk of cures the body enjoys for its physical ailments, the body claims it suffers from psychical ills that no medicine can reach. The body makes no distinction between what we might call good and bad emotions. Hope, joy and love are just as unwelcome as fear, hatred and sorrow. All are disturbances from the passive, undemanding state for which it seems the body longs. Even memory is a curse, since it means that the painful knowledge and emotions the soul forces on it cannot be forgotten. The end result of body's possession by soul is that it has become a fit instrument for sin and, by implication, for punishment.

Then we have the final enigmatic coda.[26]

> What but a Soul could have the wit
> To build me up for Sin so fit?
> So Architects do square and hew,
> Green Trees that in the Forest grew.

The associations raised by the contrast between the green trees and the buildings hewn from them are both complex and ambiguous. One thinks first of a contrast between nature and art. The 'natural' body is implicitly on the side of nature, the 'green tree'; the more sophisticated soul, whose business it is to form and command the body, is, presumably, the architect. But which is more valuable in the end – what is free and unrestricted by artifice, or what has been crafted to human use by skill and artistic effort? The context of the coda within the complaint gives a natural bias to the 'green trees'. But is this really the attitude of the poet, or merely the point of view of the body?

Whatever value judgment one makes – and a value judgment is not really demanded – it is clear that the green trees and whatever the architect may make of them cannot exist simultaneously. One must be sacrificed for the other since there is a fundamental incompatibility between them. And perhaps this is the real point. Body and soul both long for separation, even if, in this poem, it means death. Each wishes to act according to its own nature, and these natures, as in a bad marriage, are incompatible. In this it differs profoundly from the medieval debates, where it is only sin and wickedness that had made soul and body incompatible. There good souls and bodies parted at death with regret, and expressed a longing for reunion at the last day.

What Marvell has really done is to dramatize our inmost conflicts in this life. We would, and we would not; we long for peace, to 'grow naturally', and we long for achievement and recognition, to 'square and hew' our works to a satisfactory design. The conflicts are unresolvable.

The Appearance of the Soul in the Debate Literature

I have discussed the origins, ideas and general concept of the soul that inform this literature of conflict. But what of the appearance of the soul? In the previous chapter it was a beautiful woman, and some residue of this tradition is found in the debate literature as well. The soul that appears to Hildebert, and then debates with him as if he were body, certainly fits this category. So does James Howell's soul, which begins as an aetherial spark, but gradually resolves into the shape of a 'veild Nunn with a flaming cross on the left side of her breast'. However, this feminine appearance is the exception here. The physical image of the souls in the dialogues and debates is not by any means consistent, and it seems often to be determined by function rather than by real visual imagination. In some of the dialogues such as Andrew Marvell's, there is no physical description at all.

In the fourteenth-century Cambridge manuscript of the 'Visio' both body and soul are clearly, if naïvely, visualized. Drawn in brown and red ink, the series of illustrations of cadaverous body and childlike soul has a strange, raw power. The body struggles as it summons up the energy to speak; the soul raises its hands in horror. Significantly, it is the soul in these drawings that appears the more 'human' and is clothed in flesh; the body has already decomposed into a fleshless skeleton. Soul, on the other hand, is almost chubby, with its round face topped by unruly sprigs of hair. The hideous devils, one with an additional face on his abdomen, drag the soul with a pole and rope towards hellmouth, which, as usual in medieval painting, is literally a gaping mouth.

And what of the sex of this soul? The drawings give little clue. There are certainly no genitals, and only in the first of the illustrations might there be a suggestion of breasts. Crashaw's translation, from which I have quoted, sometimes refers to the soul as 'she' and says it ought to have been 'mistress' of the body. Similarly, references to the body's wife in the text would indicate that in life the individual was male. But sex does not seem to be a very important matter here. The soul is relatively unformed and childlike – a miniature, undeveloped body.

The childlike soul finds its ancestor in the thirteenth-century French dialogue, 'Un samedi par nuit'. The appearance of the soul in this poem that takes place on a Saturday night some time after death, when the soul is briefly released from torment, is indeed extraordinary: 'The soul that issued forth seemed to me quite naked, in the appearance of a child. . . . The creature was a tiny figure . . . green as a chive.' As far as I know, this is the only soul specifically described as green in the whole of literature! Apart from its unusual colour, the childlike, sexless and miniature appearance of this soul links it to that in the 'Vision of Saint Bernard'. We shall meet it again in the separation scenes of Chapter 6.

In an illustration of soul attached to one of the body and soul ballads the soul is of adult size, but still, as far as one can tell given that a rope is tied around its waist and between its legs, sexless. It stands in an attitude of prayer (manifestly too late), while devils with pitchforks prepare a fire for it. Again, however, while deprived of sex, the soul retains its distinctive humanity.

What is the significance of this type of soul? The feminine soul was easier to explain. One possible suggestion is that the anonymity of the features and the sexlessness indicated the common nature of the human soul, and the universality of its plight. The soul that appeared to Saint Bernard (or Philibert), though ostensibly attached to the corpse before him, *might* be his soul. The moral lesson strikes home.

Earlier bodies and souls tend to be less visualized. The soul in the 'Homily of Macarius'[27] is distinguished only by its evil smell. But what might be a purely naturalistic detail turns out to be linked to the moral state of the soul. Physical characteristics become outward signs of an internal state. Much later, in the eleventh century, we find a manuscript in which the soul addresses the body after death (Vercelli Homily IV) that links the state of the soul not to the smell of its body but to its appearance. In one of these, for the sake of contrast, there is both a good soul and body and a wicked one, and both address their respective bodies in turn. As the wicked soul berates its body, the body itself grows physically uglier. But when the good soul thanks its body for having endured suffering during life, its body is transformed and becomes beautiful.[28] This may remind us of the connections between goodness and beauty in the last chapter, and indeed there are similarities. In this case, however, it is not that the external appearance is an infallible marker for the internal state, but rather that the acknowledgement of moral goodness or wickedness literally changes appearance.

CONCLUSION

The modern reader may be forgiven for thinking both the form and the macabre content of this literature are of antiquarian interest only. Most of us do not spend so much of our lives worrying about what will happen after death that we would be likely to have a vision of elements of our being debating in some afterlife. The separation of the individual into two 'persons' that are pictured in this way seems intolerably naïve to us.

Yet early in the twentieth century, William Butler Yeats in 'A Dialogue of Self and Soul' used the general concept to debate two completely different ways of living life and valuing it. Here the soul is an ascetic, urging the individual to the steep ascent of learning, to a life of wisdom and resignation that will deliver the self from the endless cycle of passion, birth and death. But the self (which here, unusually, has the characteristics of body), prefers to remain attached to the life of flux and human events, even if it means miring itself in a physicality that is aesthetically repulsive. Rather than abnegate life, the self wishes to understand it, to follow action and thought to their sources, and having done this to be able to forgive itself for everything arising from this imperfect, human condition.[29] The terms of this debate are different from those of earlier centuries, but the basic notion of arguing out within oneself the deepest issues of life has not changed.

A modern example of this kind of dialogue is found in Jane Roberts' collection of poems, *Dialogues of the Soul and Mortal Self in Time*. Here the 'mortal self', encased in body, debates with her soul, claiming that the soul simply doesn't understand the limitations and constraints of life on earth.

> Perfection isn't human
> and here all creatures die.
> The leaves fall downward, not up
> for all your holy talk,
> and I've never seen
> one small corpse of a bird
> pick itself up again and fly.[30]

The soul responds in a rather superior and condescending tone ('Oh my, what metaphysical conceit'), and initially the mortal self chooses to cast its lot with the flesh, which 'speaks a living alphabet'. It casts doubt on the soul's insistence that 'we sculpt our lives out of our thoughts'. In 'Dialogue Four: The Body's Warm Home', the poetess describes in dreams leaving the body, rushing 'outside my bones I like smoke'.

> Once I breaststroked
> through the clear night air
> while my waiting
> skeleton flashed white warning.
>
> (p. 16)

Yet in the end she snuggles back 'into this heated nest of skin and blood I that I call home'.

> It may be perilous, hung
> between birth and death,
> but this body's mine,
> and dammit, loved.
>
> (p. 17)

Jane Roberts' sequence of poems concludes with a reconciliation between soul – a being that she says looks 'so much like me I that I

107

get confused' (p. 46) – and the mortal self. They simply cannot be disengaged from one another. As the soul says, 'I'm the you | from which your you-ness | constantly appears' (p. 100). To deny the Soul is, ultimately, to deny the very identity of self.

Other concerns present in the medieval dialogues also surface in our current thinking. Sophisticated as we may believe ourselves, I would claim that the general fear of death and even more the fear of a misspent life, a life directed to the wrong ends, is with us today. And we still externalize our temptations and fates. 'The devil tempted me', is usually said jocularly today, and we have largely given up believing in and burning witches. But 'something got into me' is frequently a more serious expression of what we claim has led to an action. The most common modern way (and probably the one that is most analogous to the body and soul dialogue) of shedding responsibility for action is to plead abnormal brain chemistry. Here the chemicals, hormones or receptors in the brain are the uncontrollable elements that are not amenable to reason and force the person to act in a way for which it can be argued he/she as a whole person cannot be held accountable. Thus these elements within the brain, in the popular imagination, take on an independent life of their own, causing us to act in ways that are not directly under the control of the will. All we lack is an artist or poet to give them a physical shape.

As it happens, in 'An Anatomy of Migraine', Amy Clampitt has done just that. Here it is not body and soul that is the seat of conflict but the double-hemisphered brain, 'at the very core a battle; so the neurobiological | dilemma of the paired, the hemispheric | re-ramifies— bright, dark; left, right; | right, wrong—' that fights against the integration of the self, the 'precarious sense of *I am I*'. The pairings or words she uses here can be seen as implicitly moral, though divorced from any specific frame of reference. And these opposing forces, recognized by Plato, Galen and Descartes – and dimly by our medieval dialogists – extend like a destructive force throughout the universe, 'as though | the cosmos repented of itself, of all those | promises, all those placebos'.[31] The soul or the brain – we continue to need a metaphor for the conflict that is at the very heart of our being.

FOUR

The Soul at Play

Mankinde-is bed schal be under the castel, and there schal the sowle
  lye under the bed tyl he schal ryse and pleye
('Mankind's bed shall be under the castle, and there the soul shall lie,
  under the bed, until he shall rise and play.')

The Castle of Perseverance

Even more remarkable than the body and soul dialogues for their
insistence in seeing the soul as a concrete entity are the plays
that actually portray it as a character on the stage. Bizarre as it may
seem, from the time of the English mystery plays of the fifteenth and
early sixteenth centuries, through the Spanish *autos sacramentales*
(sixteenth and seventeenth centuries) up to some extraordinary
examples from the twentieth century, this has taken place.

I have made cursory references in previous chapters to some of the
reasons/justifications that writers have given for portraying the soul
in physical terms.[1] It seems, however, that before presenting the
most concrete of all representations of the soul – that as an actor on
the stage – this convention that gives to the soul in literature the
attribute of physical presence and visibility now needs to be looked
at in more detail.

THE SOUL AS A VISIBLE ENTITY

We have seen that a good number of the Church Fathers believed that
the soul had a shape that was in some way visible, probably
resembling that of the physical body.[2] Even when they did not *believe*
this theologically they wrote and painted as if it were so. A
remarkable illustration from the *Très Riches Heures du Duc de Berry*
for Psalm 25 ('Unto Thee O Lord do I lift up my soul') shows the

109

psalmist holding up a miniature of his naked self to God. Other writers and theologians, ranging from Saint Augustine to the Cambridge Platonists Henry More and Ralph Cudworth in the seventeenth century, solved the need for the soul to be 'imaginable' by insisting that it was never separated from a body of some sort – that even after death it had a 'celestial' (Augustine) or 'airy' (Henry More) body.

One of the most extensive and interesting presentations of souls occurs in Dante's *Divine Comedy* which, set entirely in the afterlife, is populated almost exclusively by souls – that is, the dead who have already been assigned to one sphere or another, though they all still await the final judgment. Dante and Virgil (the latter also a spirit) travel painfully through hell and purgatory before Dante alone reaches paradise. (Virgil, as a good man but a non-believer in Christ, returns to his assigned sphere of Limbo before heaven is reached.) The overall structure of the *Divine Comedy* is based on the move- ment towards the heavenly kingdom where Beatrice resides, but its intermediate movement rests on the familiar dead that Dante meets and whose story he hears. To do this he must recognize them, and he does. Indeed, their appearance and voices are very similar to those they had in life. Yet they are souls or spirits.

It is only in Canto XXV of *Purgatorio* that Dante asks for and receives an explanation of the contradictory elements of the physical and the spiritual in these souls. By this time he has met Statius (a Roman poet, AD 45–96) who, unlike Virgil, secretly converted to Christianity and is therefore in purgatory, and who reveals these things to him. At this point Dante, Statius and Virgil are all on the sixth cornice, where the gluttonous are being punished. Although surrounded by tempting food, the gluttonous are not allowed to eat, and consequently grow thin. But Dante asks, 'How can they grow so thin, who need no food in their new state?'[3]

This is the impetus for Statius to launch into a long disquisition on the soul. He explains its origin in the Aristotelian terms with which we are familiar: the perfect blood from the male heart becomes sperm, descends to the sexual organs, and from thence the male active blood drops on to the passive blood in the female womb. This active blood, breathed on by the power of God, forms the soul, while the passive matter becomes the body. At death, the soul is freed from the flesh 'but takes with it the essence I of its divine and human faculties' (ll. 80–1) such as memory, intelligence and will. 'Miraculously . . . I it falls at once to one or the other shore' (ll. 86–7) and in its new atmosphere, the formative parts of the soul, which formed the body in the womb, again use their powers to shape an image.

> Then, as the air after a rain will glow
> 　　inside itself, reflecting an outer ray,
> 　　and clothe itself in many colors – so
>
> wherever the soul may stop in its new hour,
> 　　the air about it takes on that soul's image.
> 　　Such is the virtue of the *formative power*.
>
> 　　　　　　　　　　　　　　　　(ll. 91–6)

This new form follows the soul eternally, as flame follows fire. It draws its visibility from the air; hence it is called a *shade*. From the surrounding air it also forms organs of sight, speech and all the other senses. Thus spirits can speak, laugh, weep and desire, and the shades change their appearance according to these emotions. It is in this way that those souls who are being punished for gluttony show all the symptoms of starvation, even though they no longer need food to survive. It is also in this way that the spirits Dante meets are recognizable by appearance and voice.

There is no Christian precedent for this representational means of portraying souls.[4] While orthodoxy states that after the Last Judgment souls will be united to their own bodies so that they may fully experience damnation or bliss, there is no indication that spirits have bodies of their own. For Augustine, any perceived representation of a soul is a mere phantasm, like an image in a dream. Aquinas does not even require the soul in torment to have a body, since its torments are spiritual.[5] But Dante's souls experience sensory pain and pleasure through their aetherial bodies. That these are not solid but 'airy' is shown by the soul's constant amazement that Dante, as one still living, casts a shadow, which they cannot do.

It would seem that this 'shade' that Dante describes owes a great deal to the most famous work of his guide, Virgil, in hell and purgatory – the *Aeneid*. The very term 'shade' goes back to Homer, and in Virgil the two terms, 'soul' (*anima*) and 'shade' (*umbra*) are both used. When Aeneas descends to the Underworld he recognizes and speaks with Anchises, his father, but the 'shade-like' nature of his form is shown by Aeneas' inability to grasp his hand – just as Odysseus could not clasp his mother. For Dante, however, the shade of the dead is not a permanent form. It mediates between life in the world and the Last Judgment, when it will be replaced by the resurrected body.

This explanation of 'airy bodies' gives Dante theological and, if one can apply the word in this age, 'scientific' justification for characterizing souls as beings that can be apprehended by the human senses. But there is another reason that is, perhaps, even more compelling. It does not appear overtly in the *Inferno* or *Purgatorio*, not until the *Paradiso*. At this point Dante is taking literally certain things that he has seen in the heavenly spheres, when Beatrice tries to resolve his confusion by explaining that they are to be understood symbolically. Their literalness is an accommodation (though Beatrice does not use this word) to the weakness of mortals, who cannot understand divine truth directly.

> So must one speak to mortal imperfection,
> which only from the *sensible* apprehends
> whatever it then makes fit for intellection.
>
> Scripture in like manner condescends,
> describing God as having hands and feet
> as signs to men of what more it portends.[6]

We mortals can only comprehend through our senses; therefore the spiritual must become sensible for our benefit.

Centuries later, this argument is taken up by Milton, who applies it primarily not to souls but to spiritual beings such as angels. (Milton also believed that spirits had airy bodies, but that is not the defence he makes of the way he treats them in *Paradise Lost*.) His argument centres, rather, on the need to make the events in heaven comprehensible to those on earth. How can one present to mortals the struggle between good and evil angels in heaven? Milton, speaking through Raphael to Adam and Eve, accepts the difficulty.

> Sad task and hard, for how shall I relate
> To human sense th'invisible exploits
> Of warring Spirits? . . .
> . . . yet for thy good
> This is dispenc't, and what surmounts the reach
> Of human sense, I shall delineate so,
> By lik'ning spiritual to corporal forms,
> As may express them best. . . .[7]

Analogy is to be the basis of his literary method. The battle between Satan and his cohorts and the other angels in heaven presents Milton with his greatest challenge. A cosmic struggle between good and evil between 'Spirits that live throughout | Vital in every part' (VI.344–5) is couched in terms of seventeenth-century warfare. Thus at the end of Book VI Raphael again reminds Adam and Eve that this cannot be seen as a literal description of what really happened in heaven. He is 'measuring things in Heav'n by things on Earth' (VI.893) so that they may understand them.

At one level any representational description of the battle in heaven might seem an inadequate 'objective correlative' for the theological concept. However, the implied correspondence between the earthly and the heavenly does itself make an important theological statement. Earth and heaven *are* linked (on a more trivial level, Milton insists that the hill and dale landscape of earth is modelled on the heavenly landscape),[8] and the likening of spiritual to corporeal forms has a significance beyond that of mere poetic necessity.

THE SOUL ON STAGE: MEDIEVAL AND RENAISSANCE PLAYS

The medieval theatre was born within the confines of the church. The earliest dramas were simple actings out of Bible stories. The

113

Quem Quaeritis plays, so-called from the opening words of the Latin text: 'Whom do ye seek', were tableaux of the women visiting the empty tomb on Easter morning. Eventually, these plays became much more elaborate and formed cycles that dramatized the whole history of mankind, from the creation of the world to the Last Judgment. They moved out of the church and were staged in innyards or on carts that were drawn through the streets of the town or city, stopping at various 'stations' for a performance. It was possible to stand on a medieval street corner and see the whole history and meaning of human life unfold before your eyes in the course of a day. These cycles of plays were called either 'mystery' plays, because each was sponsored by a different craft guild or 'mystery', or Corpus Christi plays because they were most often played on the Feast of Corpus Christi.

Alongside these 'mystery' plays there also grew up 'morality' plays. These differed from the mysteries in that they dealt not with the Biblical history of the world, but with how man ought to live. Typically, a central character representing mankind would be tempted in various ways. Usually he would nearly succumb to these temptations, only to be rescued at the end by Good Deeds, Mercy, or some such allegorical character representing an abstract virtue. These morality plays were highly allegorical, with virtues and vices represented by suitably costumed figures on the stage. Not surprisingly, it is in one of these plays that we first meet a character that is the human soul.

The Castle of Perseverance

The first known play in which the soul makes a stage appearance is *The Castle of Perseverance*, a morality play dating from about 1425.[9] We have a sketch of the stage set, which shows the Castle in the centre of a round playing space, with five scaffolds to be occupied by the World (West), the Flesh (South), the Devil (North), Covetousness (North-East), and God (East). Mankind, advised by both a good and bad angel, is attacked by the World, the flesh and the Devil together with their attendants, the Seven Deadly Sins. The

Castle is defended by the Seven Virtues (Meekness, Charity, Abstinence, Chastity, Industry, Generosity, Patience), and the Four Daughters of God. At first Mankind is persuaded by the arguments of World and ascends the scaffold of Covetousness, but eventually Shrift (confession) and Penance persuade him to come down, repent and enter the Castle of Perseverance itself, where he will be protected from the attacks of the Seven Deadly Sins.

The Devil and his cohorts plot to regain Mankind's loyalty and attack the Castle, initially without success. But eventually Covetousness persuades Mankind to leave the Castle with him, despite the pleading of the Virtues. At first he is more than content with the riches that Covetousness offers him, but before long Death enters and strikes him with his dart. Seeing Mankind dangerously wounded, World then turns on him, tells him that all his goods will be lost, and wishes him quickly dead. After cursing World for his infidelity, Mankind realizes the folly of his life and lies down on his bed to die. Once he is dead, Soul crawls from beneath his bed. Soul stands by the bed and begins to upbraid the body in terms similar to those in the dialogues of the last chapter. After venting his rage against the dead Mankind for his life of iniquity, Soul changes and pleads with the Good Angel for Mercy. Alas, the Good Angel says he is unable to help because Mankind was in thrall to Covetousness; there is no option for him other than hell. Then Soul calls on Mercy. But before Mercy can intervene, the Bad Angel carries Soul on his back to the scaffold of the Devil (hell).

Next the Four Daughters of God (of whom Mercy is one) appear and argue among themselves whether Mankind should be punished or saved. Truth and Righteousness take a hard line, but Mercy and Peace beg for clemency. They ascend the scaffold of God, their Father, and appeal to him. God decides for Mercy and Peace. The Daughters of God then rescue Mankind's Soul from the scaffold of the Devil and lead it to the throne of God.

The play is intended as an exemplary lesson for its audience. Mankind is seduced by the pleasures of the world until Death precipitates the crisis that leads him to turn from these transient things to God. As such, it has much in common with the best known of the morality plays, *Everyman*. But the appearance of the Soul on the stage is unique. It is regrettable that although we are told how each of the Daughters of God is to be clothed, there is no indication as to what Soul should look like. It is worth noting that this Soul, crawling out from under the bed at the time of death, seems to have no role to play within life. This is the immortal part of Mankind, only set free at the dissolution of the body.

The Welsh Soul and Body

The next appearance of Soul on the stage in Britain occurs in a Welsh play that dates from the early sixteenth century but is really medieval, not Renaissance, in concept. *Soul and Body* belongs in type to the earlier moral plays dealing with the coming of death, and the unhappy end of a life given over to pride and lust.[10] The Body addresses the audience and makes it clear that the play is to warn them against vainglory, haughtiness and frivolousness. The action begins with Body and Soul debating just before the time of death. As usual, each blames the other for the misspent life they have led. The Body (here masculine) accuses the Soul of being 'mistress' over him, commanding him to do evil. The Soul claims evil was the body's idea. In the midst of these conventional accusations, however, there is a delightfully human moment when the Body, acknowledging the presence of the audience, says plaintively, 'Many here are listening | To thee saying this, | That I was troubling thee.'[11] The self-pitying and justificatory tone for a moment lifts the play out of the realm of stereotype and into the sphere of real characterization and emotion.

At the end of the unresolved debate, the Soul departs from the Body, and the Devil and Michael struggle for it. Jesus and Mary appear, and Mary asks that the Soul be weighed in order to settle the matter. Eventually the Soul is saved, for those who repent even at the hour of death will not be punished. The grappling of devils and angels for the Soul, and its being weighed are new features in this drama, but as part of the process of death and judgment we shall look at them in more detail in the chapter on the soul at the time of death.[12]

The Soul at Play

Spanish Plays: Farsa rational del libre albedrío

It was not in England but in Spain that the soul had its longest run on the stage. In England the Reformation put an end to the mystery and miracle plays, which were dying out in any case as more sophisticated forms of drama became popular. But in Catholic Spain the Church continued to encourage religious drama so that it had a much longer history, flourishing well into the seventeenth century with some plays continuing to be staged into the eighteenth. Here too the rigid dogmatic restraints of the moralities were cast off, and the plays developed with a freedom and humour that contrast with their northern counterparts. A good example of such a play featuring both soul and body is *Farsa racional del libre albedrío* ('The rational farce of free will') by Diego Sánchez de Badajoz,[13] published in 1554.

The central theme of the play is the temptation of Free Will by Sensuality and Error. This struggle between good and evil is in the same tradition as *The Castle of Perseverance,* but the characterization is at once freer and more clearly visualized, with a generous element of humour. Free Will, dressed as a man fully armed, enters and boasts of his power, his riches and his appearance. He wants to marry, and naturally, for a person of such grandeur, he wants 'the most beautiful, perfect wife | to be found in the whole world'. At this opportune moment, Body, dressed as a shepherd, comes on stage with Soul, dressed as an angel, tied to him and dragged along by him. Body has the answer to Free Will's desire for a wife: his very own daughter, one Sensuality (who will later appear dressed as a tart), will do nicely. Body sings the praises of his daughter, who is the prettiest, most lovely young girl in the whole world. But Free Will is not impressed. Body, dressed as a shepherd, is wearing such dirty clothes! This man can hardly be the father-in-law for him!

Free Will asks him who he is. 'I am the Body, and this is the Soul | who spoils all my pleasures.' At this the captive Soul pipes up saying that she shrinks from him because he pursues only perishable things. She wishes to ascend to God but is constantly held down by Body's weight. Free Will, witnessing this scene, is puzzled because, he points out, in the perfect state, body was subject to the soul and reason.

117

But Soul explains how the sin of Adam has changed all that. Free Will then turns to Body and admonishes him to subject himself to the Soul and God, but Body breaks out in harsh defiance. Soul reminds him that God is merciful, and Free Will reiterates this, 'but on condition I that you turn from ugly to beautiful'. Soul urges Body to penance, but when Free Will mentions the effort required to turn from evil to good, Body can only joke about the effort of dancing to the music of guitars, the greatest difficulty he can manage.

Eventually, however, Body does express a desire to learn how to restrain his evil deeds, and then Free Will brings out the Ten Commandments for his edification. But Body soon tires of instruction and reverts to form. Soul wishes to fast, Body wants a feast; Soul want to go to Mass, Body to play. He complains of Soul, who is still tied to him, 'How she tugs, the wretch! How cross she is, how she struggles!' Free Will intervenes, seizes Body's own hand, and beats him with it. Body calls out to his daughter, repeating his praises of her and his desire to make a gift of her to Free Will. This time, Free Will shows some interest and asks who she is. 'She is my Sensuality, I She will drive you crazy if you see her.' At this, Sensuality enters, singing and playing a tambourine. Soul then compels Body to leave, and the focus of the rest of the play shifts to the temptation of Free Will by Sensuality.

This stage version of the conflict between soul and body during life recapitulates many of the themes in the body and soul dialogues – the paradox of their incompatibility and union in life, and the need for proper subordination between them. However, the images of the two as rather grubby shepherd and pure angel, coupled with the literal yoking of them together adds a new element to their characterization. There is no real evidence that the union between them in this play is a marriage (in which case, Sensuality would be the offspring of Soul as well), but the struggle between them and the impossibility of Soul's escape certainly suggest this.

Spanish Plays: El Pleito Matrimonial del Cuerpo y el Alma

A century later an allegory of marriage is precisely the situation that Calderón, one of Spain's leading dramatists, uses for his *auto*

1 The soul-bird in the Egyptian Book of the Dead, Egyptian Museum, Cairo (see pp. 5–6, 137). *(The Bridgeman Art Library)*

2 Mummified food for the king's *ka*-soul (see p. 2). From *The Illustrated London News*, illustrating an article on 'Tutankhamen's larder', 1923. *(The Bridgeman Art Library)*

3 As Prokris is slain by her husband, Cephalus, her soul, as a bird, flies upwards (see p. 2). Attic red-figured krater, fifth century BC. *(British Museum)*

4 Attic black-figure amphora depicting Orpheus playing his lyre to Athena, *c.* sixth century BC (see pp. 9–10). *(Ashmolean Museum, Oxford/The Bridgeman Art Library)*

5 Hermes entrusting the infant Dionysos to Silenus. Attic crater, *c.* 440–435 BCE (see pp. 10–11). *(Gregorian Museum of Etruscan Art, Vatican/ photograph © Scala, Florence, 1990)*

6 Charon ferries souls across the Styx (see pp. 173–4; cf. Plate 37). Marble relief from a sarcophagus, third century, AD. *(Art Resource)*

7 The soul, on death, returns to its own star (see pp. 21–2). Illustration to Dante's *Paradiso* by Paoli. *(British Library, Yates/Thompson MS 36)*

8 Butterfly held in the hand of a skeleton and inscribed 'Psyche', from a silver cup found at Boscoreale (see p. 49). *(Musée du Louvre/photograph © RNM – Hervé Lewandowski)*

9 Jupiter, with Mercury and 'Virtus' (or Virgo), creating souls as butterflies by painting them, by Dosso Dossi (*c.* 1479–1542) (see p. 49). *(Kunsthistorisches Museum, Vienna/Art Resource)*

10 Psyche and Eros in *biga* (see pp. 49–50). Relief fragment from Taranto, *c.* 430–410 BC. *(Ashmolean Museum, Oxford)*

11 Winged Psyche (see p. 49). *(Musei Capitolini, Rome/Art Resource)*

12 'The Soul Exploring the Recesses of the Grave'. The soul, unlike the mortal youth on top of the cave, is privileged to see death (see pp. 72–3). Illustration by Louis Schiavonetti after William Blake, for Robert Blair's 'The Grave'. *(National Gallery of Victoria)*

13 'The Reunion of the Soul and Body' (see p. 72). Illustration by William Blake, for Robert Blair's 'The Grave'. *(Mary Evans Picture Library)*

14 'The Soul Hovering over the Body Reluctantly Parting with Life' (see p. 73). Illustration by William Blake, for Robert Blair's 'The Grave'. *(Mary Evans Picture Library)*

15 Philibert the hermit has a vision of soul and body debating in the dead of a winter's night (see pp. 84–7). From *Visio Philiberti*, Cambridge University Library MS Add 3093, fol. 1v. (*Cambridge University Library*)

16 The body raises itself with groans and replies to the soul's accusations (see pp. 84–7). From *Visio Philiberti*, Cambridge University Library MS Add 3093, fol. 3r. *(Cambridge University Library)*

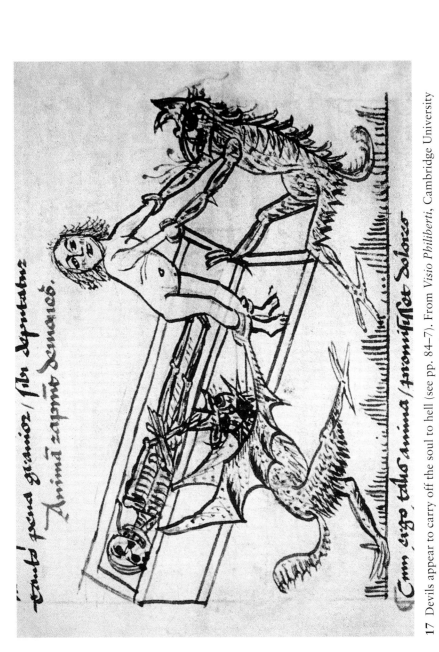

17 Devils appear to carry off the soul to hell (see pp. 84–7). From *Visio Philiberti*, Cambridge University Library MS Add 3093, fol. 5v. (*Cambridge University Library*)

18 The soul is dragged towards hellmouth (see pp. 84–7). From *Visio Philiberti*, Cambridge University Library MS Add 3093, fol. 6v. *(Cambridge University Library)*

19 Emblem by Andrea Alciati, *Nupta contagioso* (A Woman Married to an Infected Man), Padua, 1621. The plate depicts King Mezencio, who has ordered his daughter to be bound with a man suffering from the plague (a forced marriage). In *El Pleito*, Soul laments, 'And finally, my torment is the torment of the tyrant who bound together a living and dead person, since I suffer the filth of their lewdness, desires, appetites, anger, gluttony, and imprudence' (see p. 119) *(Photograph courtesy of the British Library)*

20 Stage setting for *The Castle of Perseverance* (see pp. 114–16). From *Chief Pre-Shakespearean Dramas*, ed. Joseph Quincy Adams (London: George G. Harrap & Co. Ltd, 1925), p. 264.

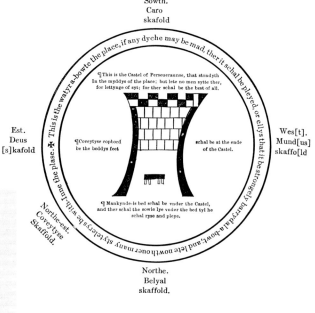

Sowth.
Caro
skafold

This is the watyr a-bowte the place, if any dyche may be mad, ther it schal be pleyed, or ellys that it be strongely barryd a-bowt, and lete nowth ouer many stytelerys be with-inne the place.

¶ This is the Castel of Perseueraunse, that stondyth In the myddys of the place; but lete no men sytte ther, for lettynge of syt; for ther schal be the best of all.

Est.
Deus
[s]kafold

¶Coveytyse copbord be the beddys feet

schal be at the ende of the Castel.

Wes[t].
Mund[us]
skaffo[ld

¶ Mankynde-is bed schal be vnder the Castel, and ther schal the sowle lye vnder the bed tyl he schal ryse and pleye.

Northe-est.
Coveytyse
Skaffold.

Northe.
Belyal
skaffold.

21 Drawing of an Indian spirit guide (see pp. 130–1). From Ruth Brandon, *The Spiritualists*, p. 38.

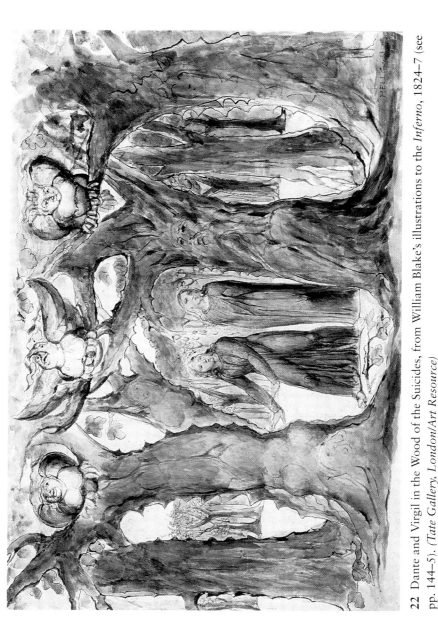

22 Dante and Virgil in the Wood of the Suicides, from William Blake's illustrations to the *Inferno*, 1824–7 (see pp. 144–5). *(Tate Gallery, London/Art Resource)*

23 'The Soul Visiting the Mansions of the Dead', by Paul Nash (see pp. 141, 211–12). From *Urne Buriall* and *The Garden of Cyrus*, ed. John Carter, with thirty drawings by Paul Nash *(London: Cassell & Co., 1932)*. (© Tate London, 2003)

24 *My Soul is an Enchanted Boat*, by Walter Crane (see pp. 143–4). *(The Bridgeman Art Library)*

25 Dante and Virgil in the eighth circle of hell, the 'stinking ditch' of the souls of the alchemists and falsifiers. Botticelli's illustration of Canto 29 of the *Inferno*. (*Art Resource*)

26 Good and evil angels struggle for possession of a child. 'Good and Evil Angels', by William Blake, 1795/?c. 1805. (*Art Resource*)

sacramentale about Soul and Body: *El Pleito Matrimonial del Cuerpo y el Alma* ('The Matrimonial Strife between the Body and the Soul').[14] Calderón's work was a Corpus Christi play, written in honour of the Holy Eucharist. These *autos* have some similarities to the medieval mystery plays, but they have a tightness of form and an ability to deal with more complex religious problems that sets them apart from the medieval mysteries. *El Pleito* was probably written before 1640, but was not published until 1655.

As the play opens, Body and Soul are about to be united in marriage. The first characters on the stage are Sin and Death. We are given no physical description of Sin, but Death bears the conventional scythe, and makes his entrance by cleaving a tree in which he has been encased. Sin and Death begin by abusing one another, but they soon make common cause, recognizing that, firstly, they are related (Death is the offspring of Sin), and secondly, both of them envy and hate man. Sin admits that he, in the form of a serpent, wished to be united to the noble and beautiful Soul, whose home is in the mind of God. But instead the Soul has the idea of 'entering the shapeless embryo of a faceless, formless corpse, into which she will breathe life and awareness – the body of an uncouth peasant, made of impure matter, a mud of earth and saliva, so rough and rustic himself that without the soul he can undertake nothing, achieve nothing, think nothing'. The Soul, Sin recognizes, is an intermediate kind of being. It is neither without beginning nor end (as God is) nor *with* beginning and end, as the Body is, but with a beginning yet without an end. As such she may unite herself to a lower nature. To their marriage Soul will bring her Powers (memory, will and understanding), while Body brings the five senses. It is, of course, a forced marriage, and it has been suggested that the play evokes Alciati's emblem *Nupta contagioso*, which depicts the king Mezencio ordering his daughter to be wed to a man suffering from the plague.[15] Having described the desirability of Soul and the appalling nature of her union to Body, Sin suggests to Death that, while they two cannot prevent the marriage, Death can annul it by his intrinsic power of separating Soul and Body. Then Sin will carry Soul off to his underground prison where, presumably, he can enjoy her.

Next a cave is revealed in the side of a rock. Inside is Body, asleep. Sin boasts of his power to make the crack in the rock widen, so that the womb-like boulder may 'spit him out', 'abort him'. He points out the circularity of Body's fate: just as he comes out of the centre of the earth, so will he return to it as his grave. To be born and to die are thus united actions. Body in his cave is helpless, with lips that cannot taste, eyes that cannot see, and so forth. To add to Sin's chagrin, he can see Soul, the intended bride of this unattractive lump, seated above on a throne of glory. There is a real element of social comedy in this play: 'What is a nice girl like you doing marrying a creep like him?'

Body, against all probability, because he has not yet been united to Soul and should, therefore, be inanimate, begins to speak. And the content of his opening remarks are even less likely for the oaf he is presented as being than the fact that he can speak at all. He debates, rather like a primitive Hamlet, whether he wishes to be or not to be – that is, whether he should be united to Soul. In the end he decides that not being will be worse than the worst that can happen by living. Death comments, sardonically, 'He is making every effort to develop himself'!

Body's decision having been made, Soul descends, protesting that she enters into this marriage unwillingly. As she reaches earth, she immediately trips and falls into the arms of Sin. She is filled with fear, but cannot escape original sin, and asks, 'Is this to be born, or to die?' To this Sin replies, 'Is not to be born the same as to die?' Meanwhile, Body is taking on new strength and new desires. He leaves the cave, but as he does so he, like Soul, trips and falls – in his case into the arms of Death. He asks the same question as Soul, and receives, from Death, the same reply.

As they are joined in marriage Life enters with a torch; the united Soul and Body will survive as a human being as long as the flame lasts.

At first Body is enamoured of the beautiful Soul, and seeks instruction from her on how to use the senses. Soul introduces him to her powers of Memory, Will and Understanding. (The other two characters are not described, but Understanding is a fashionable young man.) Understanding, seeing that Soul has been sullied by Sin, invites her to wash – symbolic of the sacrament of baptism. This does not banish Sin entirely, but changes him from Original to Present Sin.

Death snatches the flame from Life, and by gaining control of it leaves Body and Soul in uncertainty as to when their dissolution will come. But Understanding promises a food that he will serve at their wedding banquet that will save both Life and Soul. All go out to the feast except Will, who stays behind, grumbling about 'geriatric Understanding', and resolving to make certain that from now on everything that Body does displeases Soul. At every point it is the support of Will that determines who dominates. This recalls both the orthodox theology of the Church Fathers and the philosophy of classical philosophers, for all of whom will was the decisive element in moving desire to action. Now Sin enters and conspires with Will to bring about Soul's ruin.

When everyone returns from the feast Body is vocal in his dissatisfaction, since the only thing Understanding offered him to eat was 'a piece of bread without flavour or substance'. (This being the Roman Catholic Eucharist, poor Body didn't even get a taste of the wine.) Soul and Life remonstrate with him, but he summons Will to prepare another banquet, one that actually has some proper food. He also orders rich garments, and as guests, Beauty and Idleness. Sin begins to prepare the banquet. Soul recalls banquets from the Old Testament that led to disaster, and says, rather puritanically, 'All banquets end in tragedy.'

Then Body plays his trump card: 'As you are already my wife, you must obey me.' This sets up a conflict between Soul's role as wife, which demands subordination to husband, and that as Soul, which demands dominance over Body. Soul threatens to leave Body, and there is talk of an annulment. But Life swoons at this, and Body becomes weak, so they decide to patch things up for the present. 'Marriages in which there is inequality are never happy,' says Soul. 'I am yours, but even if you cry I shall have my own way,' replies Body. Music and song reinforce the message that the incompatibility within the marriage is such that only their child, Life, holds them together.

All go to the new banquet prepared by Body except Under-standing, who refuses to participate in vanity. Death then enters, carrying the flame of Life that he has stolen, and offers to help Understanding by reminding Man of his mortality through Sleep, Death's minister.

Soul comes running in, deserting the banquet, because Under-standing was not with her. Body, having partaken of the banquet, falls asleep just as Death has planned. At this, the powers of Soul and Life also wane. Death says he has brought this about so that Body will believe in his mortality. Here Death, unlike Sin, is impartial, and does not necessarily wish Man ill; Sleep is a warning. When Body wakes he is torn between the desire simply to enjoy life and the wish to reform. At first Pleasure wins this contest, but after a long plea from Soul and an appeal from her to God for Justice, Body is less recalcitrant. Annulment of the marriage between Body and Soul is no longer a possibility, because Soul on occasion has gone along with Body's desires, assenting to them. Therefore there will only be a divorce – and that will last simply until the time for a reunion at the last day.

Now the flame of life burns low; Death appears, and Body repents. As Death's axe falls, Body goes back into the cave from which he came. Soul is left with Sin, who once more threatens her. But then wind instruments are heard, and an altar appears with the Host and Cup, and above it, on a throne, the Christ Child. At this the Soul ascends back into heaven, Body remains in the cave, Sin sinks into the flames of hell, and Death disappears back into his tree. All will await the Last Judgment and the reunion of Soul and Body at that final day.

This play is in a completely different league from most of those discussed in this chapter. While it remains schematic in its outline and in the introduction of the sacraments of baptism, marriage, penance and the Eucharist as the way to eternal life, there is much subtlety and real psychological insight in the portrayal of the relationships between the characters. Body's simple declaration: 'Well, let us be content with living, I have no need of more,' beautifully sums up a whole Epicurean attitude to life that has not ended with the seventeenth century. The courtier-like struggle for influence between Will and Understanding, the revulsion Soul feels for her uncouth bridegroom (who, after all, has just climbed out of a rock!) are all beautifully conceived.

Naturally, there are contradictions and difficulties in presenting what are essentially abstractions, parts of human nature, on the stage. But Calderón humanizes them, and tries to explain away anomalies (such as Body speaking before he is united to Soul) with considerable success. The marriage relationship, with its mixture of love and hate, dependency and individualism, and its inherent power struggle, provides an apt metaphor for the relationship between body and soul.

These plays by Sánchez de Badajoz and Calderón are intended to be enjoyed as well as to make a point. Particularly in Calderón, there is real social comedy in the marriage between the beautiful bride and the vulgar swain. Indisputably, the body is 'beneath' the soul in intelligence, morals and social class. But are we not supposed to laugh at the soul's sententiousness as well? 'All banquets end in tragedy.' The most frightening, ultimate questions are posed and remain, but within a context that makes them not just bearable but entertaining.

An Italian Opera: Rappresentatione di Anima et di Corpo

Calderón had a remarkable ability to give thoughts and ideas a tangible form and endow them with human characteristics that make for good theatre. No one else in the period had quite this combination of gifts. However, there is a most interesting early play with music that survives from Italy and was first performed at carnival time in the year 1600 – Emilio de' Cavalieri's *The Representation of Soul and Body*.[16] Here we find that soul takes on a role rather similar to that of conscience.

The work begins with a prologue between Prudence and Caution, who discourse on the dangers of living in the world. Act I opens with Time commenting on the swift passing of life and the necessity to do good. Then in Scene iv Body and Soul appear. Interestingly, Body here (masculine, sung by a baritone) seems genuinely fond of Soul (feminine, sung by a mezzo soprano). He enquires solicitously why

she is so sad, and attempts to comfort her with things he finds
delightful – the joys of the senses and earthly honour – but Soul
rejects them all. Body is distressed.

> If you are always
> Wayward and unhappy
> We shall always be weeping.

Soul then tells Body the only thing that will make her truly happy –
reposing her own (and Body's) trust in God. Body is torn:

> My senses transport me:
> My flesh tries me,
> Eternity affrights me.

Eventually he opts for God and eternal life, and the chorus rejoices.

In Act II, Pleasure again tempts a fickle Body with his music:

> Soul, at the sound of these songs
> I feel myself to be moved
> Like a leaf in the wind.

But the steadfast Soul repulses Pleasure and appeals to Heaven,
which, in an echo song, tells them to flee earthly things and fly to
God. Further temptation comes from the World and Earthly Life, but
these too are overcome.

Act III clinches the argument, with Intellect and Counsel adding their
persuasion to that of Soul to overcome the desires of Body. The contrasts they describe between Heaven and Hell are shown graphically as
first Hellmouth, complete with damned souls, opens and then Heaven,
arrayed with the souls of the blest, appears. The play ends with the
triumph of Heaven, and the whole chorus rejoices in song and dance.

The characterization here is vocal as well as representational. The
blessed soul, as one would expect, is a soprano; the damned soul is a
bass. The plot lacks the real conflict and inventiveness of Calderón's
auto, and while the work has been recorded, it has rarely been staged
in modern times. But it does provide yet another example of the

widespread appearance of souls – in life, or after it, blessed or damned – on the stage.

The Soul's Warfare

The Soul's Warfare by Richard Tuke, published in 1672,[17] must have been a strange anomaly in post-Restoration England. This contemporary of Wycherley and Farquhar bases his play on the conceit of two warring kingdoms, that of Satan and that of Empirea, the Soul, who is represented as a queen.

Empirea rejects all crude attempts to seduce her by Profit (born in America!), or Pleasure. Satan then manages to gain the support of Reason, who more subtly takes the Aristotelian line of moderation in all things. Specifically, Empirea should not force Caro (the Flesh) to severe fasting and suffering since God is God of the Soul *and* the Body. But Empirea resists; Flesh is no longer a handmaid to the soul and deserves no consideration. Act II presents a garden of earthly delights, designed to tempt all the senses, but still Empirea remains steadfast. In Act III, despite Slander's accusations of hypocrisy, she welcomes Sickness because he will provide an escape from the world. Even when Satan suggests that the foundation of her faith may be sand, she resists. She says farewell to the World, the Flesh and Satan, taking Faith and Charity with her. Hope is left behind because having been fulfilled, it is no longer needed. The Epilogue presents a triumphant Empirea in heaven.

As drama this is sorry stuff, the dying flicker of a form that has outlived any vitality it once had. The Soul itself is removed from the richness of its associations by being confined within the character of Empirea, a queen, and such conflict as there is in the drama is very one-sided. There will be no more such plays until the first half of the twentieth century when, curiously enough, the Soul, perhaps trying to ward off threatened extinction, makes a renewed appearance on the stage.

THE SOUL ON STAGE: TWENTIETH-CENTURY PLAYS

The twentieth-century plays that present the soul on stage fall into two categories: those that consciously imitate earlier plays, some of which have a rather Gothic flavour, and those that attempt to be unashamedly modern. I do not claim necessarily to have uncovered all examples of this genre, and there is no evidence that any of those I have uncovered has had a particularly successful stage history, for reasons that will become apparent. But they have their fascination as examples of more recent 'imaginings' of the soul.

Body and Soul

This play, written by and published for Elizabeth Marsh in Boston in 1920,[18] displays the greatest antiquarian interest of any written in the twentieth century. Dedicated, enigmatically, 'To the Eyes that Foresee', it begins with the body of Lord Bacardon being brought into a chapel. We quickly learn from one of the Bearers that the unfortunate Lord did not believe in God during his life. So where will he go?

At this point the Soul of Lord Barcardon appears on stage 'as a vaporous form'. (How the director is to achieve this is left to his own invention.) The Body on the bier does not want to be disturbed, but the Soul rouses it with appeals to save it. Alas, the dissolute Body does not even know who the Soul is. The Soul enlightens him: 'Thy youth, and thy desires, thy dreams, thy deeds, | Thy soul, – and lost.'[19] The Soul rather dislikes the whole struggle and would prefer to enter into the Body again and fall asleep, but since this is impossible, it wrestles with the Body, raising it to a sitting position. One cannot help wondering whether Elizabeth Marsh had access to medieval illustrations of 'Saint Bernard's Vision', so exactly does this scene replicate them.

The Body is unsympathetic to the pleas of the Soul. After all, it was this same Soul that was a burden, keeping him all night before the crucifix when he was young. The Soul has exhausted him. Soul cries out to Body, 'My home, my home!'[20] In response, Body urges Soul to find another home – the body of an acolyte, asleep in the chapel. Soul reluctantly agrees and possesses the acolyte. From now on the 'vaporous form' will be supplanted by the appearance of the acolyte.

In the next scene Soul, in its new guise, is begging alms for masses for Lord Bacardon: 'I am one that comes to the living from the body of the dead.'[21] The response is not encouraging; Lord Bacardon is not loved by his vassals. Soul returns and brings the sad tidings to Lord Bacardon's Body in the chapel – no one will pay for the repose of his Soul. In this sad situation, Soul wishes to be buried with Body, but Body still refuses, and sends Soul on a final errand to Abbot Paul, his inveterate enemy. The Abbot will not pray for the Soul, and indeed accuses it of being a spirit of perdition, but hearing the lord is dead, he no longer wishes to pursue him or wreak vengeance. Hearing of this softening on the part of his old enemy, Lord Bacardon realizes he must be dead indeed.

Finally, Body gives Soul a ring from his wife as a token for him to take to her. Constance, the wife, after seeing the token, eventually agrees to make any payment for the repose of her lord's Soul. The play ends as the Soul rushes back to the chapel with the wife's assurance just as Lord Bacardon's body is being buried. Then, in the person of the acolyte, whose body Soul still possesses, he preaches a rhymed moral to the audience, thanking God who has given him everything of value in life:

> 'Twas God who gave me all again,
> The voice of friend, the kiss of wife,
> The soothe of death, the song of life.
> And all my ways, through trackless space,
> No longer lost before His face.[22]

Despite one's feeling that it exists in the wrong century, this play demonstrates some things of interest. Soul and Body are not inveterate enemies. Cast out of Body, Soul longs for the familiar, the return to Body, rather like a return to the womb. It is a sentiment we have already encountered in the 'in life' dialogues between Soul and Body by Jane Roberts.[23] Ideas that a Soul is capable of possessing a Body that is not its own, and that it needs alms for prayers for its repose after death are medieval and/or Roman Catholic. It is worth noting, however, that there may be a practical reason for the Soul's possession of another body; it gives the Soul the specific form of a particular character on the stage and removes the need to present a 'vaporous form' throughout the play.

127

As drama, one cannot imagine that even in 1920 this work would have had a very wide appeal. It is a throwback that seems to feed on romantic attachment not only to the trappings of the Middle Ages but to its theology as well. Yet it says something about the continued appeal of these things in the early part of the last century, even if this appeal was not widespread.

Psyche and Soma

In *Psyche and Soma*, written by Wellen Smith in the first decade of the twentieth century, we return to the conceit, handled so brilliantly by Calderón, of Soul as wife and Body as husband. Unfortunately, the psychology in this play is much cruder than in Calderón. Soul (Psyche) is wholly a saint, and Body (Soma) is a boor. (This Psyche, it must be pointed out, has nothing to do with the Psyche of classical mythology.) The play seems to be as much a commentary on the attributes of masculinity and femininity as on those of Body and Soul – or rather, the author appears to find an almost complete compatibility between the instincts of the male and those of Body, and those of the female and Soul. 'Soma, endowed only with all the potentialities of manhood, in union with Psyche, whose spiritualities find satisfaction only in the contemplation of Divine ideals, constitutes a warfare which was not unknown in the experiences of Patriarchal and Classic times, in Buddhistic efforts after passiveness, in the raptures of mediaeval mysticism, and in these days of concrete dogmas and of free-thought,' Wellen Smith boldly asserts.[24]

Things begin well with a joyous marriage feast, and the hope of children, but after seven years we find there are no children and Psyche has rejected Soma for her devotions. When Psyche says to Soma, 'And I will be the fragrance upward borne | Like incense pleading for thee in the skies,' he replies bitterly, 'Yes, thou the Fire, and I the Sacrifice.'[25] Soma attacks Psyche, who retires to a hermit's cell and then a convent. Soma at his castle meditates on what he has lost, but, tempted by Satan, he soon falls in love with Thyma (Passion). While Psyche sings rapturously at the organ in her convent, Thyma replaces her in Soma's castle. But Thyma is unfaithful, and when Soma is attacked by an unknown rival, it is she who stabs him in the back, both literally and figuratively! Soma, wounded, dies in his chamber in the castle, but not before there is a grand reconciliation between himself and Psyche, who comes to him dressed in white. (This is the only indication of what Psyche's appearance on stage should be like.) 'As Psyche cannot die they ascend haloed with light in each other's embrace, while spirit voices are heard singing the same strain they sang to her in the Hermit's cell.'[26]

Quite what one is to make of this naïve and serious piece of theatre it is hard to tell. It emphasizes the fundamental incompatibility of Body and Soul (a very Platonic idea), but draws on Christian doctrine and symbolism to emphasize the sinful nature of Body when free from the influence of Soul. There is no real exploration of the subtlety of psychology of this incompatibility or indeed of temptation, except that the incompatibility is analogous to that between men and *good* women, and the temptation comes in the form of a *bad* woman. At one level it might be seen as an example of what happens in a marriage when a wife is *so* good as to be emotionally inaccessible. But this does not appear to be the playwright's intention. The reconciliation between Soma and Psyche before death gives us the optimistic ending that is characteristic of these dramas, in contrast to the endings of the dialogues in Chapter 3. Finally, the courtly setting throws a romantic and distancing gloss over the whole play, removing it from any immediacy of moral purpose it might have been suspected of having.

The Soul of Nicholas Snyders

Here we have a play that takes a rather jocular look at the soul. This is the only twentieth-century play that one can imagine having had a successful stage history, just as it is also the only one written by someone whose reputation has endured – Jerome K. Jerome. The idea behind the drama is quite simple: it is possible to exchange your soul for that of another, and if you do so you take on the personality and memories of the person whose soul you have acquired. Nicholas Snyders is an old miser who fancies his young assistant, Christina, who is betrothed to a young man, Jan. Snyders, to whom Jan's parents are deeply in debt, persuades Jan to sell him his soul in exchange for forgiveness of the debt. This will enable Jan to inherit his father's ship and make a living to support Christina. Alas, once the exchange has taken place, a personality change also occurs. Jan becomes unbearably stingy, while Snyder becomes affable and generous. As a result, Christina transfers her affections from the young Jan to the aged Snyders. The reversal in fortunes and personality seems complete. However, some of Snyders' old memories remain in him. 'I bought – Jan's soul,'[27] he confesses. In the end Jan recovers his soul – and his fiancée – and all is well.

There is no actual portrayal of the soul on the stage, but the fact that it can be exchanged like a piece of property ('May my soul pass into him, may his soul pass into me')[28] implies, however jocularly, its existence as a real entity dwelling within man. But the chief thrust of this play is not dogmatic or doctrinal; it uses the idea of the exchanged souls as a device to create an amusing few hours on the stage.

'His Soul': A Farce in One Act

The next play moves even farther into the realm of comedy, or farce, as its title indicates. Jack Burrows, an artist, spends most of his time making many sketches of the same woman, to his possessive wife's great distress. She assumes, not unreasonably, that this obsession is linked to a desire to be unfaithful. So to assuage her jealousy, Jack carves a wooden American Indian girl for a cigar store. His friend, Bob, complimenting him on his achievement, says that the Indian has 'soul'. 'Of course she's got soul. My soul. She's all I've got left.'[29] At this, to Jack and Bob's complete amazement, the statue comes to life. When asked who she is, she replies, 'Your *soul*.' Jack protests, but she insists: 'Me Wanda: Last of race. Your *soul*.'[30]

Jack responds vehemently, 'But I tell you, you're not. You're not. I haven't any soul. I never had a soul. And by George, if I had it wouldn't look like you.' He tries to send her away, but she won't go. She constantly refers to Jack as her 'Chief'. As Jack is phoning Information to try to discover where to send 'lost souls', Betty, his wife, comes in. Predictably, Betty, who has been suspicious of mere drawings of another woman, becomes hysterical about a female statue he has carved that has come to life. Faced with a choice between Betty and Wanda, Jack chooses his soul. At this Betty attacks Jack with a penknife, but Wanda shows her loyalty to Jack by intervening and taking Betty's blows. The play ends in what must be the only possible way: Jack wakes up and finds the whole thing has been a dream. Relieved, he says, 'But I want it distinctly understood that I haven't a Soul. I never had a Soul and come what may I don't want a Soul.'[31]

It would be a mistake to draw too much serious matter from this slight and amusing one act play. However, the form the soul takes, that of a cigar store Indian, may be of some significance. In spiritualist séances in nineteenth-century America, a native American Indian was frequently the human form that emerged as the medium's 'spirit' or 'control'.[32] But why dead Indians in this role? It has been suggested that it originated with the Shakers, who alleged that at their meetings they were taken over by spirits who caused them to shout, whoop and dance wildly and speak in tongues or, as they termed it, to 'talk Indian'. From this it was a short step to the assumption that the possessing spirits *were* Indian. The cigar store Indian is a humorous parody of these Indian 'souls' or spirits.[33]

Apart from this, the play is jocular, and the focus is really more on the notion of an artist obsessed with his works of art, into which he puts his 'soul', than anything of a doctrinaire nature about the soul itself. With this farce and its protestations against the possibility of the existence of soul, blasphemous in an earlier age, we move into a view of the soul on stage that attempts to take account, however unsuccessfully, of what, in the early part of the twentieth century, were 'modern' notions about the soul.

The Theatre of the Soul *and 'The Human Soul'*

The Theatre of the Soul attempts to translate into drama the theories of Freud and others who saw the soul not as indivisible but as composed of several selves with different natures. The author is Russian, and the translator reports, 'One compatriot of his tells me he is a mere *poseur*; another that he is more profound than any other living Russian dramatist'.[34] After reading the play I am in no doubt about on which side of this divide my own judgment lies!

Three characters, M1, M2 and M3 represent the three divisions of the soul. M1 is reason, M2 feeling, M3 the psychical or eternal self. All of this is explained by the 'Professor' who stands before the curtain with a blackboard and chalk. When the curtain rises one sees what purports to be the interior of the human soul. In the background is a glowing red space that appears to pulsate. This is the heart, and in front of this the three entities of the soul appear at different levels. All three are dressed in black, but their costumes differ. M1 (Reason) wears a frock coat; M2 (Emotion) an artist's blouse, and M3 (Eternal self) a well-worn travelling dress. M1 is a person who wears spectacles and has a quiet, sober manner; his hair is grey and carefully brushed. His lips are thin. M2 has a very youthful manner. His gestures and movements are quick, lively and a little exaggerated. His hair is untidy, his lips are full and red. M3 wears a black mask. He slumbers in the foreground, his bag under his arm, in the attitude of a traveller, worn out by fatigue.[35] This characterization of sober reason, and young, volatile emotion makes some sense, even if only in a very one-dimensional way. But what are we to make of the poor eternal soul, sleeping on the pavement like a tramp?

The conflict in the play is between the faculties of the soul, M1 and M2. M2 wishes to leave his wife and children for a beautiful young woman; M1 tells him to desist. The seductive singer he desires appears on the stage, and is exposed as a fraud when her wig and false teeth are removed. The wife appears, nursing their child, but M2 says there is no poetry, joy or passion in her. There is a fight between the wife and the singer, which the singer wins. Then M1 intervenes and boxes the singer's ears. M2, in revenge for this, kills M1. This leaves the guilty, emotional M2 in despair, and he telephones his 'Self' (apparently a holistic entity that lives at the end of a telephone wire) to commit suicide. A shot is heard, and a hole opens in the heart that forms the background to the set. At this M3, the eternal soul, rouses from his sleep on the floor. A Porter appears and tells him to change trains. Repeating 'I have to change here,' he goes off stage, putting on his hat and taking his bag.

It may be felt that such a sorry attempt at drama is not worth reading, never mind discussing. But its very crudeness shows the difficulty of making concrete the idea of a divisible soul that, while going back to Plato at least, suddenly gained a new prominence through the work of early twentieth-century psychology. Here visualization fails, and fails badly. We have a conflict between elements of the 'soul' or 'person' that ends in the destruction of the whole, but the issues over which they contend are so simple in concept and so crude in expression that no real interest or sympathy can be generated.[36]

The title page of this play claims that it was played at the 'Little Theatre' on 8 March 1915, and again with a different cast at the Alhambra, 18 November 1915. We learn, however, in a decidedly ill-tempered introduction, that the second performance never took place. The Lord Chamberlain passed the play, but after the dress rehearsal in the morning (the play was to be performed as part of a charity matinée) the manager said it was not to take place. Apparently this was because of the 'repulsive' incident of a woman's wig being removed to display her bald head. I wonder.

'The Human Soul' exists in typescript in a copy in the British Library. Whether it was ever performed is uncertain, but it was copyright in the United States by the author, J.A. Schwenk in 1934 and in Canada two years later. It claims to be based on the life of Dr Adolph Berrich, an American scientist who 'took the life of his young wife with his secret drug to prevent the discovery of his crime, and in the interest of science to see her soul pass from her body'.

The interest of the writer is in proofs of immortality, and the influence of early twentieth-century science and spiritualism are present in almost equal measure. On the title page he enumerates various professors and doctors who have seen souls or restored people to life. Some have duplicated the soul-seeing experiment attributed to Dr Berrich successfully with animals. Another restores life by prodding the heart to action by means of an electric needle. And 'Dr. Cryle . . . has developed the brilliant theory that each living cell in the human body is a tiny electric battery, worn out by poisons and bodily injuries sustained in the course of living. Perhaps through this electric force still untapped, we may some day discover the secret of immortality.'[37]

The play centres on the divided loyalties of Barbara Morgan, who is engaged to be married to the young and attractive Dr John

Glendale. But Glendale sees the soul only as a physical entity, and Barbara, encouraged by the ghost of her mother, abandons him for the aged Dr Berrich, who, while unattractive, does share her belief in the immortality of the soul and longs to gain evidence of this by seeing a soul. Barbara allows herself to become the subject of his experiments. On the first occasion that she leaves her body she claims death is a birth into a new and more perfect life. 'My spirit rose over my dead body and then you brought me back.' Eventually, however, his experimentation kills her. But then Dr Glendale, the young rejected suitor, produces an antidote that brings her back to life, and her soul is seen to return. Dr Berrich becomes blind, but is still convinced of eternal life. (In other circumstances one might see this as a metaphor, but here one cannot be certain.)

Notes and diagrams at the back of the play detail how super-natural effects are to be produced. 'The Human Soul appears in the following form: "An indistinguishable shadow gathers rapidly above the body, assuming the outlines of the human form, most perfect in its symmetry, bearing the likeness of the dead, most beautiful beyond description." The delicate, clear, and ethereal being floats gently in the atmosphere with eyes closed. The process of nature is complete, as it passes out of sight. The soul re-enters the body in the same way.' The appearance of the soul in this drama is really quite conventional. Separated from the body, it still retains the likeness of the person it has just left. It is 'beautiful beyond description'. To differentiate it from earthly matter, it is diaphanous, and floats gently with eyes closed, signifying its separation from sensual things.

The interesting thing about this play which, in contrast to the previous one, contains human beings, is the way in which crude science mingles with ideas of the visibility of spirits, the appearance of ghosts who speak to the living, and other apparatus of the spirit world. It seems that the author starts with a firm belief in the reality and immortality of the soul, but in the scientific climate of the period felt these things must be substantiated in a way that will satisfy the material senses. There is a paradox here, and it a paradox that is at the heart of this whole discussion: the things of the spirit must be confirmed by the evidence of sense. It does not make for good drama, but it does give us a notion of the confusion of ideas that were current in the period.

SUMMARY

These portrayals of Soul on the stage begin by making visible its struggle with temptation in life. This temptation may be represented by personified qualities, such as Lust, Worldly Goods, Lechery, etc., or it may be represented collectively by Body, which contains within itself all these worldly desires. The very early plays are schematic and dogmatic. By the time of the Spanish playwrights, however, a richness of character and situation, together with a less solemn approach incorporating comedy, gives rise to plays that are entertaining quite apart from their 'message'. The common analogy between body and soul, husband and wife, assists in this enterprise, since the soul can be set in the context of a familiar relationship that is itself often treated with a blend of seriousness and comedy.

This lightness of touch disappears in the twentieth century when, apart from the one farce and the work by Jerome K. Jerome, the plays are either solemnly antiquarian in feel or vainly attempting to be 'modern' and 'scientific' without having quite decided how these attributes relate to traditional beliefs or, just as important, how they can be portrayed within the structure of an entertaining piece of stagecraft. All the twentieth-century plays I have discussed date from before the Second World War. None has had a particularly successful stage history. The soul on the stage cannot be subtle. Once it is costumed and sent out to speak its lines it exists within certain prescribed limits. Perhaps the complexity of our doubt and knowledge (evident to some extent in 'The Human Soul') makes this kind of drama impossible any longer. Perhaps we are now interested in different things; we do not personify and visualize abstractions of any sort in the way the Middle Ages did. In the last two plays discussed, the image of the soul (or elements of it) retreats into cartoon-like stereotype or becomes vague as vapour. The conceit of the Soul as a visible actor in the drama of life has run its course. Indeed, the remarkable thing about the appearance of Soul on the stage is not that it ceased, but that it ever occurred at all.

FIVE

The Soul is Like . . .

The most natural way to visualize the soul is by analogy. No one can really know what a soul looks like – or even if it has an appearance at all. Once one moves away from the most common image – the soul as an airy replica of the person it has inhabited – it can appear in innumerable guises. What often happens then is that it is visualized not in a literal way, according to what the writer or artist believes a soul *actually* looks like, but rather according to some aspect of its reality as this is perceived by the artist or writer. The soul is *like . . .*

This propensity to see the soul in terms of its likeness to something else is deeply rooted in a view of the world that, from early Christian times through the Middle Ages and even the Renaissance, saw the world as symbolically organized by God himself. The material world is a sign of the immaterial, and Richard of St Victor, writing in the twelfth century, could assert that *all* material things have some likeness to the immaterial. This world is a sign, writ large, of the eternal world. God is the origin of all things, and every effect is a symbol of its cause.[1]

Of course, not all analogies operate on this exalted theoretical level. Most are based on partial similarities – one aspect of the thing to which the soul is likened illuminates a particular feature or characteristic of it. In the previous chapters we have already seen many analogies in practice that range between the extremes of the 'true' analogy described above, and the partial, more arbitrary analogy, which is more common. The soul is like a beautiful woman; the soul is like a bird; the soul is like a wife married to a boorish and recalcitrant husband; the soul is like a husband married to an insubordinate wife. Outside the realm of the 'true' analogy, since the comparison is only with *one aspect* of the thing to which the soul is

136

likened, consistency is not to be expected. It is a bird, a butterfly, a grasshopper, a hand using a tool, and so on. There is no hope of examining all of these analogies, because they are as infinite as the faculties and possibilities of the soul can be conceived. But in this chapter I shall look at a good number of them and try to bring some kind of order and logic to the plethora of images.

There are two main categories of analogy: those that compare the soul in isolation to something else – a bird, a snake, a jewel, smoke; and those rather more complex analogies that see the soul in its relation to something else – God, the body, the world – as like some other relationship. The first type of comparison illuminates a quality or qualities of the soul, while the second usually deals primarily with its role and function. I have therefore separated the discussion into two parts, each dealing with one of these two types of analogy.

ANALOGIES DEALING WITH THE SOUL ALONE

The Soul as a Bird

The most common analogy for the soul is that of a bird. We have found it as far back as an early Egyptian drawing and the writings of Homer. It appears in *Oedipus Rex* by Sophocles, when the chorus, bewailing the misfortunes that have come upon the people of Thebes, chants:

> There are no growing children in this famous land;
> there are no women bearing the pangs of childbirth.
> You may see them one with another, like birds swift on the wing,
> quicker than fire unmastered,
> speeding away to the coast of the Western God.[2]

The Egyptian *ba*-soul is depicted as a human-headed bird, and the souls leaving the bodies of the dead in Homer flutter as they fly free.[3]

If the bird is the most common analogy for the soul, it is also one of the most suggestive. A bird, first of all, is free. In an age when men were bound to the earth, a bird could soar above it. Its passage was visible, but it was essentially its own master, unable to be tracked or pinned down. Similarly the soul, casting off its earthly habitation in death, must be able to soar to the afterlife.

It is not only human souls that are compared to birds. The Holy Ghost is usually depicted as a soul-bird, a dove, emanating from the glory of heaven, its rays of light streaming down to the earth. In pictures of the annunciation, these rays from the dove are frequently directed towards the head of Mary, sometimes specifically to her ear, impregnating her with the divine Logos, the soul of the infant Jesus.[4]

The dove also appears frequently in early Christian funereal iconography. Here it represents the souls of the just, particularly of Christian martyrs. It is commonly engraved on the tombs of early Christians with an olive branch in its beak, signifying purity and freedom – and possibly also alluding to the hope brought to Noah by the dove returning to the ark with an olive branch in its beak. We have a specific account of how the martyr Eulalie exhaled with her last breath a dove whiter than snow that flew towards the sky. And St Gregory the Great reported that St Benedict learned of the death of his sister, Saint Scholastica, by seeing her soul climb to heaven as a dove.[5]

Of course birds are not always symbols of hope and freedom. Sometimes they are caged, and the bird in the cage becomes a metaphor for the soul enclosed in the body. Francis Quarles, in the seventeenth century, wrote a short poem that amplifies the picture of a caged bird in his book of *Emblems*. It begins 'My Soule is like a Bird; my Flesh, the Cage'.[6] Significantly, the bird in the cage in the accompanying illustration has a human head. Outside the cage an angel turns the latch to release it, and hanging from a tree branch above is another cage with its door already standing ajar, while in the distance a bird flies free.

A much earlier poem from the fifteenth century, 'Lovely lordynges, ladys lyke',[7] presents a more complex picture of the soul's/bird's wishes. While walking in the forest, the author sees a brightly coloured bird with wings as glorious as those of an angel. The bird flies away, and the poet follows to search for it. When the poet finds it again he grasps it by the wing and, holding it in his hand, asks it what it wants. The bird asks the poet to go away. Here it is at least free 'as wyld fowle and nothing tame' instead of in a cage, as it once was, where it raged with its fears. Yet it seems far from happy, and laments, exclaiming, 'Be dere God, woo is me!' The poet asks the bird its trouble. Perhaps he can make it a new cage in which it will be happy. The bird asks, sceptically, what sort of cage this might be, and most of the rest of the poem is taken up with an elaborate description of this cage. It will be physically exquisite, with floors of silver, posts of cypress, windows of jasper, and a perch of carbuncle. But in addition to this it will be a holy place. The gold pinnacles will have *Veni Creator spiritus* and *Gloria in excelsis* inscribed on them. Other birds surrounding him will have a religious function as well: the 'throstelcoke Gabrielle', which greeted Mary with a *'Gracia plene'*, and the nightingale which will, appropriately, sing *'Benedicite'*, will be in his new cage with him. There may be more than one inter- pretation for this allegorical poem, but the most plausible to me seems to be that the bird is the soul that was first encased in a body (the poet's?) that gave it grief and pain. Having escaped, it had the joy of freedom, but an even happier state would be to be reunited to a glorified body, one that would assist in bringing it to God rather than separating it from Him. This is what the poet appears to be promising the bird in his long description of the 'cage' he will offer it.

It is a short step from the rather supernatural bird that speaks in the fifteenth-century poem to other poetic birds that are products of artifice as much as of nature. In Andrew Marvell's poem 'The Garden' the soul becomes a bird with silver wings that casts 'the body's vest aside' in preparation for its final abandonment of earth for heaven:

> Casting the Bodies Vest aside,
> My Soul into the boughs does glide:
> There like a Bird it sits, and sings,
> Then whets, and combs its silver Wings;
> And, till prepar'd for longer flight,
> Waves in its Plumes the various Light.[8]

Here the bird with artificial wings that nevertheless is 'natural' enough to sing, seems prepared to remain for a time, uncaged and content, within the green and growing garden. It will leave earth eventually, but not just yet.

Marvell's bird, part natural and part artificial, prepares one for the even more complex figure of the soul-bird in W.B. Yeats' poem 'Sailing to Byzantium'.

> Once out of nature I shall never take
> My bodily form from any natural thing,
> But such a form as Grecian goldsmiths make
> Of hammered gold and gold enamelling
> To keep a drowsy Emperor awake;
> Or set upon a golden bough to sing
> To lords and ladies of Byzantium
> Of what is past, or passing, or to come.[9]

The fact that Yeats refers to the bird as the 'bodily form' he will choose after death might seem to confuse the issue. It appears, however, that this 'body' must be, in effect, the visible form of the soul. It is 'out of nature', eternal as only something that has transcended the world of change and decay can be. Yet it is, paradoxically, both *in* time (it can sing, an activity that is sequential and emotional), and *out of* time since its song is not limited to the present, or even the past, but at once encompasses and holds in an eternal present 'what is past, or passing, or to come'.

In the later poem 'Byzantium', the central stanza presents an image of an artificial bird that stands outside and above the world of 'mire and blood' that represents the human passion of life.

> Miracle, bird or golden handiwork,
> More miracle than bird or handiwork,
> Planted on the starlit golden bough,
> Can like the cocks of Hades crow,
> Or, by the moon embittered, scorn aloud
> In glory of changeless metal
> Common bird or petal
> And all complexities of mire or blood.[10]

140

The bird in this poem, significantly, does not sing but can only crow 'like the cocks of Hades'. Despite its status as 'miracle' and able, in the glory of its eternal 'metal', to scorn 'common bird or petal' there is something deeply disturbing about this bird. Its superiority may after all be illusory. Permanence is not the only good to be desired, and the poem returns in its last stanza to the rough reality of life with all its complexity and passion, just as, in 'The dialogue of Self and Soul', also by Yeats, the dominant self wishes to remain attached to the life of flux and humanity.[11]

In this image of the artificial bird, we have moved a long way from the unambiguously free and joyful soul-bird, winging its way towards another world. Yeats' scornful piece of golden artifice may be unchanging but lacks the vitality that is to be found chiefly in the impermanence of earthly life. The versatile analogy of the soul as bird can be used to present the limitations as well as the joys of the eternal soul.

Insects, Animals and other Natural Objects

Other analogies from the natural world – particularly with insects or animals – also occur, though with less frequency and less complex resonance. One of the most common and ancient of these is the butterfly. We have already seen its portrayal on early tombs, and Psyche herself was usually pictured with butterfly wings.[12] The concept unites the free flight of the bird with an aetherial delicacy. Further, the butterfly develops out of a chrysalis stage, thus symbolizing the transformation of ordinary life into something of wonder and beauty. Other winged insects, such as bees, wasps and dragonflies also function in a similar way as analogies for the soul.

Rather more puzzling is the image of the grasshopper that is used by Paul Nash in one of his illustrations for Thomas Browne's *Urne Buriall*. The soul – or rather the souls – in the woodcut are portrayed as stylized grasshoppers. So far my researches have found no logical explanation for this image. The grasshopper, like the insects above, is agile and emerges from a larval state, but it scarcely represents beauty or elegance. Is it simply an arbitrary image, or does it contain a particular personal meaning for the artist?

The snake as an image of the soul may be initially more surprising, but is actually more readily explicable. We think of the snake as a disguise of the devil, tempting Eve in the Garden of Eden and cursed by God for doing so, but the snake is also a creature that has the ability to renew itself and to grow by shedding its skin. It is this transformative ability of the snake that is the primary connection between it and the soul. In addition, the shape of the serpent identifies it with the marrow of the individual, and since it was anciently believed that new life sprang from the marrow, the snake, by association, became identified in this way as well with renewal of life. Thus in ancient Greece, a man's life-soul, that which lived on after death, might assume the form of a snake and is represented as such on some tombs.[13] In Ovid's *Metamorphoses*, he states, 'Some people also believe that when a human body is shut up in the tomb, and its backbone rots away, the marrow changes into a snake.'[14]

Even the mouse, unlikely as this may seem to the modern imagination, has been seen as a form of the soul, particularly of the soul leaving the body at the time of death. A red mouse indicated a pure soul, a black mouse a soul darkened by the pollution of sin.[15]

Literary Analogies

Some of the comparisons described above are rather one-dimensional, but in the hands of a great writer or poet the soul can appear clothed in an array of complex allusions. This is John Donne, personifying the soul and making it the actor in a little vignette to illustrate a sermon:

> What would a dejected Spirit, a disconsolate soule, opprest with the weight of heavy, and habituall sinne, that stands naked in a frosty Winter of desperation, and cannot compasse one *fig leafe*, one colour, one excuse for any circumstance of any sinne, give for the *garment of Righteousnesse*?[16]

Here the disconsolate soul that looks in vain for a 'fig leafe' in the deserted, frosty landscape, is a new Adam, cast out of Eden, seeking in vain to return. It is winter, and the white landscape affords no solace of leaf to cover or colour to divert him as he stands shivering in the desolate scene.

The image of the soul as a traveller occurs again in one of Donne's Holy Sonnets:

> Oh my blacke Soule! now thou art summoned
> By sicknesse, deaths herald, and champion;
> Thou art like a pilgrim, which abroad hath done
> Treason, and durst not turne to whence hee is fled.[17]

Unlike Bunyan's Christian, also a pilgrim on a journey, this pilgrim-soul has committed treason during his time abroad (that is, on earth) and therefore cannot return to the heavenly home from which he has issued. Other associations (which may or may not have been in Donne's mind) crowd upon the reader – most notably that of Mowbray, exiled from his native land in Shakespeare's *Richard II*, which would have been written only a few decades before this poem.

In nineteenth-century Romantic poetry the soul travelling on its journey through life is frequently seen not as a pilgrim (too narrowly religious) but as a boat. One of its most notable evocations in this guise is found in a song from Shelley's 'Prometheus Unbound':

> My soul is an enchanted boat,
> Which, like a sleeping swan, doth float
> Upon the silver waves of thy sweet singing;
> And thine doth like an angel sit
> Beside the helm conducting it,
> Whilst all the winds with melody are ringing.[18]

Here the image of the boat floating through life is combined with the image of the swan – pure white and silent until it sings its first and last song in death – and of the maiden, whose figuring of the soul we have already looked at in detail in Chapter 3. Boat and swan float tranquil and passive in a backwards motion that takes them from 'Age's icy caves, | And Manhood's dark and tossing waves . . . Through Death and Birth, to a diviner day'. The end of the journey is paradise, and a state that, given the progression described above, would seem to end in a retreat to any idyllic prelapsarian state, 'peopled by shapes too bright to see l . . . Which walk upon the sea and chant melodiously'.

The idea of the prelapsarian soul leads to the image, also found chiefly in the nineteenth century, of the soul as an infant. The French 'Poème de l'âme' by Louis Janmot (1881)[19] with its accompanying illustrations, portrays the newborn soul as a baby, cradled in the arms of an angel, being brought down to earth. The innocent, child-like soul, emerging pure and only gradually corrupted by the world, is also to be found considerably earlier in Wordworth's 'Ode on the Intimations of Immortality'.

If there is something almost too sweet and cloying about this romantic image of the soul either emerging from a scene of bliss or retreating effortlessly to a paradisial past, a most effective antidote is to be found in the poetry of that medieval master of hell and paradise, Dante. The masculine vigour of his imagination has produced what may be the most curious and original image for the soul ever penned when, in the *Inferno*, he envisages the souls of the suicides as thorny trees:

> Its foliage was not verdant, but nearly black.
>   The unhealthy branches, gnarled and warped and tangled,
>   bore poison thorns instead of fruit . . . .[20]

The wind, blowing through one of the trees, gives it a voice with which it can explain its origin:

> When
>
> out of the flesh from which it tore itself,
>   the violent spirit comes to punishment,
>   Minos assigns it to the seventh shelf.
>
> It falls into the wood, and landing there,
>   wherever fortune flings it, it strikes root,
>   and there it sprouts, lusty as any tare,

144

> shoots up a sapling, and becomes a tree.
> The Harpies, feeding on its leaves then, give it
> pain and pain's outlet simultaneously.[21]

From the branches of these soul-trees the bodies will dangle to the end of time. Since the suicides have deliberately thrown the body away, it cannot be united to them at the judgment day. The fundamental association here is probably the use of trees as a means of suicide by hanging. But the ingenious transformation of the soul into a blackthorn tree that Harpies nest in, providing both punishment and the voice to lament that punishment, is one that could only have been invented by someone of the genius of Dante.

In the *Paradiso*, however, Dante paints a very different picture of the souls of the blest. Here the predominant imagery is that of light, but within this light there is also room for colour and form. In Cantos XVIII and XIX Dante describes the souls of the just rulers as points of light combining to form the shape of an eagle.

> Before me, its great wings outspread, now shone
> the image of the eagle those bright souls
> had given form to in glad unison.
>
> Each seemed a little ruby in the sky,
> and the sun's ray struck each in such a way
> the light reflected straight into my eye.[22]

The eagle stands for nobility and justice, so it is appropriate that this form should be made up of a composite of the souls of the just and temperate rulers.

At the end of the *Paradiso* we have another significant image formed by the souls of the saved. Here 'all those who had won return to Heaven's height' form a vast white rose with a golden centre: 'Into the gold of the rose that blooms eternal, I rank on rank, in incenses of praise I it sends up to the Sun forever vernal I . . . Beatrice drew me.'[23] This is the glorified soul, unimaginably resplendent, but nevertheless conveyed in terms of the best our mortal senses can conceive.

These images bring us to a kind of correspondence that is more sophisticated than most of what has been described hitherto. It is based not on a single point of contact between the soul and the object but primarily on the position that the rose and the eagle occupy in their individual hierarchies. It suggests a 'real' analogy of the sort outlined at the beginning of the chapter rather than an arbitrary and partial one. The rose is the chief of flowers, as the eagle is the chief of birds. It is therefore appropriate that these species, at the top of their particular orders of being, should correspond to the perfected souls of the blessed.

ANALOGIES DEALING WITH SOUL IN RELATION TO BODY

Frequently the soul is seen not in isolation but in its relationship to the body. On this earth, the two are a composite, but with differing roles and functions. To some extent each is therefore defined in terms of the other. Again, comparisons and images clarify this relationship.

External/Internal

The most obvious aspect of the relationship between body and soul is that of the external to the internal. The body is external, apparent to our senses; the soul is not. Yet for much of the history of Western thought, the soul, despite its hidden nature, has seemed more 'real' than the body. From this relatively simple perception come comparisons, some of which merely restate them, and others that add new dimensions through their own connotations.

The analogy that expresses the internal/external relationship in its simplest form is that of the body as a garment and the soul as a living being clothed in that garment. The basic idea is very ancient, and is variously attributed to Galen or even Aesop. But many changes can be rung on this single idea. When the seventeenth-century writer Thomas Beverley compares the body to a garment, it is to show the ease with which it can be cast aside. The soul 'values the Body no more, than the Body does a Garment . . .'.[24] In contrast, when Thomas Adams, a divine from the same period, compares the

146

body to the skin of a serpent, he is not thinking chiefly of its ability to be cast aside but, as in the simple analogy between soul and snake above, of the way this gives it the capacity for renewal. Just as the serpent, by shedding its skin, gains perpetual youth, so we 'shall put off, not the skinne, but this *mortall body*: and so be *clothed with immortalitie* and eternall life above'.[25] And we have already seen the soul-bird in Marvell's 'Garden' casting aside 'the body's vest', in preparation for 'further flight' – presumably to eternal life.

There are many variants on the garment/self theme. One of these is that of the house/inhabitant or house/precious goods stored inside. Sometimes the metaphor becomes quite elaborate: the body is a house of clay, the bones are timbers, the walls flesh, the windows eyes.[26] These images may emphasize the confinement and limitations the soul endures in this life, or they may portray the body as a fortress for the soul, vigilantly securing it from harm.[27] Other examples emphasizing the confinement motif range from the cage/bird analogy that we have encountered earlier in this chapter, or those that see the body as a prison or a grave for the soul. Rather more unusual is the image used by John Woolton, the sixteenth-century Bishop of Exeter, when he describes the soul in the body as a candle in a lantern. When the candle is removed from the lantern, the lantern is dark, but the candle itself burns more brightly.[28] Similarly, the body is lifeless when the soul leaves it, but the soul then comes into true life.

The internal/external idea also manifests itself in relation to Christ and the Church. Christ is the soul, the essence of religion, and the Church is its outward manifestation. This outward manifestation is particularly shown in church worship. Here the body is seen as analogous to the external forms of worship and the soul to the internal intent of the heart. 'As the outward worship without the inward is dead, so the inward without the outward is not complete, even as the glorification of the soul separate from the body is not, nor shall not be consummate till the bodie be again unite unto it.'[29] For Donne, the soul is to the body as Christ himself and his merit are to the clear and outward profession of his truth.[30] Doctrine is to language as the soul is to the body or essence is to existence: 'In this case . . . the matter, that is, the doctrine that we preach, is the forme, that is, the Soule, the *Essence*; the language and words wee preach in, is but the Body, but the *existence*.'[31]

One of the most tantalizing images of the spatial body/soul relationship is also among the most ancient. In an Orphic poem called 'The Net', the formation of a living creature is likened to the knitting of a net. The image, alluded to by Plato in the *Timaeus*, suggests that the body is analogous to the material of the net, and the soul to the air in the interstices between the material.[32] This is a particularly subtle image, since it represents the soul as something 'real' but nevertheless invisible and not subject to investigation by human senses. It also suggests the simultaneous growth of soul and body. As in the weaving of the net, fabric and the spaces between the fabric are created at one and the same time.

Plotinus, writing hundreds of years later, says that the soul is to the body as light is to air. The air, he insists, is in the light rather than the light in the air.[33] He is not so much stating a scientific idea here (after all, he hardly had an inkling of modern wave and particle theories) as he is asserting that it is the soul that is radiant and all-encompassing. The air is simply the medium through which its radiance moves.

All these analogies either explicitly or implicitly assume the superiority of soul to body. Sometimes the latter is a decidedly negative influence as when it is a cage or prison for the soul. But at others it is either neutral or positively helpful in enabling the soul to manifest itself in the physical world.

Actor/Agent: Form/Matter

This leads us to another category of analogy that depends on the differing functions of soul and body. The form/matter analogy goes right back to Plato and Aristotle, although the two understood the relationship in very different ways, as we saw in the first chapter. Form is that which gives shape and meaning; matter is the medium through which that shape and meaning is expressed. This could be extended (as Plato did) to seeing the form as permanent, eternal, and the matter as changing and transient. By the seventeenth century this distinction, when applied to body and soul, took on a religious dimension. Thus John Donne could say, 'That though in my matter, the earth, I must die; yet in my forme, in that Image which I am made by, I cannot die . . . it is . . . the Image of God himselfe.'[34] In the context of the whole passage from Donne's sermon, matter and image, body and soul, are further enriched by being associated with north and south, mortality and eternity.

It is an easy step from the analogy with form and matter to that with actor and agent. Just as form shapes matter, so the actor works through the agent. The soul is to the body as a mariner is to a ship, directing it across the sea. This comparison occurs frequently; we have already encountered in Guillaume de Deguileville's *Pilgrimage of the Life of Man*.[35] Also, the body and soul are like a tool and the craftsman who directs that tool – an idea that goes back to Aristotle. 'The body, and the senses are but the tooles, and instruments, that the soule works with; But the soule is the art, the science that directs those Instruments.'[36] Or the soul is to the body as a riding master is to a horse – a comparison that has clear affinities with Plato's image of the horses and rider in the *Phaedrus*, though here there is a single horse, and the comparison is between soul and body, not between different faculties of the soul.

Another analogy on this theme with ancient roots is that which sees the body as a musical instrument and the soul as the player of the instrument. Just as the soul gives life to the body, so the player strikes the instrument into harmony. This simple analogy is capable of a surprising number of variations. It may be used to show the closeness of body and soul, and to show the good that body may do soul, just as the instrument gives pleasure to the player of it. It can also explain why the soul leaves the body at the time of death. 'As the Musitian ceaseth to play when the Instrument is vnstrung, so the soule ceaseth to giue life vnto the body, yea, flyes out, when it is destroyed.'[37] The lute remains, like the body of a dead man, after it has ceased to be played. Ultimately though, it is the soul or the player of the lute that remains superior. The player may be hindered by a poor instrument, but his ability to play is undiminished; the soul may be frustrated by the 'ill habit' of the body, but its latent powers are unimpaired. And, as Plotinus pointed out, when the time comes, the wise man (soul) can give up the lyre (body) entirely and sing unaccompanied.[38]

Accomplices/Antagonists

A more direct and active relationship between body and soul is implied in those analogies that see them either as accomplices or antagonists. When they are accomplices, they are usually up to no good. The parable of the blind man and the lame from the Talmud, cited in Chapter 3, is one example of this.[39] Donne characterizes them as Herod and Pilate, who together conspire to crucify Christ.[40]

Most of the comparisons, however, deal with them not as accomplices but as antagonists. Since this idea has been explored in some detail in Chapter 3, it does not need great elaboration here. The cosmic image of the *primum mobile* and the inner planets struggling against one another as they move in contrary directions[41] is one of the most powerful analogies for the struggle between body and soul. Many others are allegorical interpretations of Bible stories. Esau and Jacob, the twins who strove against one another even in the womb, are seen as body and soul or flesh and spirit respectively.[42] The story of Ishmael and Isaac, the son of the bondwoman and the son of the free, are similarly understood figuratively.[43] One (Isaac, the soul) must inherit, while the other (Ishmael) must be cast out. And the self-tormenting and mutually destructive nature of the body/soul relationship is wonderfully captured in an analogy from a seventeenth-century sermon that claims the soul can kill the body just as a sword cuts its own scabbard.[44]

Proper Subordination

The concept of proper subordination is a natural outgrowth of the notion of the conflict between body and soul. Subordination, if carefully observed, should prevent conflict. The idea is a pervasive one and analogies for body and soul based on this idea exist on all levels – the political, the personal, and the domestic. Fundamental to this idea is the Aristotelian form/matter distinction – which, as we have seen, spawned its own group of analogies. According to this distinction everything, while a limited 'end' in itself, functions as a means to an end for something higher on the scale of being. This hierarchical 'tidiness' results in analogies that liken man to a household or a kingdom. In both the emphasis is on good government and proper subordination. The King is to the kingdom as the soul is to the body. Thomas Adams asserts, 'In man there is a *kingdome* . . . The minde hath a Soueraignty ouer the body. Restraine it to the *Soule*: and in the Soules kingdom . . . Reason hath a dominion ouer the affections.'[45] Analogies based on the kingdom can relate to faculties within the soul as well as to soul and body. The mind (reason) is king; the will is a privy councillor, and the heart is the obedient community.[46]

The analogy with the well-governed house is just one step down and follows naturally from that with the kingdom. Within this house, the soul should be the mistress and the body the servant. Sometimes servant and mistress are not anonymous but are linked to biblical prototypes such as Hagar and Sarah or Rachel and Leah. The latter pair form part of an elaborate allegorizing of Jacob's household by Richard of Saint Victor. Here the simple soul/body: mistress/servant relationship is expanded to include the hierarchical relationship among many of the faculties within the soul. Jacob is analogous to God, Rachel to Reason, and Leah to Affection.[47] The maids of Rachel and Leah signify Imagination (which is servant to Reason) and Sensuality (which is servant to Affection). The whole is worked out in interminable detail, with great seriousness and tediousness.

A final example of the soul/body: mistress/maid analogy is found in a dramatic dialogue by Richard Brathwait. 'A dialogue betweene *Death*, the *Flesh*, and the *Soule*' exploits most possibilities of this concept. This elaborate dialogue almost moves into the realm of the dramas we have looked at in the previous chapter. Both Flesh (who has all the attributes of a physical body) and Soul are women, with Flesh a young damsel and the Soul her mistress. When Death knocks on their door, Flesh, the maid, is frightened and refuses to open it. An exchange follows that is a typical 'death and the maiden' piece, with Flesh refusing to submit her beauties to the embraces of Death, and Death insisting on his right. The maiden pleads her charms, but Death is impervious to them:

> I care not for thy *temples* faire and high,
> Though deckt with fragrant flowrs most curiously.[48]

151

Death catechises the maiden about how she spends her time, and discovers that she flirts and is totally possessed by the world. When Soul is angry with her, Flesh tempts and wins her. The Devil, interestingly, points the moral: 'It seemes, then, that the mayd her mistresse sways.'[49] The Devil then seizes Flesh, who calls on Soul for help. Soul begins by berating her and pointing out that if she is taken away and separated from her (Soul), she (Flesh), will be nothing but a carcass. But soon Soul turns to comfort Flesh, explaining that Death will actually be a boon to them both. She persuades Flesh that now sense must submit to reason, thus emphasizing the need for the proper subordination that Flesh has overthrown. Soul instructs Flesh and prepares her for death, reminding her of the grain of wheat that must die before it rises.

Soul/Body: Husband/Wife

From the kingdom to the household it is a short step to the final group of analogies with body and soul – that between husband and wife. This analogy has already been touched on in relation to the conflict between body and soul in Chapter 3 and as the basis of some of the Spanish plays in Chapter 4. But its history extends well beyond the boundaries of a single country or a single interpretation. The two basic components of man and the basic unit of society were seen to correspond in many ways both as ideal types and as fallen, sinful counterparts. The marriage relationship, believed to be divinely ordained, but observably imperfect and fallen from its original state, was ideally suited to present this dual perspective on the condition of man himself. It combined elements of stark realism with abstract concepts. Marriage is not merely a theoretical relationship but an actual one with all its passion and pettiness as well as its joy. So when writers thought of body and soul as living friends or antagonists, indissolubly bound together for good or ill, rather than as theological concepts, it was in terms of marriage partners that they envisaged them. And just as the analogy with marriage gave an added concreteness and 'imaginability' to the soul/body relationship, so the soul/body relationship gave an archetypal significance to that between husband and wife.

The ideal and unchanging type of the marriage relationship is that between Christ and the Church, which has already been seen to be analogous to the relationship between soul and body. But the historical archetype of marriage is the relationship between Adam and Eve. Created perfect but yet fallen, Adam and Eve present both an ideal and a counter-ideal, and the latter can only be measured by the gulf between it and the former. Their actions provide not only a pattern for the diverse relationships between soul and body, but an historical explanation for those that are antagonistic. The Fall of Adam and Eve is the cause of our own fallen nature, and their struggle and discord have become internalized in our own being as the struggle between body and soul.

> And so the Serpent robbed the Woman, and robbed her Husband, and robbed all their Posteritie, of that godly affection, that holy appetite and desire, which the Lord had furnished Mans nature withal. Euer since which . . . all the whole many of vs are peruerted in our wills, and so corrupted in all our desires, that now the inclinations of our nature are no longer desires . . . but they are lusts and concupiscences, nothing els but lewd and inordinate affections.[50]

One of the fascinating things about this analogy between body and soul, husband and wife, is the way in which it is possible either for husband to be analogous to soul and wife to body or for it to work precisely the other way round, with the wife analogous to the soul and the husband to the body. There are several reasons for this variation in the identification. Chapter 2 has shown the way in which the soul was frequently visualized as a beautiful woman, a source of guidance and inspiration to men. In the chapter on plays featuring souls we also found the soul usually portrayed as a woman. In the case of the play by Calderón, the body and soul were specifically identified with husband and wife, with the husband playing the oafish body and the wife the pure soul that descended from heaven to marry him. However this play, significantly, is written in a language in which the word 'soul' is feminine in gender – as it is in all Romance languages, Greek and German. But the English language is not gendered. There is no linguistic pressure to make the soul either masculine or feminine. And there are other reasons why writers might see the soul as the masculine partner in the relationship.

Firstly, in the identification of soul and body with Adam and Eve the soul is usually seen to be like Adam and the body like Eve. While some writers (notably Milton) saw the chief sinner to be Adam because of his uxoriousness, the conventional interpretation is that Eve tempted Adam in much the same way the body, through the senses, tempts the soul. When Eve offers the apple to Adam in the Garden of Eden, she places herself in the position of wily, fleshly temptress, thus reinforcing this identification. Less important, but still a factor among the more learned writers, was the Aristotelian belief that at conception the semen of the father contributed the soul while the mother gave only the matter or body. Finally, and probably most importantly, we come back to the issue of hierarchy and proper subordination. The husband ought to control the wife, just as the soul ought to control the body. 'The dominion of a man over his wife is no other than as the soul rules the body,' writes that most moderate of Anglican preachers, Jeremy Taylor.[51] He goes on to expand the analogy, showing that as this rule of proper subordination is carried out or ignored, so the union of soul and body or the marriage may be happy or wretched.

> For the woman that went before the man in the way of death, is commanded to follow him in the way of love. . . . For then the soul and body make a perfect man, when the soul commands wisely, or rules lovingly, and cares profitably . . . [for] that body which is its partner and yet the inferiour. But if the body shall give lawes, and by the violence of the appetite, first abuse the understanding, and then possesse the superiour portion of the will and choice, the body and the soul are not apt company, and the man is a fool and miserable.[52]

For these reasons, in English and within the context of the analogy, the soul is universally masculine and the body feminine.[54] The soul in isolation, of course, is a different matter, as I have amply shown in the second chapter.

154

In other languages, where there is linguistic pressure for the soul to be feminine, there is no such consistency. In the Old French poem 'Un samedi par nuit', discussed in Chapter 3,[54] the soul is most certainly feminine and the body masculine. But, alas, it is notable that the woman, even when soul, still gets the worst of the argument. 'You were my lady,' the body says. 'When you spurred me, I ran. You whipped me so that I could never rest.' Here the feminine, controlling soul, similar to the cruel mistress in a medieval romance, is a malign influence.

SUMMARY

What, finally, do these analogies say about the way we have envisaged the soul? Those that deal with the soul in isolation emphasize its desire to be free, and its sense of entrapment in our present life. As such, they look to the future with optimism; there is that in us that will survive. But the present, with the constraints we as human beings feel upon ourselves, is less than ideal. The 'compromise' images by writers such as Yeats and Marvell that present the soul as partly belonging to the natural world and partly to the world of art can be seen as encompassing our dual desire to have eternity and the joy of change and transience at one and the same time.

Analogies that focus on the soul in its relationship to the body are even more varied. They usually show the soul as the controlling partner in this life, that which is ultimately responsible for our well-being here and our future fate. But they also show the need of the soul for the body, without which, in a material world, the soul can ill perform its functions. It is marriage, with its joint sense of dependency and antagonism that provides the most versatile analogy for the soul and body relationship. And just as the marriage relationship can only be severed by death, so death also separates body and soul. Indeed, for much of Western history, the separation of body and soul has been the definition of death. In the next chapter we shall see how the soul fares in this extreme situation.

SIX

The Soul at the Time of Death

Indeed, it behooves each man that he himself should examine his
   soul's fate,
   how it is grave when death comes and severs the kinsmen who
   formerly were together, the body and the soul.
      'The Damned Soul' from the Exeter text of The Soul and Body

eath is the inevitable end of every man. Within the Christian
tradition this inevitability is linked to the first sin of Adam and
Eve, which tainted mankind. In a miniature from a fifteenth-century
manuscript of Augustine's *City of God* we find a picture of God
showing Death to our first parents. And Aquinas reinforces this view:
'The necessity of dying is a deficiency brought upon human nature by
sin.'[1] Death is a time of high drama for the soul, since it is then that it
must leave the body. Indeed, the philosophical and theological
definition of death, up to the time of our own more scientific
definitions, has been the separation of the soul from its body.

If there seem to be inconsistencies and contradictions in ideas
about death and its aftermath, even within a given culture, it may be
because of the difficulties of 'imagining the unimaginable'. We are
entering 'a realm of thinking where thinking cannot really be done,
and where there is no experience'.[2] The Greeks coped imperfectly
with the parting of body and soul at death and somehow continued
to see a link between them. They were not alone in this difficulty. So
much of the material in this chapter acknowledges the separation,
but still visualizes a soul that may care for its body, berate it, and
come back to visit it. Our conception of what happens at and after
death is inevitably limited by our restricted knowledge and sense
perceptions. We can only go so far in extending the boundaries of
our vision beyond the world we know.

The Soul at the Time of Death

THE SEPARATION OF BODY AND SOUL

Ancient, Medieval and Renaissance Writers

From the Greeks to Freud, death, particularly the death of the young, could have erotic elements. *Eros* and *Thanatos* were closely linked; uncontrolled passion could lead to death. Conversely, the two represented the two conflicting poles of human desire, for life or death. In the Renaissance 'to die' was a euphemism for sexual activity, a figurative connection that became literal in the belief that intercourse actually shortened a man's lifespan.[3] The eroticism did not have to be heterosexual or even limited to humans. In Greek culture a young man might be snatched by the gods through erotic desire, since heaven is incomplete without mortals.[4]

Greek souls flew instantly out of the mouths of their possessors at the time of death, with no indication of fear or difficulty. Egyptian and Christian souls had a rather harder time of it. Most of us do not want to die. In Shakespeare's *Measure for Measure* the saintly Isabella may urge, 'Be absolute for death', but it is Claudio's impassioned, 'Sweet sister, let me live', that reverberates through the ages. So it was assumed in the Christian culture of both the Eastern and Western Church that the soul would not leave the body voluntarily but had either to be persuaded to leave or dragged out by force. The visualization of these scenes in the Coptic Gospels of Egypt, written very early in the Christian era – probably before the third century – and in later Christian writings leaves no doubt that the emerging soul was seen as concrete, a semi-physical entity that could be visualized.[5] It should be emphasized that these Egyptian ideas concerning the soul are centuries later than those concerning ancient, pre-Christian Egypt discussed in the first chapter.

As far back as these Egyptian writings, there is an assumption that souls leaving the body may be 'good' or 'evil', and a distinction is made between the good soul and the wicked soul. The good soul is usually enticed from the body by persuasion, while the wicked soul is removed forcibly by physical instruments – a whip, a hook, or a trident. In the earliest Egyptian Gospels one angel, Death, removes the souls of all men who die. But later, in other texts, the angel

157

Michael, or Jesus himself, or other angels may remove the soul.[6] Some of these angels were cruel and malevolent and became associated with devils, an association that had a profound effect on medieval visualizations of deathbed scenes.

When the soul is finally released from the body it begins its ascent to heaven, but this is hindered by spirits who come to confront it with its various sins. It must prove its innocence of these sins before it is allowed to ascend farther. Also, it is often given a tour of the universe, of heaven and hell, so that by seeing both it may be either properly grateful for the pains of hell it has escaped, or remorseful for the joys of heaven it has lost. This tour, however, is not the same as the visit to heaven and hell in classical literature or the Middle Ages. It takes place at the time of death rather than during life, it lacks the detailed descriptions of heaven and hell in these other accounts, and since the soul does not return to earth these tours can scarcely provide information for the living.[7]

The aspect of these ancient beliefs that most fully captured the Christian imagination was the actual moment and method of separating body and soul. This was what was decisive – the culmination of life on this earth and the beginning of a new life of salvation or damnation. The ceremony of extreme unction – anointing various parts of the body with holy oil at the time of death – continues to be practised in parts of the Christian Church to the present day. While the ceremony as presently practised appears to derive from rituals of anointing for the purpose of healing, it is believed by some critics also to have a connection with these ancient separation scenes. By this means the good soul was freed from the sins of the individual members of its body.[8] Similarly, the evil soul had its members pricked in anticipation of even greater punishments to come. As Christianity came to emphasize the possibility of repentance and salvation for all, it was the ceremony of anointing that came to be used universally. Thus even Emma Bovary's sinful members can be anointed as she dies, a suicide, in Flaubert's nineteenth-century novel.

One of the oldest accounts of the separation of body and soul is found in a Latin prose legend, which is a free rendering of a sermon attributed to one Alexander, a disciple of Macarius of Alexandria, whose 'legend' has already been mentioned in Chapter 3 in connection with the body and soul debates.[9] The Latin prose legend describes the separation of an evil soul from the body by demons. This removal is done with great violence. The demons, blacker than Ethiopes, crowd around the dying man, saying, 'Pierce his eyes that coveted all they saw, cut the ears, pierce the heart that knew neither mercy, nor pity, nor goodness; tear off the feet and the hands, so quick to do evil.' The soul reproaches the body for having caused its present desperate situation, but to no avail. The devils carry the soul off on their black wings. After being taunted by being shown the joys of paradise, the soul is conducted to hell. There a demon in the form of a dragon first swallows him up, and then spits him out into the fire.[10] Following this, the good soul of a monk leaves its body peacefully, through the mouth. As it departs it thanks its body for helping it during life and assures it that it will rest for some time in peace in the earth and then rise to be reunited with it in glory.

Sometimes the devils actively impede the departure of the soul from the body. In an Irish homily, probably from the twelfth century, the soul tries to escape through various orifices of the body – the mouth, the nose, the eyes, the ears. But at every exit death meets it and drives it back. Finally it escapes through the crown of the head. When it has done so it is astonished to find that it is surrounded by a garment of perturbed air. It protests, saying, 'This is not my own garment at all. Where is my garment? the bright, beautiful garment I put round me at first when I entered into this corrupt body. . . . [This garment] is murky, filthy, dimmed, horrid, frightful now . . .'. The soul asks who has torn its original, glorious dress, which it wore when it entered the body, from it. The demons give the answer. With horrible imprecations they tell the soul that the garment was given by them; it 'has become foul itself as thou art foul'.[11]

In other separation scenes there is an actual struggle between angels and devils for the soul as it emerges from the body. We have seen that this occurs at the end of the early sixteenth-century Welsh play.[12] But its most impressive form is found in lurid illustrations. One splendid example is to be found in a book, *Complaynt of the*

Soule printed in the early sixteenth century by Wynken de Worde. Here anxious friends and family gather round the bed of the dying man, while St Michael removes a tiny, sexless replica of him from the crown of his head. Both the dying man and his widow hold a large lighted candle, a symbol of Christian hope. But dancing around the foot of the bed are the most horrible, scaly devils shouting imprecations such as 'Heu infame', 'Spes nobis nulla'. Presumably the 'lost hope' in this case is the devils' own, as they despair of attaining the soul they believed was their own. They are furious and show their outrage in violent gestures. In other illustrations, where the souls are indubitably evil, devils actually tear them, represented as miniature bodies, from the mouths of the dying.[13]

Depictions of scenes like these are so common in medieval art and particularly in illuminated manuscripts that it is possible to look at only a few representative samples. In one, from a manuscript in the Bodleian, a small, white sexless soul kneels in the centre of a circle surrounded by piles of rocks that mark the bleak landscape. On the soul's right an angel pleads for it, while on its left stands a hideous devil holding out papers containing, presumably, lists of sins. A notable feature of this particular devil is the hideous faces on its chest, arms, knees and even genitals. Since the face is a sign of the head, the seat of reason, it seems that these displaced faces indicate the removal of reason from its rightful place and its dominance by fleshly appetite. While the fate of this particular kneeling soul hangs in the balance, the picture does provide some reassurance. In the sky above, a benign God the Father presides, flanked by two angels who hold a sheet in which another tiny soul, almost like a newborn, peeks out at the scene below.[14]

One of the most famous separation scenes is that in the *Rohan Book of Hours*. This picture is frequently described as a 'Last Judgment', but actually it is the immediate, provisional judgment that takes place at the time of death. Here there is nothing of the *en masse* separation of the good and wicked souls characteristic of the Doomsday pictures that will be encountered in the next chapter. Rather we have a single, emaciated man lying on an embroidered cloth in an open landscape with only a diaphanous loin cloth covering him. Skulls and bones of others long dead surround him. He breathes out his soul (again a sexless miniature), with the words 'Into thy hands, O Lord, I commend my spirit'. This soul has initially been seized by a devil, but flying down from the left-hand corner of the picture a red-clad St Michael, sword in hand, has grasped the devil by the hair and appears to be ready to free the soul from his grasp. Filling the upper right-hand corner of the painting, a compassionate God the Father, holding a sword and orb, signs of power and judgment, looks down at the dying man and says, in the vernacular, 'For your sins you shall do penance. On Judgement Day you shall be with Me.'[15]

The really wicked may be characterized by the abnormal manner of the separation of their souls and bodies. In a fifteenth-century Italian picture of Christ on the cross with thieves on either side, the soul of the evil thief is emerging from his mouth feet first. This appalling death (or birth) is assisted by a devil tugging to free the soul.[16] These sorts of scenes are doubtless in the back of the mind of John Donne when, in the course of a deathbed meditation in 'Of the Progresse of the Soule', he writes:

> Thinke Satans Sergeants round about thee bee,
> And thinke that but for Legacies they thrust;
> Give one thy Pride, to' another give thy Lust.[17]

Donne's advice to the dying is to circumvent the wiles of the devils by giving them not his soul but his vices, which were given *by* devils in the first place.

Depictions of separation scenes did not die out with the Middle Ages, or even with the early seventeenth century. An eighteenth-century French woodcut illustrating a seventeenth-century text, *A View of Human Life*, shows two cherubs, one holding a scales, flying down to receive the spirit of a man who lies on a pallet in what appears to be a large open tomb, surrounded by symbols of the vanity of life – sword, wreath, book, crown.[18] And a nineteenth-century Italian painting by Gabriele Smargiassi (1798–1882) also shows a separation scene. Here, in a typically romantic nineteenth-century landscape, against the background of the setting sun, the soul of the dead man, which appears to be a replica of his body lying inert on the ground, stretches up to a resplendent angel who holds up a host in her hands.[19]

The parting of soul and body, from ancient times, has frequently been seen as a source of regret to the soul – despite an opposed tradition, encountered in earlier chapters, in which the soul desires only to be free of the body. The regret that the soul may feel at parting from the body has been acknowledged from the time of the Greeks onwards. There is a picture on a fifth century BC lekythos of a soul mourning its body at the graveside. And in the Vercelli manuscript of the Old English 'Address of the Soul to the Body' the soul similarly returns to the grave of the body to comfort it. 'The soul willingly seeks with joy the clay vessel it formerly wore for a long time.' It speaks 'in good words, wisely, triumphantly. . . . "Dearest companion, although the worms yet greedily attack you, now your soul has come from my father's kingdom, fairly clothed, wound about with joy . . . I would then say to you that you should sorrow not, because [when] we are gathered at God's Judgement, we must then afterwards enjoy together . . . and be of high rank in heaven."'[20] And as late as the seventeenth century, the metaphysical poet Henry Vaughan imagines the soul comforting the body at the time of their separation:

> But thou
> Shalt in thy mothers bosom sleepe
> Whilst I each minute grone to know
> How neere Redemption creepes.
> Then shall wee meet to mixe again, and met,
> 'Tis last good-night, our Sunne shall never set.[21]

When the soul and body have been wicked in life, the case is somewhat different. Then the soul may still regret its separation from the body, because this separation marks the beginning of its own eternal punishment, but this regret will be combined with anger against the body for having participated in or (as the soul perceives it) initiated the evil they have done in life.

In a tract published in 1639 and rather laboriously entitled *The Soules Progresse to the Celestiall Canaan, or Heavenly Jervsalem*, we find this combination of sorrow and recrimination in a deathbed scene unrivalled since the Middle Ages. First come the devils to fetch the soul, which then 'feeles the body begin by degrees to dye, and ready, like a ruinous house, to fall upon her head'; yet she is afraid to come forth from the body 'because of those hell-hounds which wait for her comming'. Seeing all her pleasures gone, the soul addresses herself to those members of the body that in the past have delighted her – the eyes, the ears, the feet, the hands. None can help or give her pleasure now. Then the soul addresses the body as a whole and reviles it, yet acknowledges a mutual responsibility that is usually absent in the medieval addresses: 'But O corrupt carkasse, and stinking carion, how hath the divell deluded us? and how have wee served and deceived each other, and pulled swift damnation upon us both!' When the soul finally does come forth, trembling, it is seized by the fiends 'who carry her with violence *terrenti simili* to the bottomlesse lake, that burneth with fire and brimstone, where shee is kept as a prisoner in torment, till the generall judgement of the last great day.' At that time the soul will greet the flesh with even greater imprecations than before, and both will be punished, 'that as they sinned together, so they may be tormented together eternally'.[22]

This sort of thing will doubtless seem pretty foreign to a modern reader. The literal depiction of the separation of body and soul and the accompanying dramatic paraphernalia can be seen merely as 'medieval' in the pejorative sense. But I believe it is much more than this. It is really 'an externalising process, as the workings of the conscience guide the meditations and exclamations of the soul, and is, in short, the self-judgment of the soul'.[23] The dying person looks back and assesses his life. What he finds may not be consoling. The trappings of devils and angels make the abstract concrete in a particular way that is alien to the modern imagination. But we still assess our lives and judge ourselves, even if it is without the benefit of visible spirits egging us on.

Of course there is an extent to which we *do* die differently today. Modern medicine often means that the boundaries between life and death are blurred, so that there is never a moment when we consciously 'die'. Drugged and tubed, we slip imperceptibly from one state to another. We do not *decide* the manner of our death in the way that Donne allegedly did, crossing his hands and arranging his body so that nothing needed to be done afterwards by others. Struggles of angels and demons, even fear at the imminent approach of death, are a bit incongruous in the modern intensive care unit. Yet we do die; we fear death; we hope it is not extinction. The trappings have changed, but the reality has not.

William Blake

Some of these concepts continued into the supposedly rational eighteenth century, and are particularly notable in the works of William Blake. We have already seen Blake's visualizations of the soul as a beautiful woman. But this was not his only concept of the soul; the depictions change to fit the context.

Blake believed in forces of good and evil, even though he did not interpret them in a particularly orthodox way. In his writings good is energy and the life of the imagination; evil is matter and those things that pull man down to a state of bestiality. In some of his paintings and engravings, particularly those illustrating the literary works of others, the visualizations of this contrast between good and evil are depicted in ways similar in content, though not in style, to those of medieval writers and artists. One such illustration shows good and evil angels struggling for the possession of a child as its soul leaves its body.[24] In another picture (this part of a series of engravings for Blair's poem 'The Grave') we have dramatically paired and contrasting pictures of 'The Death of a Strong Wicked Man' and 'The Death of the Good Old Man'.[25]

The Good Old Man lies in a state of perfect repose, one hand on a copy of the Bible, which is open to the New Testament. Surrounding him at head and feet are a group of young men and women (angels?) praying. On a table beside the bed sit a chalice and loaf of bread – signs of the Eucharist. Behind the bed there is a large, open window through which two figures in long flowing robes and wings (indisputably angels!) conduct the soul of the old man. This soul, a replica of the figure on the bed, floats upwards with eyes raised and hands clasped in prayer. The atmosphere is one of peace and serenity.

In contrast, the 'strong wicked man' writhes in agony on the bedclothes. Two women are his companions, one leaning over him, one standing at the head of the bed. Both are in extreme distress. A cup lies broken, spilling its contents beside the sick man's pallet. As with the good man, there is an open window through which the soul of the dead man (again an exact replica of the individual) is flying. But the landscape outside is mountainous and bleak; he holds up his hands in horror as if to ward off the realm into which he is moving, and he appears to be enveloped in and almost propelled by diaphanous flames that rise up from behind the bed. If one were in any doubt as to the message of Blake's engraving, Blair's accompanying verses are all too explicit:

> Strength too! thou surly, and less gentle boast
> Of those that loud laugh at the village ring!
> A fit of common sickness pulls thee down
> With greater ease than e'er thou didst the stripling
> That rashly dar'd thee to th'unequal fight. . . .
> See, how he tugs for life, and lays about him,
> Mad with his pain! . . .
> O how his eyes stand out, and stare full ghastly!
> While the distemper's rank and deadly venom
> Shoots like a burning arrow cross his bowels,
> And drinks his marrow up.[26]

The reluctance of the soul to leave the body, as portrayed in Blair's poem, is in part sheer nostalgia for the joys of life, and in part a desire to have more time in which to amend its ways. In another illustration already discussed in Chapter 2, the soul, here pictured in isolation 'counting on long years of pleasure here', is not ready for a future life.[27]

In that dread moment how the frantic soul
Raves round the walls of her clay tenement,
Runs to each avenue, and shrieks for help,
But shrieks in vain! How wishfully she looks
On all she's leaving, now no longer her's!
A little longer, yet a little longer,
O might she stay to wash away her stains,
And fit her for her passage![28]

But death, stalking behind like a murderer, pursues the despairing female soul 'through every lane of life'. Frail and fallible, she is confronted with her inescapable fate. At last, forced 'to the tremendous verge, | At once she sinks to everlasting ruin!'

Death and the Psychics

The medieval separation scenes depicted a visible soul departing from its body, but it was only in the nineteenth century that a small group of people tried to prove this as a reality verifiable by the senses. The notion of a visible soul took on totally new dimensions with the advent of spiritualism. One might have expected the concept of the soul to become ever more abstract with the advance of scientific achievement, but such was not the case. Rather, science added a new dimension to the visualization of the soul. Previously, there may well have been credulous people who believed they actually saw souls departing from bodies, but the physical was not necessary to their faith. Now, for a small group of people, belief in the actuality of the soul and the afterlife depended on its physicality and the ability to *prove* that physicality in an unprecedented way. What was real was what could be evidenced by the senses. The whole thrust of spiritualism (despite the name given to the movement) was to materialize the soul.

The nineteenth-century spiritualist movement began in an unlikely fashion through the pranks of two sisters in upstate New York. A series of rappings was heard in the home of the Fox family, and two of their daughters, Katherine and Margaretta, then only 11 and 13, claimed that the rapping that was communicating with them came from the ghost of a peddler murdered in the house. (Forty years later Margaretta confessed that the rapping had been done by herself and her sister cracking their toe knuckles on any resonant surface!) News of the remarkable events soon spread, and with many people ready to cash in on the phenomenon, notably the girls' much older sister, Leah, there was soon a cult of mediums who claimed to be able to communicate with the dead. Seances flourished. Mediums carried their craft to Britain, and by 1852 one Mrs Hayden visited England to give sittings at a guinea a piece 'for the educated classes'.[29] Many of these mediums were demonstrable frauds, but a surprising number of 'the educated classes' were nevertheless enthralled by the notion of communicating with the dead. Henry Sidgwick, Professor of Moral Philosophy at Cambridge, no less, became the first president of the Society for Psychical Research in 1882. And if one *could* communicate with the dead, then doing so became the necessary proof of the survival of the self after death. The soul could be empirically confirmed.

The other physical manifestation of 'soul' or 'spirit' was to be found in the excrescence by some mediums of a curious substance called 'ectoplasm'. The production of this 'ectoplasm' occurred under conditions similar to those the mediums used for conjuring spirits. The medium was in a cabinet, which had been searched – as indeed had the medium's body. After a length of time, usually half an hour, during which the observers often entertained themselves by singing hymns, the medium would produce a substance from the mouth or from other orifices of the body – some of them considerably more intimate than the mouth! These excrescences often took the shape of human limbs or, in some cases, of faces. As with the mediums who communicated with the dead, some of these too were undoubtedly frauds and were exposed as such. But not all demonstrations of the phenomenon have ever been satisfactorily explained.[30]

Most of the effort of the Society for Psychical Research and that of mediums was concentrated on telepathy between two people, both living, or between the living and the spirits of the dead. But the new emphasis on the materiality of the soul had one interesting side effect: the attempt to see, quite literally and physically, the emergence of the soul from the dying body and its ascent from it. A Mr Holland actually constructed a viewing device rather like a studio camera through which he attempted to observe a soul as it ascended from a dying person and took form. This he claimed to have eventually succeeded in doing and invited an impartial reporter from the *Chicago Tribune* to observe the experiment. As the man died, an object gradually became distinguishable. 'It seemed like the vapory form of a man rapidly assuming a more perfect shape, pure and colorless as the most delicate crystal.' Gradually the distinct shape of a man was seen, and lay floating about a foot above the body on the bed, moored to the body by a slender cord. The soul's eyes were closed. Then the cord that held it to the clay parted, 'and a gentle tremor passed through the beautiful form. . . . The eyes of the spirit opened, and a ray of intelligence and of unspeakable joy passed over its face. It arose to a standing position, and cast one sorrowful look at the tenantless clay that lay so still.' At this point the reporter, not unreasonably, fainted.[31]

Even more remarkably, Mr G., in 1902, recorded the death of his wife in the *Journal of the Society for Psychical Research*. In this case, as far as we know, no special equipment was required. As his wife died, a woman about three feet tall, gold-hued, with flowing robes and a crown appeared over the bed, together with two kneeling forms clad in white drapery. 'In the air above his dying wife, extended horizontally, and moored by a cord attached to her forehead above her left eye was a perfectly shaped, unadorned spirit body. For five hours Mr. G. watched the spectral form writhe and struggle to release itself,' but until his wife died the image persisted. Then, at the moment of her death, the spirit body, the spectral trio and the mist dissolved.[32]

The notable thing about both these descriptions is the large element of purely conventional imagery in them. Mr G.'s account, particularly, with its golden woman (Mary?) flanked by kneeling spirits, leans heavily on the iconography of altar painting for its effect. The observation of a cord in each case is surely derived not just from the idea that the soul is connected to the body until the time of its release but from the customary likening of death to a new birth.

But the most astonishing thing about these accounts is that both these men wished profoundly to *see* a soul leave its body, believed that it was possible to do so, and were convinced that they had succeeded. Dr Berrick in the play 'The Human Soul' discussed in Chapter 4, takes a more extreme approach. He is prepared to kill his young wife in order to see her soul depart. (Probably he assumes he will no longer be around if he has to wait for her to die naturally.) What becomes clear from the history of the spiritualist movement is that, bizarre as the account in the play may seem, it could scarcely aspire to be more bizarre than the reality.

Another method of trying to 'prove' the existence of the soul was devised by an ingenious doctor at Massachusetts General Hospital. Dr Duncan McDougall, in 1907, attempted to *weigh* a soul. He wrote: 'If personal continuity after the event of bodily death is a fact . . . it must occupy a space in the body.'[33] So he tried to detect a sudden, inexplicable loss of matter at the time of death – the weight of the soul. To this end he constructed a bed mounted on a frame supported by sturdy platform beam scales 'sensitive to two-tenths of an ounce'. His first subject, a man dying of tuberculosis, produced a highly successful result. 'The moment that the patient succumbed, after three hours and forty minutes of observation, the beam end of the scales dropped, hitting the metal bar beneath it with a clang. This sudden and unexplained fall indicated to Dr. McDougall that the first soul to be monitored weighed precisely three-quarters of an ounce.'[34]

Alongside these attempts to 'prove' the soul in a doubting-Thomas sort of way by making it wholly visible there was arising another school of thought, embodied in the works of artists and writers, that portrayed the spiritual in general and the soul in particular in an abstract form. Their inspiration went back in part to the mystery cults of early Greece that have been described in the first chapter, imbibing along the way inspiration from the Hermeticists (a Graeco-Egyptian cult of first to third centuries AD), Paracelsus, and the spiritualist movement of the nineteenth century.

It was quite possible for the same person to be both a spiritualist and at the same time interested in physical manifestations of the soul. Madame Blavatsky (1831–91) was one such. She was deeply involved in the psychical circles described above, but also was one of the most important figures in the nineteenth-century development of Theosophy, and wrote works (*Isis Unveiled*, 1877, and *The Secret Doctrine*, 1888), which claimed that true spiritual insight came from mystical experience. So that alongside the concrete 'spiritual' showings there flourished a mindset that saw spiritual reality in arrangements of symbols and colours. Thus, in contrast to the concrete separation scenes we have just been describing, we have a painting by Marsden Hartley (1877–1943) showing 'The Transference of Richard Rolle' in abstract and symbolic terms. Rolle's monogram hovers above a desolate landscape emblazoned within a spiritual triangle against a cloud, whose whiteness signifies a transcendental world. His assumption takes him from the realm of a bleak earth to a resplendent heaven signified only by its radiance.[35] This increasingly abstract portrayal of the soul will be looked at in greater detail in the final chapter.

THE FATE OF THE SOUL

Tests of the Soul

The ultimate fate of the soul is shown at the time of death. For the separation of soul and body, in orthodox Christian teaching, is not the end of either. It is closely followed either by an immediate judgment of the soul or at least by an intimation of what its eternal state will be. This is not to be confused with the Last Judgment, which occurs at the end of the world and the reunion of soul and body at that time.

The state of the soul after death was something about which the Church had great difficulty in formulating a definite doctrine. The New Testament provides no clear guidance. Christ's words to the good thief on the cross, 'Today thou shalt be with me in Paradise', imply an immediate transition. Similarly the parable of Dives and

Lazarus[36] indicates that Lazarus is in a state of bliss and Dives in a state of torment just after their deaths. But most of the apocalyptic writings, particularly the Book of Revelation, focus on a final judgment when Christ will appear in glory and separate the saved and the damned. It is this vision that has inspired the countless 'Doom' paintings in Christian art. The truth is that the Church probably began by assuming a short interim period for those who were unfortunate enough to die before Christ's imminent return. (It was assumed that most of those who knew him on earth would still be alive at his Second Coming.) But as the years stretched to centuries and millennia, this short-term theology would not suffice. The difficulty was, there was no clear guidance towards a long-term theology. So at times artists and writers worked according to one set of assumptions, and at times according to another. If judgment was immediate and final, then how could the Church up to the Reformation justify prayers for the dead soul? The doctrine of purgatory, a place in which souls did penance for their misdeeds but with the ultimate hope of redemption, provided a constructive framework for the interim waiting period. But it could not be justified on biblical grounds.

The most common view in the Western Church, as I have stated, is that the soul at the time of death gains some intimation of its ultimate fate, and spends the intervening period between death and final judgment in a situation that reflects its status, good or evil, but that the final determination of the soul's fate takes place at the Last Judgment, the end of the world, when the soul will be reunited with its body to make its pain or pleasure more acute.[37]

In ancient Egypt there was only one judgment, and this took place immediately after death. The soul was literally weighed in the balance on a scales held by the god Anubis, in the company of Osiris and his forty-two assessors. There are many paintings of this momentous event. The dead man trembles as he sees that his heart is no longer in his breast but resting in one pan of the scales, with the feather of Truth or Justice on the other side. He defends himself, pronouncing the negative confession of ancient Egypt: 'I have not brought suffering on any person . . . I have not taken milk from the mouths of children, I have not driven cattle from their pasture . . . I am pure, I am pure, I am pure.' If the feather balances the heart this shows that the heart is not burdened with evil deeds, and it will go to the realm of the dead presided over by Osiris. But if the pan with the heart sinks against the feather, then the soul is immediately destroyed by the Devourer, who stands waiting beside the Judge.[38]

The image of the scales travelled to Greece, but there were very significant differences in its use and meaning. Instead of man being measured against an abstract principle of justice, two *eidoloi* (souls with a physical form) were set against each other, one in each pan of the scales. The sinking of the pan meant not judgment, but Death, who, in place of the Devourer, took the soul away. Thus the whole was not a judgment but 'an external affirmation of destiny'.[39]

The emphasis on judgment in Christianity meant that the image of the scales was likely to be imported into its own iconography, as indeed it has been. In Christian art, however, it is the Archangel Michael who holds the scales and weighs the soul. There are slightly different versions of exactly what is placed in the pan against the soul. Sometimes it is the good deeds of the soul, often represented by the miniature figure of the soul itself, balanced against its evil deeds. In other cases the soul, a miniature figure, is set against the redeeming blood of Christ. These two different pictures represent two quite different theologies of salvation – works versus Christ's saving grace. Both could co-exist well before the time of the Reformation.

In Guillaume de Deguileville's *Pylgremage of the Sowle*[40] during a contest for the soul between a guardian angel and Satan, Mercy, an advocate for the soul, argues for weighing the records of the sins in a balance against his good deeds. 'The balance will not lie, but without favour judge the truth.'[41] Alas, they are too heavy, but then Mercy delays the court while she goes to heaven to obtain a charter of pardon from Christ. Now the balance is set up again, and when the pardon is added to the side of good deeds it suffices to save the pilgrim from eternal damnation. Instead he goes to purgatory, where eventually he will cleanse himself of sin and be saved.

When the devil appears to be winning the struggle for the soul in the Welsh play of 'The Soul and the Body', we again have an intervention, this time from Mary, who pleads with Jesus:

172

> I pray in my necessity
> Against all the devils
> That the soul be weighed in the balance.[42]

She points out that the accused said psalms, and 'showed repentance in the hour of death, | And received Thy consecrated Body'. Further, she asks that she may place her Pater Nosters in the scales with the soul. Jesus relents:

> In spite of what he ever did against me,
> Breaking the law and the Ten Commandments,
> As you are pitiful towards him,
> Take him without refusal.[43]

Thus the soul is saved both because it repented at the hour of death and because, like the soul in Deguileville's *Pylgremage of the Sowle*, it has a powerful advocate. In both these cases, it is a friend of the soul (Mercy and Mary) who asks for the ceremony of weighing, and also in both cases the result is successful not through strict justice but through Christ's redeeming sacrifice.

Serious as the subject of this art is, the medieval mind sought to lighten it in various ways, and lurking behind the sense of doom and judgment lies the mischievous gargoyle-like humour of the artist. Thus we have many such illustrations where the devil tries to push down the pan with the evil deeds and distort the result. The devil and the artist could be jokers, both!

After the separation of soul and body and the initial judgment of the soul, there must be a passage to another world. In many of the Christian pictures discussed the passage is made by the soul in the company of angels – or devils – who guide it to its temporary abode before the great judgment at the last day. But there are many other models as well. The notion of some kind of gulf separating the two states of being, the earthly and the heavenly, is very ancient. In classical mythology Charon, the ferryman, rows souls across the river Styx on the other side of which is the Elysian abode of those who have died. Charon could decide not to ferry a soul, but this was not a matter of moral judgment: it depended rather on whether the body had been buried and whether the soul had the payment that Charon demanded for his services. The idea of Charon did not entirely die out in the Christian era. Dante has Virgil use his services in the *Inferno*, and, more surprisingly, he appears on a bronze relief on the tomb of two brothers who were late fifteenth-/early sixteenth-century Italian doctors. Here we have a variation on the visual concept of the soul: it is portrayed as a company of winged infants. The wings, as we have seen in the last chapter, connote freedom, and combined with the child they presumably indicate not immaturity but innocence.[44]

Sometimes the passage to the other world is so devised that it is itself a test and judgment. The most common form of this was the bridge that is easy to cross for the good soul, but impossible for the wicked. The bridge first appears in Persian mythology and spans the gulf between earth and heaven. While good souls negotiate it without difficulty, for evil souls it becomes 'like the edge of a razor. And he who is righteous passes over the bridge . . . [but] he who is of the wicked, as he places a footstep on the bridge, on account of affliction and its sharpness, falls from the middle of the bridge, and rolls over head-foremost.'[45] A further hazard is the doppelgänger (its own double) that the soul may meet coming in the opposite direction. This will be externally what the evil soul already is internally – foul and stinking. Horrified, the soul staggers on its uncertain foothold and falls into the abyss.[46] There are many other varied descriptions of bridges of judgment. One occurs as early as the fourth-century *Visio Pauli*, though this is now believed to be a ninth-century interpolation. In the eighth century St Boniface has a vision of hell in which he sees a traveller, the Monk of Wenlock, watching souls cross or fail to cross a river of pitch spanned by a wobbly timber plank.[47]

In the *Vision of Tundal*, written in 1149 by an Irish monk, Tundal suffers a stroke brought on by suppressed anger against a friend. For two days he lies comatose, during which time his soul leaves his body and he has a terrifying vision of hell. Two perilous bridges punctuate his journey. The first, across a deep valley, is spanned by a plank a thousand feet long and only a foot wide. He sees many souls fall down, and is himself only saved by an angel who leads him by the hand. Naturally there is a terrible creature waiting to devour him on the other side, with a mouth so wide that nine thousand armed men might ride abreast through it. He manages to escape the beast as well, only to encounter the second bridge. This is two miles long and crosses a lake filled with ravening beasts. It is only as wide as the palm of a hand and studded with sharp nails. Tundal must not only cross it, but must lead with him a wild cow, since in his life he stole a cow from a neighbour![48]

In all these cases it is not the innate skill of the soul that determines the outcome but its condition, good or ill, which enables it either to accomplish what is beyond its natural ability or not to do so.

The soul is tested in these various ways at the time of death, and a clear intimation of its ultimate fate is given. But within the tradition of the Western Church, none of this is certain until the final day, when God will come in glory as king and judge. In the meantime, the soul appears either to languish in a state of misery (as is the case with the souls who come back to berate their bodies in the debates), to serve time in purgatory (as God tells the repentant soul illustrated in the *Rohan Book of Hours*), or to spend time in some state of indeterminate bliss, not fully heaven, but certainly quite comfortable.

SUMMARY

The fear that death at best presages a complete change in our situation and at worst eternal misery or even extinction has caused people through the ages to expend a large amount of creative energy imagining what may happen. In ancient times and in the Middle Ages these imaginings focused on the actual moment of death. Death, like much else in life, was perceived in terms of a drama with all the elements of struggle, guilt, punishment and hope. If we no longer focus so precisely on the moment of death it is in part, I have suggested, because modern ways of dying have robbed it of its intrinsic drama. Yet the emotions of guilt and hope survive.

The emotive power of Kafka's *The Trial* does not lie in the uniqueness and surrealism of Joseph K's situation but in its universality. At one level Joseph K, mysteriously accused of a crime worthy of punishment by death, protests he is not guilty; at another he knows that, simply by virtue of having lived, he is. A corollary of guilt is punishment. We too, like Joseph K, may protest we do not deserve it, but at the same time we fear and long for expiation of guilt which, in all cultures, is linked to punishment and suffering. Just possibly, we fear, a lifetime of guilt *must* be repaid with an eternity of suffering.

Then there is hope. The Archangel Michael swoops in, sword in hand, and dispatches our devils. We are rescued, 'saved'. We use this word in such trivial contexts now it is difficult to feel its full import. Perhaps most of us cannot conceive of being 'saved' for eternity because both concepts – 'saved' and 'eternity' – are equally incomprehensible in their abstract enormity. So we have invented pictures, in words and on canvas. We hope they may contain some fragment of reality.

SEVEN

The Immortal Soul: Doomsday and Beyond

> We must assert that the intellectual principle which we call the human
> soul is incorruptible.
>
> *Thomas Aquinas*, Summa Theologica *I. iii.lxxv.6*

The immortality of the soul is axiomatic; the soul is that part of us that is immortal. The other essential characteristic of the immortal soul is that it should retain the individuality of the person whose soul it is (or was) in life. The Epicureans,[1] and later Averroes, denied that the individual soul survived death. Averroes, a twelfth-century commentator on Aristotle, claimed rather that a single intellect existed for the whole human race. Every individual, during life, participates in this intellect, but at death his individuality is swallowed up again in the whole. These views spare the soul the fear of punishment after death, but in its place they raise the spectre of annihilation.

The immortality and individuality of the soul, as well as the concept of its judgment, were not present in the writings of the pre-Socratic Greeks, but they do appear in the works of Plato, as we saw in the first chapter. Indeed, some of Plato's arguments for the immortality and incorruptibility of the soul are quite similar to those of Aquinas. Combined with these ideas, however, in the Greeks is the notion of metempsychosis, the belief that the individual soul can be embodied in different ways before it finally attains eternity. This, to some extent, negates the absolute distinctiveness of the soul, and especially its distinctiveness in union with a particular body. Within the Western Christian tradition the fact of a single incarnation in one body is particularly important because of the complex ideas concerning the interrelationship of body and soul in sin, judgment and ultimate fate. Therefore, within this tradition it was essential to reject the notion of metempsychosis for the belief in one earthly life that body and soul shared together followed by an eternity of bliss or damnation likewise shared.

THE SEPARATED SOUL

The separated soul after death will retain memory and character; in other words, it will retain selfhood. From the time of Descartes ('I think, therefore I am') this self is a thinking substance and is identical with the 'I'. But long before this, Aquinas identified thought as the property that belonged to the soul alone, and therefore 'the soul, having an independent activity, is capable also of independent existence, as an incorruptible substance in its own right'.[2]

But how do we think about these things? How do we conceive of a pure abstraction? How do we conceive of immortality? The Greeks conceived of it negatively: the Gods were *athanatoi*, 'not subject to the darkening of mortals', or, more simply, those who do not die.[3] This vague and shadowy definition was not sufficient for a religion like Christianity where immortality was the ultimate hope and promise – even if it was, necessarily, preceded by death, 'the darkening of mortals'. The state of immortality had to be imaginable and alluring. So even this abstract, separated soul had to become picturable and set in a landscape, just as the soul during life and at the time of death had to be imaginable.

This was not a difficulty that had arisen earlier. For the Egyptians, the soul (or souls) were so bound up with the preservation of the body after death that the notion of visualizing it other than in a symbolic form was redundant. As for the soul, the Greeks and the Romans, neither of whom believed in a resurrection of the body, had it retain a kind of visibility recognizably similar to the individual it had inhabited. It was a 'shade', able to be seen yet not sufficiently substantial to cast a shadow. But in Christianity there was a clear division between the soul joined to the body in life, the disembodied soul at death, and the soul reunited to its body at the Resurrection.

In relation to the immortal soul this raised interesting theological problems that were, to some extent, connected with a certain literalism in thinking. It was not good enough to say, 'The soul is really abstract and invisible, but I want to be able to imagine it in particular situations and doing particular things, therefore I shall picture it as such and such.' If we cannot think of abstractions, then just maybe the soul never is a complete abstraction: maybe it always has *some* kind of body, even if not the kind it was united to on earth.

This was the route certain philosophers and theologians began to take from the early days of the Christian Church. It is different from the kind of 'accommodation' I described Dante and Milton prac- tising[4] because it is not a *conscious* fiction. Dante and Milton deliberately fashioned their descriptions of the soul to the needs of literature; these thinkers actually believed the soul either was or possessed some kind of body. If there is any 'accommodation' here, it appears to be an unconscious accommodation of doctrine rather than merely of literary method to human needs.

Origen and Tertullian both, in their very different ways, constructed theologies that allowed for the soul either to *be* in certain ways a body (Tertullian) or to always be attached to an ethereal body (Origen).[5] Dante at one level appears to be using the concept of 'bodies' for souls purely as a literary device, but the realism of the 'shades' he describes, that talk, express emotion through their features, and move independently leads one to feel at times that he has uncritically (and perhaps unconsciously) adopted the beliefs of his classical literary models in matters of substance as well as style.

It would be reasonable to suppose that any *belief* in the corporeal nature of souls would have died out before or at the time of the Renaissance, but such was not the case. In the late seventeenth century Henry More, part of a group of thinkers known as the Cambridge Platonists, was arguing about whether or not separated souls had bodies. This he did against the background of the thought of two great philosophers of the period, Hobbes and Descartes. Hobbes was a pretty thorough-going materialist who attributed the belief in a separate soul to the 'demonology of the Greeks'[6] – a view that has some plausibility. Descartes, in complete contrast, asserted the absolute reality of mind and spirit over against matter. Working in this conflicting climate of thought was no easy matter, and it led More into some strange philosophical contortions.

He asserted that spirit (or soul) was immaterial, but then followed this up by denying that immateriality, by definition, excludes extension – that is, the ability to occupy space. So we could, in theory, have an immaterial soul that at the same time was extended in space, a property usually attributed only to body. However, More goes farther than this and asserts that spirits are not only extended but that they are always united to *some kind* of body. This is not a gross, earthly body but an 'airy' body, which is the habitation of the soul after death as it is the habitation of angels and demons. Thus, just as spirit can have some of the characteristics of bodies, so body can have some of the properties of spirit. The result of this is still to assert the reality of soul (against Hobbes) but to minimize the enormous gap between the realms of matter and spirit in Descartes.

One way or another souls must be visible to the imagination even after death. Because after the individual judgment that takes place at the time of death (discussed in the last chapter) the story is still not over. The soul will wait in a state of relative bliss or damnation – or it will expiate its sins in purgatory, a place of punishment, but one that allows the soul to hope that at the last day it will be translated to paradise. Once the soul is dead and separated from its body, it can no longer change its intention. The will of a soul that was evil in life will remain fixed on evil, and the will of one that was good will remain attached to goodness. Those in purgatory *appear* to change their state from one of torment to one of bliss, but that is only because, in order to qualify for purgatory, their will must be fixed on the good, though they have failed to attain it perfectly in life.[7]

Two tremendous events are yet in store for the soul. In its state of bliss, misery or trial, it waits to be united with its body and to take part in the final judgment.

The Bodies of the Damned and Glorified

The reunion of the soul with its earthly body is, as far as I am aware, an idea that is unique to Christianity and closely related religions, including Islam. In the Myth of Er we saw how souls were sent back to earth to be reunited with *some* body, but it most certainly was not the body they had left. As for those who were fortunate enough to escape the cycle of reincarnation, they would then be free of body. For Plato, freedom from the body was a good; reunion with it could only bring misery.

The Christian religion, however, is based upon a god who became incarnate, who took on body. Body therefore is not to be despised. 'If the flesh of man were not to be saved, the Author of salvation would never have taken the flesh of man upon him.'[8] It is through the body that we exercise the senses, that we accomplish good and evil. In the chapter on conflict between the soul and body, we saw how the soul reviled the body as at best the instrument of sin and, in some cases, the instigator of it. It is therefore just that whatever reward or punishment is to be meted out to the soul should be shared by the body also. So, at the last day, 'the trumpet shall sound, and the dead shall be raised incorruptible'.[9] The modern reader probably finds this implausible, in any literal sense. Even in the seventeenth century, Donne acknowledged the difficulties, but asserted that they would be overcome. 'Where mans buried flesh hath brought forth grasse, and that grasse fed beasts, and those beasts fed men, and those men fed other men, God that knows . . . in what corner of the world every atome, every graine of every mans dust sleeps, shall recollect that dust, and then recompact that body, and then re-inanimate that man, and that is the accomplishment of all.'[10] The rhetoric at least has the ring of conviction. And this body will be not a different body, but 'the same body made better'.[11]

But what is 'the same body made better'? This is a question that exercised Christians as early as the time of St Paul: 'But some man will say, How are the dead raised up? and with what body do they come?'[12] Aquinas explains how he imagines this resurrected body in the saved: 'Just as the soul which enjoys the divine vision will be filled with a kind of spiritual lightsomeness, so by a certain overflow from the soul to the body, the body will in its own way put on the lightsomeness of glory.' This body, unlike the recalcitrant body on earth, will move in complete obedience to the soul's wishes. Indeed, the term 'spiritual body', Aquinas says, means not that it is completely immaterial like air, but that it is entirely under the control of spirit.[13]

Still the reader asks, 'But what *kind* of body exactly?' It will not have escaped the notice of most of us that our bodies are not exactly a constant throughout our lives. In the midst of all this literalness, will we have the body with which we died? Not at all, says Aquinas. We shall all rise at the perfect age – thirty-two years and three months, the age that Christ was when he died. Before this, we have not reached full maturity; after this we decline. But then a further question arises. If we are all to be perfect, what happens to the female sex which, as everyone knows, is less perfect than the male? Even Aquinas, it seems, does not like the idea of a heaven entirely without women, so he argues that 'the frailty of the feminine sex is not in opposition to the perfection of the risen. For this frailty is not due to a shortcoming of nature, but to an intention of nature.'[14] Well, that's a relief.

And what of the damned? What kind of body will they have? Their bodies too will be 'proportioned to [their] souls'. Thus they will not be subject to the spirit, nor will they be agile in obeying the soul; 'rather, they will be burdensome and heavy, and in some way hard for the soul to carry . . .'. They will be 'dense and darksome'. Most important of all, just as the bodies of the just retain their use of the senses for pleasure, so the bodies of the wicked have the use of their senses to feel suffering. This pain will be eternal because, unlike on earth, they are not subject to corruption.[15]

I have quoted so extensively from Aquinas because his pronouncements were and remain in the Catholic Church the statement of its most influential theologian on the matter. But, as always, imagination does not stop at doctrine. What did people *imagine* the bodies of the saved and the damned looked like?

In the chapter on stage plays featuring the soul I stated that in plays such as *The Castle of Perseverance* and other mystery and morality plays we had no clear directions as to how the soul should be represented. This is true as far as the text of the plays themselves is concerned. But ingenious research by Meg Twycross, based on lists of costumes and props for the York and Coventry Cycle plays of the Last Judgment, has shed some light on this interesting question. In the records of the Mercers Company for the year 1433 the clothing for evil souls is listed as: two tops, two pairs of hose, two masks, and two

27 The soul leaves the body (see pp. 159–60). From *Complaynt of the Soule*, printed by Wynken de Worde. *(British Library)*

28 'The Death of the Good Old Man', by William Blake, 1808 (see pp. 164–5). From illustrations for Robert Blair's 'The Grave'. (*Mary Evans Picture Library*)

29 'The Death of a Strong Wicked Man', by William Blake, 1808 (see p. 165). From illustrations for Robert Blair's 'The Grave'. *(Mary Evans Picture Library)*

30 God creating a soul. From *Omne Bonum*, by James le Palmer. British Library, MS Royal 6E.VI, fol. 94v. *(British Library)*

31 The soul at the time of death. Two men watch sorrowfully as the soul, a small, naked body, emerges from the mouth of the dying man. It is about to be received by two angels, but a devil with a forked hook reaches out to grapple for it. From the Office of the Dead, Bodleian, MS Douce 102, fol. 116r. *(The Bodleian Library, University of Oxford)*

32 An angel and a devil struggle for possession of the soul (see p. 160). Bodleian, Gough Liturg. 3, fol. 95v. *(The Bodleian Library, University of Oxford)*

33 *The Weighing of the Heart*, from the Egyptian Book of the Dead (see pp. 171–2). *(Musée du Louvre, Paris/The Bridgeman Art Library)*

34 Hermes weighing souls (see p. 172). Red figure amphora from Nola, *c.* 470 BC. *(Art Resource)*

35 The weighing of souls by St Michael (see p. 172). Detail from the tympanum of Autun Cathedral (Saone-et-Loire), twelfth century. *(The Bridgeman Art Library)*

36 'Cherubs Come to Take the Spirit Away'. Note the scales one cherub is holding; judgment will not be long delayed. Illustration from *A View of Human Life*, by Marin Le Roy de Gomberville (1600–74), engraved by Daret. *(The Bridgeman Art Library Art Library)*

37 The souls of the deceased in the form of winged infants cross the river Styx (see pp. 173–4; cf. Plate 6). One of a series of narrative reliefs from the tomb of Girolamo and Marcantonio della Torre, by Andrea Riccio (1470–1532). (*Musée du Louvre, Paris/The Bridgeman Art Library*)

38 *Last Judgment*, by William Blake, 1808 (see p. 187). Petworth House, Sussex.
(The National Trust/The Bridgeman Art Library)

39 The dead resurrected as white and black souls (see pp. 182–3). Bodleian, MS Douce 134 fol. 52v. *(The Bodleian Library, University of Oxford)*

40 Hell. From the Limbourg brothers, *Très Riches Heures* (see pp. 187–8). *(Art Resource)*

41 Abd-er-Rhaman's soul guided to Paradise by Christian and Muslim angels (see pp. 193–4). Engraving by Paul Nash from his illustrations to *Abd-er-Rhaman in Paradise*, by Jules Tellier (London: The Golden Cockerel Press, 1928). *(© Tate London 2003; photography British Library)*

42 *Evocation (The Burial of Casagemas)*, 1901, by Pablo Picasso (see p. 210).
(© Succession Picasso/DACS 2003; Musée d'Art Moderne de la Ville de Paris/The Bridgeman Art Library)

43 *The Resurrection, Cookham*, 1924–6, by Stanley Spencer (see p. 211). (© *Tate London 2003; photography Art Resource*)

44 'Untitled No 1', 1915, by Hilma Af Klint, from the series *Altar Paintings* (see p. 213). *(Haags Gemeentenmuseum, the Netherlands/The Bridgeman Art Library*

wigs. The problem with this is that the clothing list for the good souls is identical. So all we learn is that the souls wore masks and were clad in tight tops and tights to make them look like the naked Resurrection bodies in Doomsday paintings. But one hundred years later, in the accounts for Coventry between 1537 and 1573 we discover that they were differentiated by colour: the good souls were white, and the evil souls black from top to toe. Thus the good souls portray on stage, as nearly as they can, the characteristics Aquinas lists for them, while the evil souls are, as he also states, 'dense and darksome'.[16]

Further evidence for this visualization of good and evil souls comes from pictures of Doomsday in a medieval manuscript in the Bodleian. Here again there are black and white souls, with the black on the left and the white on the right – that is, stage left and right, not left and right as seen by the audience. The white souls hold their hands together as if in prayer; the black gesture in an agitated manner.[17] These souls are taking part in the last fateful experience of their existence. They will live, of course, for eternity, but their state will in future be fixed.

DOOMSDAY

No other scene in life or death obsessed the medieval imagination as did the Last Judgment. In painting and in literature it is omnipresent. One of the greatest medieval poems has it for its subject:

> Dies irae, dies illa
> solvet saeclum in favilla,
> teste David cum Sibylla.
> [Day of wrath, that day
> Dissolves the ages in ashes
> As both David and the Sybil testify.]

It is, quite simply, the end of the world and of time as we know it. The juxtaposition of David, King of Israel, and the Sybil is particularly interesting, revealing again the medieval concern to reconcile Christian doctrine with Old Testament and classical teaching. The poem describes the dread of humanity when the Judge comes to judgment. The trumpet will sound everywhere in the sepulchral regions, driving all mankind before the throne of God. The Book by which all the world will be judged will be brought forth; nothing will remain hidden or unavenged. The poet then reverts to a plea in his own voice:

> Quid sum miser tunc dicturus,
> quem patronum rogaturus,
> dum vix iustus sit securus?
> [What then shall I say, wretch that I am,
> What advocate entreat to speak for me,
> When even the righteous are hardly secure?]

He appeals to the 'King of awful majesty' to save him on that day, and reminds Christ of his sacrifice on the cross for erring mankind. He calls on the 'Iuste iudex ultionis' (just, avenging judge) to grant remission of his sins before the 'day of reckoning'. May he be among the sheep and not the goats, set on the right hand of God.

The final section of the poem moves back to a general, third-person supplication on behalf of the sorrowful and terrified sinner, who will rise *from* the dust, thus making a circular connection with the 'dust' in the first stanza, to which the whole earth will be reduced:

> Lacrimosa dies illa
> qua resurget ex favilla
> iudicandus homo reus.
> Huic ergo parce, Deus,
> pie Jesu Domine,
> dona eis requiem.
> [Tearful that day
> When out of the dust shall rise
> The guilty man to be judged.
> Therefore spare him, O God.
> Merciful Lord Jesus
> Give them rest.]

The Immortal Soul

This is powerful writing that has survived in the liturgy of the Church and in many musical settings (including Britten's *War Requiem*) to the present day. Whatever literal beliefs one holds, its spell cannot be ignored. The short three-line stanza with its brief lines and tight rhyme scheme click together, reinforcing the sense of inevitability. Everything is now fixed forever; nothing can be changed.

The biblical precedent for this final drama is found in Matthew's Gospel, Chapter 25: 31–46:

> When the Son of man shall come in his glory, and all the holy angels with him, then shall he sit upon the throne of his glory: And before him shall be gathered all nations: and he shall separate them one from another, as a shepherd divideth his sheep from the goats: And he shall set the sheep on his right hand, but the goats on the left. Then shall the King say unto them on his right hand, Come ye blessed of my Father, inherit the kingdom prepared for you from the foundation of the world . . . Then shall he say also unto them on the left hand, Depart from me, ye cursed, into everlasting fire, prepared for the devil and his angels . . . And these shall go away into everlasting punishment: but the righteous into life eternal.

But what of those who could not read, or who were impervious to the spell of an ancient language? For them, there were the pictures, hundreds and thousands of them, in cathedrals and churches all over Europe. They looked up, week by week, and were fed with images of the righteous and the damned on the right and left hand of God. There could be no appeal. By this time everything was over except the pronouncement of the soul's fate. Unlike the judgment that took place at the time of death and was particular to the soul being separated from its body, this judgment was universal in scope. *All* the dead from the beginning of the world stood before the throne of God waiting to be judged.

The painting of *The Last Judgment* by Fra Angelico in the Museum of San Marco in Florence is both splendid and typical of these paintings and carvings. At the top of the picture Christ sits in glory and judgment, surrounded by the hosts of angels and archangels. At the

185

bottom of the circle of these heavenly beings, on the right-hand of Christ, sits Mary, intercessor for sinners, her hands clasped in prayer.[18] On the left is John the Baptist, the other intercessor, in a similar position. On either side of this central circle sit the prophets, apostles and patriarchs. Two angels with trumpets project down from this central height. They have indeed wakened the dead, and in the central lower half of the picture a series of open graves stretches to the horizon. On the right of these tombs the blessed, many of whom are monks and nuns (and even the odd bishop), stand gazing in wonderment at the scene before them. Some cast their eyes upwards towards the resplendent scene above; others gaze in apparent horror at the damned opposite them, but separated by the gulf of open tombs. These also include figures of eminence – kings, bishops and monks. One king clasps his face in his hands in a gesture of horror, as devils prod them all towards hell. Remote from this horror, on the far right, blessed souls who appear to have been in paradise long enough to have become accustomed to it, dance in a circle in a field of flowers. Yet others kneel in rapture before an opening through which streams heavenly light. Opposite, on the far left, the damned enjoy no such pleasures. One group sit bowed, hugging their knees in sullen despair; another group clasp one another in terror; yet a third are seated at a table where something distinctly unappetising is before them, and a fourth group are being boiled in a cauldron. At the very bottom damned souls writhe, drowning in a pit, while a huge devil consumes one of them and clasps others who will doubtless be eaten in turn.

These are the basic elements of the judgment scene – Jesus or God the Father dispensing justice, usually surrounded by the hosts of heaven and the saints, with those destined to enjoy paradise on his right, and those about to be cast into hell on his left. Of course, there are many individual variations on this general pattern. A twelfth-century judgment mosaic showing eastern influence in the Cathedral of Torcello near Venice, is arranged even more schematically and hierarchically, and shows Christ in his dual role as saviour and judge. At the very top and centre is a large figure of Christ holding his cross, having released from hell the souls of Adam and Eve, David and Solomon, as foretold by John the Baptist, who stands gesturing at one side. In the tier below this, Christ appears again, this time in glory and as judge, surrounded by a mandorla and flanked by Mary, John and ranks of the saints and apostles. Yet below this a rank of angels blow their trumpets, and the dead arise from land and sea. Another rank down, and the saved and the damned are separated. Michael with a scales and devils together with a raven mark the division, right and left, between the two states of the risen souls. At the very bottom we see the saved, including Abraham, clasping a soul to his bosom, enjoying the delights of paradise, and the damned in eternal fire, a fire that flows from the mandorla of Christ, thus showing that it is kept alive by his divine will. The schematic design of this mosaic is typical of the Eastern Church's vision of judgment.

A *Last Judgment* by William Blake gives us a much more dynamic scene. In place of the static ranks of angels, saints and sinners, we have a flowing mass of people moving up or down according to whether they are saved or damned. Thus those on the right side of Christ (the left of the painting) ascend in a balletic movement, while on the opposite side the damned fall headlong and disorderly, some already entwined with snakes or chains, to hell. The saved are a company; adults (male and female) clasp children as they soar upward together. Men and women share passionate embraces – though whether these are intended to represent husbands and wives or reunited souls and bodies is uncertain. The damned, in contrast, are isolated and fall alone. The joys of the blessed will be social joys; the wicked will suffer each essentially in a hell of his own.

HELL

Hell, one might flippantly say, has been God's gift to the imagination. It has provided writers and artists with a licence to give the more sadistic side of their nature free rein. The torments of the damned! What invention has gone into them throughout the ages.

The Limbourg brothers in their most famous work, the *Très Riches Heures* of the Duc de Berry (*c.* 1413), give a strange, luminous splendour to their horrific subject. In the centre of the picture is a burning grill, the flames of which are fanned by three mighty bellows, worked by devils who stand on them pumping. On the grill itself lies Satan with two miniature couples firmly grasped, one in each hand. Other tiny human figures, tormented by snakes, are trampled into the flames of the grill by his feet. At either side of the painting further unfortunate beings are pulled and herded by devils towards the flames. But most horrible of all is the stream of souls that, surrounded by fire, are violently projected upwards out of Satan's mouth. Spewn up towards the deep blue of the sky, they reach the summit only to fall back again into the flames. The colours of the painting are predominantly grey-blue, red and brown, but illuminating the whole awful scene is the gold the Limbourgs so favoured. It glows on the wings and bodies of the devils and the flames of the fire. Only the suffering bodies of the damned remain untouched by its luminosity.

In a fresco painted around 1320 by Taddeo di Bartolo in the Collegiate Church of San Gimignano, we have a compartmentalized hell with the damned suffering exquisite tortures custom-made for their individual sins. The compartmentalization, though visualized differently from Dante's Inferno, is similar in concept. But the sheer gut-wrenching horror of these pictures has no parallel in Dante. In the middle on the far right we see the punishments for lust. An adultress who is merely being lashed gets off lightly. Below her are two sodomites. One of them is impaled on a spit from his anus to his mouth. His fellow sodomite holds an end of the stick in his mouth, while a devil turns the other end over the fire. In another scene, the gluttonous (one of whom is a fat, tonsured monk), sit around a fire while devils force them to eat inedible food. Yet another vignette shows the resurrected souls pierced by knives and bound by chains. At the top of the fresco, in the position of Christ in judgment scenes, sits Satan himself. Simultaneously he eats one body (only the buttocks and legs are visible hanging out of his mouth), and excretes another whose head and arms wave about helplessly in a horrible parody of birth.

The artistic variations on these kinds of scenes are endless, and most show little real originality. The one artist who does show this quality, both in his concept of hell and in his visualization of it, is Hieronymous Bosch. In Bosch's work the horrors of hell, which in other artists have habitually reflected extreme but realistically possible tortures, take on a completely surreal quality. There is menace lurking in scenes that at first glance seem almost benign. Nowhere is this better illustrated than in the innocently titled *Garden of Earthly Delights*. There was a long tradition of painting gardens of pleasure and delight – earthly analogues of the Garden of Eden. Naturally these earthly gardens were stained to some extent through the sexuality of their fallen inhabitants – courtly love flourished in such enclosed gardens – but they were still, on the whole, innocent places, full of music, delicious food and drink, and playful dalliance. Bosch's garden is not quite like this.

The painting is in the form of a triptych, with a single high horizon stretching across the three panels, which appear to show a clear progression, almost a narrative, from left to right. On the far left God stands in a paradise-like garden, raising his hands in blessing over the newly created Adam and Eve. Around them numerous birds and animals play. Behind them a fountain creates a small pool from which a unicorn drinks. Other larger animals including an elephant and a giraffe wander in the open landscape. But then, when one looks closely, disturbing features begin to emerge. The tree at the far left of the painting is thick and tuberous, almost like a cactus. A cat walks under it complacently holding a dead rat between its teeth. The base of the fountain appears to rest on volcanic rock, and its jets are supported by a wheel with teeth – almost like a circular saw. Cactus leaves similar to those that decorate the tree jut out from the circumference of the wheel, and from a hole in its centre an owl peers out.[19] The background landscape is jagged and rough; swarms of birds sweep in and out of the orifices of rocks. And what about the boulder on the far right of the panel? Does it not have a weeping eye?

If all this is not offputting enough, the large central panel reveals much more disturbing features. Here the owl has multiplied and is found on both the right and left foreground of the painting. The scene is crowded with detail, predominantly of naked lovers in every attitude of lascivious behaviour, including sodomy. A procession of wild animals, with humans riding them bareback, circles in the central part of the background. Curiously, some fish appear miraculously to have left the water to join in the fun. Nature is no longer remotely 'natural'. Fruits of a frighteningly disproportionate size dot the landscape and are eaten by the lovers, and in some cases provide shelter for them.

In the third panel, balancing the Eden of the first, we have entered a surreal nightmare landscape. In the background dark shapes that appear to be the remnants of buildings are backlit by bursts of fire. On a lurid red lake a boat with a red sail moves. In the foreground, everything is perverted from its rightful use. A harp and a lute are being used as instruments of torture. Lying under the lute is a man with a part song written on his buttocks. Others gather around and sing from this unusual manuscript. A miser farts gold coins into a huge well. At the midpoint of the painting a cutaway crustaceous body supports itself on a dark lake with its leg in one sinking boat and its head in another. Anomalous, a human head that seems to be supporting a wooden circle with a bladder like a bagpipe on it, peers out from behind this strange creature. A huge pair of detached ears, held together by an arrow, act as supports for a knife like a guillotine between them. 'Everything in it . . . is charged with malevolent fury. . . . No scheme of Hell based on Dante, with his exactly-placed rings and pits, could accommodate the sprawling profusion of Bosch's imagination. It demanded a new syntax, a discontinuous symbolic language.'[20]

This is a world of unmitigated evil and disorder at every level. Burning on a red hot grill for eternity is not a pleasant prospect, but it is at least comprehensible. Bosch is so terrifying because he takes us not just into situations that are more extreme than any we have experienced on earth, but that relate to nothing in our experience. To be caught in the hells of most medieval artists would be to endure in one's self for eternity the pain we already know augmented to infinity. To endure Bosch's hell would be to *lose* the self irretrievably in an unrecognizable phantasmagoria of horror.

The ultimate horror of hell, of course, is that it is eternal. In a twelfth-century miniature from the Winchester Psalter, a grim-faced angel stands with a key that he is inserting into the lock of the mouth of hell. The mouth is literally just that, a yawning cavern of teeth and fangs surrounded by a bestial head. Inside souls in human form, three wearing crowns, writhe in torment as devils torture them. Above is the inscription: 'Ici est enfers e li angels ki enferme les portes' ('Here is hell and the angel who closes the gates').

PARADISE

As extreme as are the torments of the damned, just so extreme are the pleasures of heaven. One of the most delightful depictions of paradise is an illustration by Giovanni di Paoli for Dante's *Paradiso*. Here redeemed souls, Paoli's pictorial translation of Dante's 'sparks of light', leap and dive playfully in the river of light in paradise. It is the exuberant joy of these sparkling souls that makes them quite unusual. Their small, naked bodies flit in the green and gold landscape. More common is the solemn ecstasy displayed by the souls being crowned by an angel in a painting in Orvieto Cathedral. The angel looks down tenderly at the pious and solemn expression on the face of the redeemed man she is about to confirm in his happiness.

It is also worth noting how 'pastoral' many of these visions of heaven are. Despite the description in Revelation of the celestial city with its gold and pearl décor, when medieval artists painted bliss they did so most often in a garden – often an enclosed garden, but always one with trees, fountains and flowers. It is the garden of love transformed into the garden of paradise. Even in Fra Angelico's Doomsday painting, discussed above, the blessed on the far right dance in green, flowered fields. Bliss is innocence and freedom, not just order and splendour.

These pictures of hell and heaven are not necessarily to be taken literally – though it would be surprising if those in churches and cathedrals were not so taken by a large number of the illiterate faithful who gazed on them week by week. Heaven is a state of being eternally with God; hell is a state of being eternally separated from God. The pleasure and pain the soul derives from one or other of these states constitutes paradise or damnation. But the way of poets and artists must still be that of accommodating the abstract to the needs of human sense, and this must be done without compromising the spiritual status of souls. Dante's images of them as jewels or points of light composing the shape of an eagle or rose have already been discussed in Chapter 5. Above all, they are radiant:

> Long as the feast of Paradise shall be,
>   so long shall our love's bliss shine forth from us
>   and clothe us in these radiant robes you see.[21]

And this radiance will be increased, not diminished, when they are reunited with their bodies.

> When our flesh, made glorious at the Judgment Seat,
>   dresses us once again, then shall our persons
>   become more pleasing in being more complete.[22]

These Resurrection bodies, according to Anselm of Canterbury (1033–1109), will have the seven desirable qualities of beauty, agility, strength, penetrability, health, delight and perpetuity. 'There shall be none blind, lame, or defective; but such defects shall remain as would redound to the glory of the elect.' This means that defects, either congenital or acquired in life, will be corrected, unless they were acquired in the service of God. The scars of martyrs will shine 'with an especial and transcendent glory'.[23]

The joys of the blessed in paradise are repeated in art and literature with almost the same prolixity as those of hell. What one notices, however, about heaven in most of these literary and artistic representations, is that compared with hell it is rather static. (Dante's illumination of souls diving and leaping in the river of light is a notable exception.) One view of happiness is that it arises from the satisfaction of desire. Clearly, the happiness in heaven cannot be of this sort, because desire implies a lack of something. Desire and satisfaction are cyclical; they are incompatible with a constant state of bliss. So what we are called upon to imagine is a *quality* of happiness that is quite different from anything on earth. If we cannot achieve this, our experience of heaven may turn out to be less than ecstatic.

It is this concept of a static heaven that is described with a detached irony in an amusing tale, 'Abd-er-Rhaman in Paradise' written by Jules Tellier, and beautifully illustrated with wood-engravings by Paul Nash. The story is set in Algiers in winter. Abd-er-Rhaman, an old Arab scholar of Celtic origin (he is blue-eyed and fair-haired) is approaching death. In early adulthood, when the French came to Algeria, he left the teachings of the Koran for Christianity. Now in old age he again ponders the relative merits of Islam and Christianity. In the end he opts for Christianity, sends for a priest and receives the sacrament. But not content, he also sends for the iman of the mosque and is blessed. Thus 'by a strange and unknown miracle, he really [holds] two faiths, and each was whole & entire'.[24]

He dies, and finds that his soul is 'fine as transparent vapour', and 'the very image of his now untenanted body. His long grey beard & the bald dome of his forehead [are] still there. But he [is] naked now, and two wings [have] sprung on his back.'[25] Two angels come for him, one on the right hand, the other on the left. The first is white and 'of a beauty softer than words can tell'. The second is also lovely, but black as ebony. The first is Raphael, holding a palm; the second is Azrael, the Muslim Angel of Death. Abd-er-Rahman has led a very pure life, and he is now in the happy position of being able to choose between two paths to everlasting bliss. (The interesting corollary of this is that no one religion is truer than another: 'Out of your dreams during life is woven the stuff of your destiny after death. The man who believes in a religion makes it true for himself in the very act of belief; thereby is he judged.')[26]

Abd-er-Rhaman first chooses Paradise with Raphael, but eventually he grows bored. Others confess to the same malady. One tells him: 'Once long ago . . . I was famed for my melancholy, no less than my learning, above all the monks in the Abbey of Fulda. But melancholy as I was upon earth, my thousand years in heaven have made me far gloomier still. Through century after century my weariness has grown until today it knows no bounds.'[27]

However, this heaven is not really eternal. Just as destiny after death is woven of the stuff of dreams during life, so heavens and hells are 'mortal dreams, projected as it were upon the wall of the everlasting abyss'.[28] The dreams of men on earth, ceaselessly prolonged, foster the reality of heaven. When no Christian remains any longer among the living on earth, all the spirits in heaven will disappear. Even now things in heaven are becoming insubstantial. 'Long ago . . . we all had bodies that were solid and tangible; it was with keys of real iron that Peter caused the vasty gates of Paradise to turn on their hinges. But now, as you observe, we are very like shades . . . only two or three of our saints have kept their halos, and the very fires of hell have become far less intolerable than they were five hundred years ago.'[29] The reality of heaven, it seems, fades in proportion to the reality of the belief in it.

Abd-er-Rhaman leaves this heaven and summons Asrael to be taken to the Muslim heaven. In contrast to the Christian heaven, this one is full of sensuous pleasures. But as he wends his way through the various heavens to the seventh and final, he sees 'too much gold, too many precious stones . . . and many things besides that were resplendent and useless, and wearisome to the eye'.[30] Even in the seventh heaven he becomes bored with sameness. He concludes, rather sadly, that the wisest thing to crave at the end of our mortal journey is not an eternal round of pleasure, but the stillness of sleep.

CONCLUSION

The scepticism inherent in this rather tongue-in-cheek account of two paradises leads us to the final chapter concerning our views of the soul in the present day. What we have seen in this chapter on the immortal soul is that the arguments for its existence are largely theoretical and philosophical. Until the time of the Renaissance, the idea of an immortal soul – and of a resurrected body to join it – were articles of faith. Even after that time, a thinker such as Bacon was willing to make scientific speculations about the workings of the body and the lower faculties of the soul, but was wary of touching the subject of the immortal soul. He states that just as the creation of the rational soul was immediately inspired by God, so 'true knowledge of the nature and state of the soul, must come by the same inspiration that gave the substance'.[31]

By the mid-nineteenth century, however, this reverential attitude had changed. With the advent of Darwinism the need to *understand* the soul began to replace the need to believe in it. If it does exist, then surely there must be some evidence for it as there is for other phenomena. We have already seen this tendency in the spiritualists, who through séances, ectoplasm and so on sought to demonstrate what hitherto had been thought undemonstrable. Mistaken as they were, they were the precursors of more legitimate investigations. As science progressed, so the boundaries of the soul were pushed back ever farther.

At the same time, art itself came increasingly to be seen as a substitute for immortality, or rather as a substitute that conferred immortality of a different kind. This is not a new idea. No one has expressed it more eloquently than Ovid did in the first century BC. 'My work is complete: a work which neither Jove's anger, nor fire nor sword shall destroy, nor yet the gnawing tooth of time. That day which has power over nothing but my body may, when it pleases, put an end to my uncertain span of years. Yet with my better part I shall soar, undying, far above the stars, and my name will be imperishable. Wherever Roman power extends over the lands Rome has subdued, people will read my verse. If there be any truth in poets' prophecies, I shall live to all eternity, immortalized by fame.'[32] We find the same sentiments in Shakespeare, often extended not only to the poet himself but to the subject he celebrates: 'So long as men can breathe, or eyes can see, | So long lives this, and this gives life to thee' (Sonnet 18).

In the age of Romanticism, the position of the poet took on even greater significance. He was not a mere craftsman or a teller of tales; he was seen (and saw himself) as a 'maker' in his own right. Who needs a god to endow you with an immortal soul when you are yourself a creator, god-like in your gifts? Keats' 'Ode on a Grecian Urn' asserts the immortality of the urn as art object, but at the same time, by implication, asserts the immortality of the poem, which is also an art object. And surely, if the creation is immortal, the creator, the poet, must be as well.

The most explicit metaphor of the artist as God-creator is Mary Shelley's *Frankenstein*. Interestingly, Mary Shelley in her introduction says that her imagination was fired by an alleged (she herself clearly believes it to be false) experiment of Darwin's in which he 'preserved a piece of vermicelli in a glass case till by some extraordinary means it began to move with voluntary motion'.[33] Frankenstein, Mary Shelley's creation, becomes himself a creator when he brings to life the monster of his own devising. The analogy cannot be escaped; the artist not only makes himself immortal through his creation, he makes himself God – even though his work may turn out to be rather botched.

The artist also gives a sense of purpose and shape of narrative to life. We may congratulate ourselves on no longer believing in the terrors of judgment and hellfire, but these too gave life a sense of narrative and purpose. They made human existence a comprehensible and splendid story, most apparent in the cycles of the mystery plays, which moved inexorably from Creation, through the Fall, the numerous accidents and triumphs of Old Testament history, to God's act of Redemption and the sacrifice of Christ, which was to cancel out the curse of the Fall. Finally there was the Last Judgment, in which morality and faith were both satisfied, as people were justly divided into the saved and the damned. Alongside this universal pattern there was the pattern of the individual life, where birth paralleled the Creation, sin and suffering in life the narrative of the Bible, and death and judgment of the individual the end of the world and the judgment of all creation.

Why, after all, have these particular images of judgment, of heaven and hell lasted so long? Why do they still have potency to stir our imagination if not our belief? Perhaps it is because we still long to believe in narrative and meaning in life. We desire eternity. Most of us will not be great creative artists. And even Ovid's boast looks hollow when we consider the relatively short time after his life that Roman power did continue to extend over the lands Rome had subdued.

This certainty about the story of our lives is what we have lost. There are no longer clear answers, just questions and various ways of attempting solutions. These present-day approaches to the problem, where the tests of science and the resurgence of superstition struggle for supremacy, are the subject of the final chapter.

EIGHT

The Soul in the Modern Age

All our knowledge brings us nearer to our ignorance.
T.S. Eliot, Choruses from 'The Rock'

Our present desire is for certainties – and for certainties of a particular type, certainties that can be 'proven' by experimental means. These are what we (sometimes naïvely) think of as scientific certainties. Of course there were other kinds of 'proofs' in other ages. Anselm's ontological proof of God (I have in my mind the idea of a perfect being; one of the attributes of perfection is existence; therefore the perfect being I conceive of must exist) is a 'proof', and absolutely irrefutable if you accept the premises.

But this is not what we mean by 'proof'. We mean something verified by experiment, elaborate machinery that measures brain waves, mathematical equations that illustrate beyond doubt (and often beyond comprehension as far as the average layman is concerned) that such and such *must* be the case. It can be the only explanation for the phenomena. All of reality is knowable; we have made enormous strides in the last hundred and fifty years and will continue to do so. Once this reality is known (and it will be) there is nothing else.

We saw the beginnings of this movement towards experiential verification in nineteenth-century spiritualism with its séances and sticky ectoplasm. Even today, experiments in telepathy continue with varying results. We desperately *want* there to be something outside and beyond the physical. Yet, paradoxically, we have to use essentially physical means to attempt to discover this. The result is that the body has grown and the soul has shrunk – some would say to non-existence. Even when people today talk of what in past ages would have been termed 'soul', they more frequently use the word 'mind'.

197

It is a supreme irony that it has been the very desire to grasp the immortal soul, the intellectual curiosity that has led to the need to understand it, that has caused the deepest doubt about its very existence. If one wants a modern version of the Faust legend, it is to be found here.

THE SOUL TODAY IN SCIENCE AND PHILOSOPHY

There are at least three chief schools of thought on the subject of what we really consist of as persons. First, there is the scientific reductionism which claims that there is nothing outside the physical and knowable. This is the view expressed above in the second paragraph. Mind is wholly an offshoot of brain. What we think and feel, as well as what we believe, can be explained in physiological and neurological terms. Secondly, there is 'nonreductive physicalism', which concedes that the person is primarily a physical organism, but which insists that the person's 'complex functioning, both in society and in relation to God, gives rise to "higher" human capacities such as morality and spirituality', that cannot be explained solely in physical terms.[1] Finally, there is dualism, the belief that man consists of body and mind (or soul) that in this life interact with one another to make up the complete individual. Dualism itself can be subdivided according to the extent the soul or mind is seen as the 'real' person, completely separable, or as a part of the person, who normally functions as a unity.

I am not qualified, either as a philosopher or a scientist, to comment on these matters from the perspective of original research. What follows is a short summary of the main modern positions.

Dualism

This is probably the least popular of the three options outlined above. Despite its long and eminent history in Western thought (it would not have occurred to Descartes to question the body/soul division in man; the problem was how to explain their interaction) for many today it is completely untenable, and those who hold it are regarded as either moronic or crazy.

Richard Swinburne, an Oxford theologian, is demonstrably neither, yet produces a modern defence of one form of dualism.[2] His ideas belong to the 'soft' category of dualism – that is, he sees the body as part of the person, but 'not essentially, only contingently'. 'The soul . . . is the necessary core which must continue if I am to continue . . .'[3] But then it emerges that what he really means is that it is *logically* possible for the soul to continue to exist without its present body or any body at all. This seems to qualify his assurance considerably.

He equates 'consciousness' (a concept to which we shall return) with soul, the immaterial core of being. The unity of this consciousness over time would seem to suggest 'that truths about persons are other than truths about their bodies and parts thereof'.[4] In answer to the objection that damage to the physical brain can have disastrous consequences for precisely this unity of consciousness over time, he says that while without a functioning brain the soul will not function, that does not mean it does not exist. He asserts that brain states that contain beliefs and purposings can process in-built meaning, and this is something totally lacking in physical processes. Today, of course, we are less certain about this than he could be when this book was written in 1986.

In the end, Swinburne acknowledges that the only argument that can be given for the survival of the soul after death is one that goes beyond nature, the possibility that there is something beyond the natural order embodied in laws of nature. There may be a Resurrection of souls with new bodies in some other world, yet with apparent memories of their past lives. We would then recognize them by their memories and character, not their bodies.[5] This is less than a ringing affirmation for the survival of the disembodied soul.

Scientific Reductionism

This point of view has the great advantage of clarity. Man is a physical construct, evolved over the ages to have something we call 'consciousness', which makes him different from the rest of the animal species. This consciousness, however, is wholly dependent on physical elements in his makeup. The brain is the seat of consciousness, and anything that alters the brain substantially (disease, accident or chemical input or depletion) will alter consciousness. 'Mind' is the term most frequently used to describe the collective workings of the brain that go to make up consciousness. The word 'soul' is taboo, precisely because it connotes something beyond the physical.

The problem with this theory is that no one really knows what 'consciousness' is. Subjectively, each of us knows what it is to be 'conscious', but describing 'consciousness' in an objective way, much less explaining precisely what components go to make it up, is much less easy. It has been said recently by an eminent scientist that absolutely nothing worth reading has been written about consciousness. Despite that, there is now a learned journal devoted exclusively to the subject.

Susan Greenfield gives her own definition of consciousness as follows: it is 'spatially multiple, yet effectively single at any one time. It is an emergent property of non-specialised groups of neurons (brain cells) that are continuously variable with respect to an epicentre, where an emergent property is taken to be a property of a collection of components that could not be attributable to any single member of those components'.[6]

Unpacking this, what I understand her to mean is firstly that consciousness is something more than simple brain activity, in which there is a centre for seeing, one for hearing, one for memory, and so on. We now know that most of these functions do not take place in only one centre in the brain anyway. But consciousness is more than the sum of its parts. It surpasses the mere processing of information by the brain.

Secondly, however, consciousness is generated in the brain. Though it may surpass what we understand about the functions of individual parts of the brain, there is nothing mystical about it. There is no seat of the soul, no mini-brain within the brain, as she says at another point. In a striking image, Susan Greenfield describes it as 'like a dimmer switch', being turned up in the womb.

Not implicit in the definition above, but clearly part of her view of consciousness, is its individuality. The connections between neurons are 'sculptured to our individual biases, prejudices, memories, fears, hopes, fantasies, and experiences'.[7] Further, chemicals released in the brain influence the direction that neurons are going to grow.

This view of 'consciousness' has many elements in common with 'soul'. It is unique to the individual, and it gives him his sense of self-hood. It is the centre of what he is. Where it differs from traditional concepts of soul is that it is entirely dependent on physical elements, and therefore, by definition, cannot be eternal or separable from the body whose consciousness it is. At the same time, it is a view that has great plausibility in our present age. We know the alterations that can take place in 'consciousness' in the short term through the taking of illegal drugs and alcohol, and what is more we also know with some accuracy what changes in the brain occur to produce these effects. We also know the long-term effects that come from taking prescription drugs that, less dramatically but possibly more insidiously, are deliberately mood and mind-altering, such as Ritalin and anti-depressants. The effects of these drugs may be benign, even beneficial, but taking them inevitably leads to a view of the human *psyche* (in both the modern and traditional sense of the world) that is physical.

At a more profound level, it can raise serious questions about identity and selfhood. Who am I? The person on anti-depressants who sees life as, on the whole, a fairly worthwhile experience, or the person not on anti-depressants who cannot understand why the entire human race does not run collectively like lemmings into the sea? Am I the impossible child, hyperactive and underachieving, the despair of parents and teachers, or am I the more sober, diligent child on Ritalin, able to please others at school and at home?

Scientific Non-Reductionism

Scientific non-reductionism would assent to most of the arguments of reductionism, but would wish to add on to these elements certain things that it claims cannot be wholly explained by the physical. Those who support this position point to such things as our ability to have a theory of other minds, our future orientation, moral and ethical values, including altruism, and our ability to have complex relationships, not only with other people but with God. None of these things has yet been explained in terms of a physical construct or brain-event. But neither is that any proof that they absolutely could not be explained in such terms. The reductionists can say, 'Just wait a few more years – or decades – and all will be explained.' The non-reductionists can reply that some of these abilities are unlikely ever to be fully explained and quantified by the action and reaction of neurons and brain chemicals. In the light of the difficulties that research in these fields is encountering – not the least of which is the ethical restraints on experimentation on a live human brain – the non-reductionists may be right. The case for one side or the other may never be proven decisively, or at least not for a very long time.

In the 1970s Benjamin Libet, a neurophysiologist at the University of California, discovered that there is a mental time lag between brain waves indicating action is going to occur and the conscious awareness of a decision to perform an action – in this case to flex a finger. The brain activity occurred a third of a second *before* the individual consciously decided to flex his finger. What does this indicate? It could mean that while we believe such actions to be voluntary, they are in fact determined by non-volitional brain activity, and we invent reasons for them after the event. Or it could mean that there is some other seat of decision-making that triggers the brain's activity before we *consciously* decide. Or . . . At the moment, we simply don't know.

Roger Penrose discusses Libet's experiment that seems to show that free will involves some kind of time delay, and admits that this is a puzzling experiment. 'It might be,' he suggests, 'that something funny is going on in these timings because of quantum non-locality and quantum counterfactuals'.[8] What he is talking about here is the difficult concept that in quantum physics there are what he describes as 'non-local effects' – that is, there are effects that are not dependent on physical proximity. 'It seems to me that consciousness is something global.'[9] Penrose's own workings towards a theory of consciousness focus on the microtubules within the neurons in the brain, where he believes there may be 'large-scale, quantum coherent activity, somewhat like a superconductor'.[10]

Penrose is, in general, reluctant to embrace a hard-line reductionist approach to the mind. 'There is something in the physical action of the brain which evokes awareness . . . but this physical action is something which cannot even be simulated computationally.'[11] In some respects, he is unashamedly a Platonist with his own version of innate ideas. Discussing how a child learns numbers, he observes that the child does this not by computational rules but by abstracting the notion of natural numbers from numbers of things presented to it. 'Somehow, the natural numbers are already "there", existing somewhere in the Platonic world and we have access to that world through our ability to be aware of things.'[12]

Indeed, apart from such evangelical atheists as Richard Dawkins, there is a decided disinclination among most people to embrace a theory of mankind and the universe that is wholly physical. The noted scientist and theologian, John Polkinghorne, would espouse the physiological basis of most mental processes. But he would use the term 'soul', not just 'mind' to describe the end product of these processes as they exist in an individual. The soul stands for 'the real being'. It is a complex, information-bearing pattern, and, rather like Susan Greenfield's image of consciousness as being gradually turned on with a dimmer switch, he sees the soul growing in complexity through life as it acquires more information and more complex information-bearing patterns. What is unique about the individual soul is precisely this dynamic, developing pattern. It is the personal signature that assures identity. This pattern is not just *within* the person, but extends to relationships with other people that change and modify it. However, this soul is not, of its nature, immortal. Death is real and encompasses the whole of the individual.

Within the context of his Christian belief, however, Polkinghorne asserts the hope that God will remember the pattern of the individual and recreate it at the last day. This would give both immortality and individuality, but assurance of it is dependent on faith, not proof. It offers a rational explanation of the soul and selfhood in this life in the light of modern science, but it does not guarantee or *prove* immortality. In the end, the assurance of immortality is substantiated by a belief that transcends science.

This debate is active and ongoing. Indeed, new revelations and arguments are appearing with such speed that anything I write now may well be out of date by the time this book is printed. Recently Francis Crick, the eminent co-discoverer of the structure of DNA, published a controversial paper in Nature Neuroscience (February 2003) stating that he and a colleague, Christopher Koch, have found a neural 'seat of consciousness'. A small set of neurons, projecting from the back of the cortex to parts of the frontal cortex, express actual consciousness and can explain it in 'philosophical, psychological, and neural terms'. Crick is not innocent of an agenda in publishing these discoveries. Since the mystery of human consciousness has been one of the persistent arguments in favour of a non-physical element in individuals, Crick sees this as further proof that the idea of a soul is simply nonsense. An outspoken atheist, he has said that humanity will inevitably come to accept that the concept of the soul and the promise of eternal life are deceptions. He sees his recent work as hastening this day.[13]

Even more recently, the Reith Lectures for 2003 shed some interesting light on the 'soul' question. Asked in the question and answer session at the end of Lecture 5 whether or not he believed in the soul, Vilayanur Ramachandran said, 'Well, I don't believe there is another thing in the conventional sense called soul that survives bodily death. . . . Like most scientists I'm agnostic.'[14] And in the very first lecture he stated, 'All the richness of our mental life – all our feelings, our emotions, our thoughts, our ambitions, our love life, our religious sentiments and even what each of us regards as his own intimate private self – is simply the activity of these little specks of jelly in your head, in your brain. There is nothing else.'[15]

Not all scientists would agree with these positions, but as more and more is discovered about the physiological basis of thought and action they are becoming widely accepted. But there are some who, like Polkinghorne, while accepting the physical basis of consciousness, still believe there is something more.

Other Considerations

Closely related to the question of the soul and consciousness is the extent to which we have or do not have free will. This is something that was not questioned in earlier centuries; it was assumed that, of course, we were free agents because not to be such would undermine not only the justice of God's system of salvation and damnation but human systems of justice as well. Indeed, free will was seen as one of the defining differences between humans and animals. Animals, as Donne reflects in one of his Holy Sonnets are free from sin because they are incapable of reason and will:

> If poisonous mineralls, and if that tree,
> Whose fruit threw death on else immortall us,
> If lecherous goats; if serpents envious
> Cannot be damn'd; Alas; why should I bee?
> Why should intent or reason, borne in mee,
> Make sinnes, else equall, in mee, more heinous?[16]

The whole basis of Chapter 3, 'The Soul in Conflict', is that the individual has free will and is ultimately responsible for his actions.

Now this absolute responsibility has been called into question from many angles. There is Libet's rarefied experiment referred to above that shows our brain 'intends' action before our consciousness is made aware of this. But there are other more mundane questionings about the completeness of free will. Firstly, there are the psychological arguments that would see environment in the broad sense – not just physical and social living conditions, but the spectrum of relationships within and outside the family – as largely determinant in much behaviour. Then there is the genetic argument that sees the human being 'programmed' by hereditary factors not just for appearance and intelligence but for characteristics of personality such as temperament, sociability, susceptibility to mental as well as physical illness, and so on. Recently a neurologist, Michael Persinger, has claimed to be able to induce mystical experience – a sense of the religious – by surrounding the skull with an electromagnetic field produced by having the subject wear a magnet-laden helmet. Does this imply that all religious experience is as physically induced as a desire to scratch?

These are specific instances of the more general scientific question as to whether the world itself is a deterministic construct, or whether chance is built into the system, which might leave a place for choice as well. Einstein's understanding of the universe was essentially deterministic. Matter and energy could be converted into one another, but the total was a constant, and the conversion took place according to certain immutable laws of physics. Quantum physics, while it has a certain consistency within its own micro world, operates largely according to rules of probability or chance. In some cases the very act of observing an event seems to change its outcome. And reconciling this view of the universe with Einstein's view, produces a host of incompatibilities. Indeed, possibly the greatest challenge to modern science is attempting to reconcile these two views of the universe, which coincide with whether one looks at it in macro or micro terms.

The scientific contradictions are not the only ones that trouble modern thinkers. There are those who would argue that there *is* no objective truth to be discovered. They argue that the world is not 'an innocent perception'. Rather it is in part a construction, an interpretation that we help to create.[17] If one goes down this road far enough one can dispense with the idea of objective truth altogether. Our beliefs and imaginings about the human soul, as about anything else, are not just imperfect representations of reality but mere illusions. 'The human soul anticipates its future course of being, willing in fantasy a future of autonomy and choice, and presumes that such virtues have indeed accompanied him thus far.'[18]

These views may have some philosophical plausibility, but if there is anyone who can manage to sustain even one day's activity with them constantly in mind, I have never met that person – any more than I know anyone who can consistently think of the desk at which he works as a collection of whirling atoms rather than a solid object. Whatever we may speculate about the nature of reality, we live mostly according to commonsense appearances. And once one moves out of the realm of physics and philosophy, it is surprising how little our beliefs and imaginings about the soul have changed.

THE SOUL IN POPULAR CULTURE

Many people – perhaps most, particularly in North America – would still assent to the idea of the soul. To deny it would seem tantamount to denying themselves, their very identity. And their orthodoxies concerning it have remained much as they were hundreds of years ago.

Eight years ago a popular American television cartoon series featured an episode in which the son of the family sells his soul. It all begins when the son's best friend is threatened by the minister of his church with ravenous birds who, in hell, will pick out his tongue if he does not tell the truth, and he reveals, under this pressure of eternal torment, that it was not he who substituted bawdy words for the morning's hymn – rather it was the prankster son. Of course, both boys must be punished, and while they are working off their punishment by cleaning the organ pipes, they discuss the soul. The trickster son simply doesn't believe there is any such thing. He claims that it is just a story made up to scare kids. But his friend stands his ground. Surely, he argues, *all* religions wouldn't merely *pretend* there was a soul; what would they have to gain?

Indeed, the friend has his own decided views on the soul. It resides in the breast – straight from the Greeks, this – and when you sneeze it is trying to escape. If you say 'God bless you', it is forced back in. When you die, it flies out of your mouth and away. But our hero persists in denying that he has a soul, that his friend has a soul, and that there is such thing as a soul at all. Then his friend issues the ultimate challenge: again if he is so certain there is no such thing as a soul, why doesn't he sell this non-existent soul to him? Why not, indeed? The challenge is accepted, and the soul changes hands for five dollars.

His smart younger sister, however, is horrified when she hears of what he has done, even though she has more sophisticated ideas about the soul than either of the boys. She claims that the soul is the most valuable part of any person. Even if it is not physically real, it stands for everything that is good about the person. In desperation she tells her brother that the soul is the only part of him that is truly good and will last forever, and that his friend, to whom he has sold it, could therefore own him for eternity – and all for five dollars!

Gradually, our soulless hero begins to notice that he is different. His pets growl or hiss at him; his breath does not form vapour; automatic doors don't open for him. Worst of all, he no longer feels anything; he doesn't even have a sense of humour. He dreams that his friends' souls are translucent blue replicas of themselves, and the children and their souls play together happily. Only he is left out. He becomes desperate to recover his soul, and eventually, through the efforts of his altruistic sister, he succeeds.[19]

Of course this is intended as a parody of views of the soul. But it is a fascinating compendium of many ideas, ancient and modern, that we have encountered. The soul here is clearly not just immortal, the best part of the individual; it is associated with breath, and is the seat of the emotions. The fact that automatic doors no longer open for the boy when he is soulless would seem to show that he has in some way become insubstantial, unreal.

A more sophisticated, but still quite imaginary, view of the soul is found in Alice Sebold's recent novel, *The Lovely Bones*. At the moment Susie Salmon is brutally murdered by a sex offender, her friend Ruth is crossing their school parking lot. 'Suddenly, down out of the soccer field, I saw a pale ghost coming toward me,' she tells her mother. 'It was female, I could sense that,' Ruth said. 'It flew up out of the field. Its eyes were hollow. It had a thin white veil over its body, as light as cheesecloth. I could see its face through it, the features coming up through it, the nose, the eyes, the face, the hair.'[20] The aspect of this soul, escaping from its body, is for the most part familiar to us. The soul retains the sex and appearance it had in life, except that its 'eyes [are] hollow'. This view of the soul, with its veil of cheesecloth is not notably different from the floating souls drawn by Blake for 'The Grave'.

As for Susie, she describes her exit from the body thus: 'Once released from life, having lost it in such violence, I couldn't calculate my steps. I didn't have time for contemplation . . . . When you begin to go over the edge, life receding from you as a boat recedes inevitably from shore, you hold on to death tightly, like a rope that will transport you, and you swing out on it, hoping only to land away from where you are.'[21] As she streaks by Ruth, her hand leaps out 'to touch her, touch the last face, feel the last connection to Earth'.

In heaven, she sits in a gazebo (she has longed for one on earth) and watches what goes on down below. Then, gradually, she spends less time in the gazebo and walks the fields of heaven. But she is still preoccupied with what is happening on earth. If she wanders too far, she finds herself back again in the cornfield where she was murdered. 'My head would throb and the sky would darken and it would be that night again, that perpetual yesterday lived again. My soul solidifying, growing heavy. I came up to the lip of my grave this way many times but had yet to stare in.' But then she thinks that if this were *really* heaven she could meet her grandparents, and that if she could be with them, she 'would feel only joy and have no memory, no cornfield and no grave'.[22] She is told she can have this, but in order to achieve it, she has to 'give up on Earth'. In this view, coming to terms with heaven can only be achieved gradually and painfully, after a process of closure with those one has loved on earth.

Despite its use of some conventional imagery, this book does not give a picture of the 'easy' heaven that the soul longs to escape to. Rather it centres on the grief of the loss of earth and its simple joys. At one point in the novel, as part of her desire to experience what she missed on earth so that she may leave it, she possesses the body of a friend and uses it to experience sex with her old boyfriend. In its comparative views of life and the afterlife this book has more in common with classical literature than with the Christian one. There is a 'heaven' for Susie, she retains identity and is immortal, but this is small comfort for the things of earth she has never had the chance to experience in her short life. Underneath the surface conventionality of the beliefs expressed lies an ill-concealed sense of doubt and loss.

One more popular manifestation that is frequently used to 'prove' the existence of the soul in the present day must be mentioned. This is the 'near-death' experience, or what Harold Bloom rather scathingly calls, 'not dying'.[23] The experience of near-death is a frequently told modern story, probably because it is a modern experience. Medicine now has the ability through machinery to keep people alive in some circumstances when technically 'dead' and to bring them back. The tales of these experiences usually have certain elements in common. There is often an ability to hear the doctors pronounce the death sentence, but this is not accompanied by feelings of fear or distress. Somctimes the person appears to float above the 'body' on the bed or operating table and observe his/her former self dispassionately.

Occasionally extraordinary powers are displayed by the disembodied person or soul; one woman, blind from birth, recounted how she saw her body for the first time. After this, there is usually a passage through a tunnel at the end of which there is a bright light. Passage to the light brings great joy. Sometimes it is accompanied by meeting dead friends or family; sometimes Christ or angels are the greeting party. But in all cases the soul is made to understand it must return to the body. Frequently this is done with great reluctance. Sometimes it is accompanied by the great and natural pain of being in an extremely ill body. But those who have this experience are nearly all convinced that it is a foretaste of what final death will be like.

No one would dispute that it is a real and profound experience for those who have had it. For some, it has been genuinely life-changing in terms of their goals and values. Nearly all feel that it affirms the existence of life after death. There is no way of proving or disproving this. What is certain is that 'near-death' remains precisely that – *'near death'*. While the brain may be inactive during the period of 'separation', it cannot be dead, because death implies an irreversible process. If the person can be revived, then the condition of irreversibility has not occurred. Like so many of the devices we have looked at in this chapter that seek to 'prove' immortality or an after life, it may bring subjective assurance, but 'proof' it cannot be.

THE SOUL IN MODERN ART

Up to the beginning of the twentieth century there were fairly conventional ways of representing the soul in art. It was a miniature of the individual, a beautiful woman, a sexless child, or, more symbolically, a bird, a boat, a butterfly. These ways of portraying the soul have never entirely disappeared. In 1901 Picasso, in *Evocation (The Burial of Casagemas)* depicts the soul of his friend, a naked replica of his body that lies on the ground at the bottom of the picture surrounded by sobbing women, mounting a white horse that is eagerly waiting to carry him away into the sky.

A quarter of a century later, Stanley Spencer's *The Resurrection, Cookham* is entirely representational, bearing a striking similarity to many medieval and Renaissance pictures of the Resurrection. The dead awaken, slowly stretching themselves to new life. Spencer says, 'No one is in any hurry. . . . Here and there things slowly move off but in the main they resurrect to such a state of joy that they are content.'[24] Some are clothed in garments that indicate the period and station in which they died – women as brides, men suited or cloaked. One wears a ruff; others are naked. The tombs themselves range from the ancient to the contemporary open book on which the artist himself is lying. Apart from the fact that the God who presides over the scene is a benevolent woman, holding two children in her arms, the scene differs little in its essentials from the souls arising from graves in the *Rohan Book of Hours*.

Similarly representational in a very stylized way is the figure of a soul cut from cardboard and photographed in the 1930s by Frantisek Dritkol. This soul is an elongated, slender dark shadow of a woman, swooping down in a curving motion from circles of darkness towards the light.

Paul Nash's illustration 'The Soul Visiting the Mansions of the Dead', from the series he did for Sir Thomas Browne's *Urne Buriall* is symbolic rather than realistic, but it is still definitely representational. The passage he is illustrating describes the flight of souls to the mansions of the dead. 'Before Plato could speak, the soul had wings in Homer, which fell not, but flew out of the body into the mansions of the dead.'[25] The soul itself is represented by grasshoppers, surrounded by a nimbus. These souls are housed in a kind of geometrical bookcasing, translucent, floating in the clouds. Three of them fly about; a fourth sits on an aerial perch made out of suspended framework. These open tiers of platforms 'seem to sway on their supporting and interpenetrating clouds, while above them a towering framework extends the perspective backward and upward into the heights of heaven'.[26] It seems that Nash executed the picture without reading *Urne Buriall* with any thoroughness. The phrase to him 'suggested only aerial habitations where the soul like a bird or some such aerial creature roamed at will perching now and then on these convenient structures in the clouds or in the pure upper air'.[27] Later he realized that Browne's concept of the 'mansions of the dead' would almost certainly have been under the earth. But while the illustration he produced may thus lack some authenticity in relation to the text, it remains a glorious evocation of freedom after death. I confess a certain perplexity about the choice of grasshoppers as the winged creatures who roam this airy kingdom. But the picture as a whole conveys an overwhelming impression of heavenly space and light.

Other artists in the early twentieth century felt that the 'spiritual' in art could best be expressed in a non-representational way. Perhaps the representational is too limiting, presenting the soul and the spiritual in general in too specific and confining a way. The spiritual is fed by an internal impulse, and this impulse might not necessarily wish to express itself in recognizable objects from the physical world. Wassily Kandinsky's treatise, *Concerning the Spiritual in Art*, makes precisely this point: 'That is beautiful which is produced by internal necessity, which springs from the soul.'[28] The two means the artist has at his disposal for externalizing this internal necessity are form and colour. But mere beauty of form and colour is not enough. 'The artist must have something to communicate, since mastery over form is not the end but, instead, the adapting of form to internal significance.'[29] He believes that 'after a period of materialistic temptation, to which the soul almost succumbed, and which it was able to shake off, the soul is emerging, refined by struggle and suffering'.[30] He speaks favourably of Madame Blavatsky and the Theosophical Society, which consists of 'groups who seek to approach the problem of the spirit by way of *inner* knowledge'.[31]

But how is this inner knowledge or spirit to be communicated to the observer? Kandinsky talks at length about the effect of colour, both a single colour on its own and in combination with other colours, but he is at his most interesting when he discusses shape. 'The life of the spirit', he asserts, 'may be graphically represented as a large acute-angled triangle, divided horizontally into unequal parts, with the narrowest segment uppermost. . . . The whole triangle moves slowly, almost invisibly forward and upward. . . . At the apex of the highest segment often stands one man.'[32]

This triangle represents, primarily, the ascent of humanity to an ever higher spiritual life, and the small number of those who succeed in reaching the peak, but the triangle as an art shape recurs with surprising frequency in paintings of artists who are similarly concerned with the spiritual. We have already seen the extraordinary ascension and translation of Sir Richard Rolle,[33] and there are many other examples. An untitled painting by Hilma Af Klint from a series described as *Altar Paintings* shows a triangular form of rainbow colours in strips leading up to the apex, which ends in a circle of gold, green and mauve. It is not difficult to see it as an ascent leading to the circle of eternity.

The triangle was by no means the only shape that had significance for these painters. Spiritualism, particularly the influence of people like Rudolf Steiner and Madame Blavatsky, was a strong force in the work of many of these artists, and the symbolic world of the occult found its way into their paintings. The mandala, other Jungian archetypal forms, and the circle are only a few of the most common among their large vocabulary of symbolic forms. These forms were not chosen arbitrarily; many of them had been used in the ancient past. The artists were not interested in the aspects of theosophy that attempted to make spirit manifest in a physical way to 'prove' its existence, but rather in the notion that the whole world was imbued with spirit that could be discerned by those who worked to initiate themselves. Further, since the reputed origin of theosophy was the rediscovered wisdom of figures from the past, such as Pythagoras and Plato, these artists felt they were carrying on a sense of historical continuity in a period of great change.[34]

While some persisted in using a wide variety of occult symbols in their work, others moved ever farther into the abstract, where communication and reality could be expressed as 'vibration'. 'The world reverberates; it is a cosmos of spiritually working human beings. The matter is living spirit.'[35] If Roger Penrose is right, and there are effects that are not dependent on physical proximity, this may be a case of art, in a general way, intuiting scientific reality. Suzanne Duchamp attempts to make this concept visible in a painting she titles, *Vibrations of Two Distant Souls*. A yellow double tetrahedron, rather like an old-fashioned street lamp, balances in the centre of the picture. Suspended delicately from the tetrahedron is a grey web-like shape, with a red and black dot at its centre. The background of the painting is also yellow with cones and rays of green, red, blue and white streaming across it, connecting to the whole.

Here we are moving into a realm where it is impossible to say, 'This is . . .' or 'This means . . .'. The effect is communicated at the level of emotion, not intellect. Nevertheless, certain forms, directions and colours do stand for certain things. In theosophical texts, the vertical line stands for male spirituality, leading heavenward. Many of Frantisek Kupka's paintings are based on such vertical lines. 'All imply upward movement consistent with the principle of levitation, a principle common to the artist's continuing activities as a medium and to the theosophical idea of ascent from the world of matter to that of spirit.'[36]

It is noticeable that these artists talk of 'spirit', and the 'spiritual', an abstract force moving through everything, rather than 'soul', a localized and particular thing. Going back to Paracelsus, they assert that all the elements of nature are invisible and spiritual.[37] Dissolving the corporeal form becomes a way of ascending to the spiritual. In this there is a turning back not just to ancient wisdom but to the ideas of such philosophers as Plotinus. The real is the non-physical. Kandinsky struggles with the question of what is to replace the missing object in abstract art, but his answers are general and evasive. One must experience visual forms purely, but exactly how this translates into paint on canvas is unclear. On the one hand, these pictures are supposed to communicate to everyone at an instinctive, subliminal level; on the other they are much more comprehensible to those initiated into the world of mystical thought that the artists inhabited than to the average observer. Yet as belief in the soul in any literal way is more and more intellectually suspect, references to and representations of the 'spiritual' retain a satisfactory combination of both vagueness and transcendence. Whether it is really what we desire is unknown – possibly even to ourselves.

CONCLUSION

The idea of the soul is deeply bound up with our very humanity. We are mortal, and we *know* we are mortal. It is a fact we find profoundly disquieting. '*Timor mortis conturbat me.*' It is also what sets us apart from the rest of nature. Added to this, we have the ability to conceive, in some dim way at least, of an eternity. The idea of eternity and the fact of extinction are on a collision course throughout our lives.

Then there is the mystery of physical death itself. Medically, of course, it is not a mystery at all, but what the observer sees – the sudden shift from vitality and activity to a mere object that (for a brief time) will continue to resemble the person in appearance only – is difficult to absorb. What happens? 'Personhood' has fled. Where has it gone? These were the kinds of questions that troubled the Greeks when their heroes died in battle; something vital must escape. What exactly is it? Can it be seen? Identifying it with breath is a natural thing to do, because ceasing to breathe is one of the infallible signs of death – or was in the ancient world.

Breath can be felt but not usually seen. So if the soul is breath, the question of what it looks like still remains. We want not just the certainty that it exists, but that certainty substantiated by the most dominant of our senses. The attempts in the nineteenth century to 'see' the soul are both absurd and heartbreaking. We understand what they wanted while we deplore their naïveté. Imagination is better.

We have seen how we have imagined the soul throughout the ages in multiple ways so that it can minister to our multiple needs. It is a miniature self, reinforcing our sense that we can retain our identity. It is a beautiful woman, implying moral and physical perfection. It is male, because it should rule and be superior to the body. It is a bird, because it is free, not bound to the earth. It is all of these things and more. It is our selfhood.

For most of the vast span covered by this book, while the nature of the soul might be in doubt, its very existence was not – or at least not by the majority of people. The desperate 'proofs' that came into vogue in the late nineteenth century were not a sign of confidence in the soul but quite the reverse. What is certainly known does not *need* proof. But as modern science expands the realm of the physical and explicable, the realm of the spiritual and inexplicable naturally diminishes. Some find this cause for rejoicing and assert the same quite passionately. Jonathan Miller has said that religion (and therefore presumably belief in a soul) is 'a form of mental illness'.[38] If a belief that one will survive forever is empowering, so is a conviction that one can predict the future down to the last incinerated fragment of an imploding universe.

Yet the desire to believe in something beyond the physical exists. It spends itself in astrology, in rigid fundamentalism, in meditative exercise, in vague references to the numinous, in a passionate desire for past certainties. On the date of issue nearest to All Souls' Day (by design or accident?) the following poem appeared in the *New Yorker*.

The Second Space

The heavenly halls are so spacious!
Ascend to them on stairs of air.
Above white clouds the hanging celestial gardens.

A soul tears away from the body and soars.
It remembers that there's up and down.

Have we really lost faith in a second space?
They've dissolved, disappeared, both Heaven and Hell?

Without unearthly meadows how will one meet salvation?
Where will the gathering of the damned find its abode?

Let us weep, lament the enormous loss.
Let us smear our faces with coal, disarrange our hair.

Let us implore, so that it is returned to us,
The second space.[39]

The opening picture is of a heaven that takes us back to antiquity – or our own childhood. We are invited to ascend to the spacious halls of heaven through white clouds on stairs of air. The hanging celestial gardens stand as images of a traditional paradise, and the soul that 'tears away from the body' will still know that there is 'up' and 'down', not just in the physical but in the moral and hierarchical senses. Does no one, the poet asks, still believe in this 'second' space, governed not by the laws of physics but by the laws of faith? Without the 'unearthly meadows' (a phrase that joins neatly the physical and the conceptual), how can we find a heaven, or its antithesis, a hell? Landscape itself is a necessary element in the vocabulary of salvation and damnation. The loss is 'enormous', and the envisaged mourning – faces smeared with coal, dishevelled hair – is Old Testament in its extravagance. Finally, we are urged to 'implore' – a word with its own resonance of ancient religious fervour – for a return to us of this world built on images and concepts that are deeply unfashionable, and deeply desired.

The purpose of this book has been to give some shape and understanding to the 'why' of ideas and imaginings that have been developing over thousands of years. At every point there is a tension between the need to 'know' and a desire for the kind of apprehension that scientific knowledge is unlikely ever to provide. No one could deny both the practical benefits and the intellectual satisfaction that 'knowing' at all levels has given us. Yet if its result is the extinction of anything beyond 'knowing', perhaps we should indeed 'weep, lament the enormous loss'.

> Give back to us what once you gave:
> The imagination that we spurned and crave.[40]

Notes

Introduction

1. C.G. Jung, 'Spirit and Life', *The Structure and Dynamics of the Psyche*, quoted by Edward F. Edinger, *The Living Psyche: A Jungian Analysis in Pictures* (Wilmette, IL: Chiron Publications, 1989), frontispiece: 'The psyche consists essentially of images. It is a series of images in the truest sense . . . a structure that is throughout full of meaning and purpose; it is a "picturing of vital activities . . .".'
2. A.E. Crawley, cited by William Ellis, *The Idea of the Soul in Western Philosophy and Science* (London: George Allen & Unwin, 1940), p. 23.
3. Sir Francis Bacon, 'De Augmentis', *Works*, ed. J. Spedding, R.L. Ellis and D.D. Heath (London, 1857–74), p. 406.
4. See I.A. Richards, *Coleridge on Imagination* (London: Routledge & Kegan Paul, 1955), pp. 57–9.

One

1. Emily Vermeule, *Aspects of Death in Early Greek Art and Poetry* (Berkeley: University of California Press, 1979), p. 75.
2. Ibid., p. 18.
3. See David B. Claus, *Toward the Soul* (New Haven: Yale University Press, 1981), pp. 54–6.
4. Jan Bremmer, *The Early Greek Concept of the Soul* (Princeton: Princeton University Press, 1983), pp. 21–2.
5. Homer, *The Iliad*, trans. Richmond Lattimore (Chicago: University of Chicago Press, 1951). All citations of *The Iliad* are to this edition.
6. Michael Clarke, *Flesh and Spirit in the Songs of Homer* (Oxford: Clarendon Press, 1999), p. 147.
7. Homer, *The Odyssey*, trans. Albert Cook (New York: W.W. Norton, 1974). All citations of *The Odyssey* are to this edition.
8. Bremmer, *The Early Greek Concept of the Soul*, pp. 93–4.
9. Hesiod, *Works and Days*, 170f, quoted by Vermeule, *Aspects of Death*, p. 72.
10. Hesiod's account of the four ages of man's life on earth – Golden, Silver, Bronze, and Iron – is a splendid example of that philosophy of life according to which 'everything gets worse and worse'. The men of the Golden Age were created in the time of the Titans, during the reign of Cronos. They remained eternally young, didn't have to work, and spent their time feasting and playing. The men of the Silver Age who succeeded them turned from the gods and were hidden by Zeus in the earth. Only in the Bronze Age did violence and death proper occur. However, during this age we also have living the Heroes (see above), who alone have an afterlife similar to their forbears of the Golden Age. Finally, in the Iron Age (in which Hesiod places his own generation) there is a universal moral decline.
11. However Herodotus, the first Greek historian, notes the similarity between the Orphic sects and Egyptian mysteries. See Erwin Rohde, *Psyche*, trans. W.B. Hillis (London: Kegan Paul, Trench, Trubner, 1925), p. 335.
12. M.L. West, *The Orphic Poems* (Oxford: Clarendon Press, 1983), p. 4.
13. See ibid., p. 32.

Notes

14. Whether the ascetic practices leading to purification were part of the ritual of the early Orphic cults or only arose much later, in the early Christian era, through a Neoplatonic interpretaion of Orphism, is a matter of debate.

15. I am indebted to M.L. West for this very abbreviated account of the birth and death of Dionysus. Details vary considerably in the different theogonies. This summary is largely from the *Rhapsodic Theogony*, the last of the theogonies, which is itself a compilation of earlier accounts.

16. See W. Ellis, *The Idea of the Soul in Western Philosophy and Science* (London: George Allen & Unwin, 1940), p. 30.

17. Clarke, *Flesh and Spirit in the Songs of Homer*, p. 288.

18. Ellis, *The Idea of the Soul*, p. 47.

19. Ibid., pp. 49–50.

20. See Bremmer, *Early Greek Concept of the Soul*, pp. 25–31, 33–4, and Rohde, *Psyche*, pp. 301–2.

21. Ellis, *The Idea of the Soul*, p. 47.

22. Plato, *Phaedo*, 66b, trans. Hugh Tredennick in *The Collected Dialogues of Plato*, ed. Edith Hamilton and Huntingdon Cairns (Princeton: Princeton University Press, 1961), p. 49. All further references to the *Phaedo* are to this edition. References are given in the text.

23. This is a not unreasonable fear, given what we have learned of the disappearance of *thumos* in Homer, and the very tenuous existence of *psyche*. Also, the *Hieronyman Theogony*, an Orphic work from the third century BC, claims that animal souls blow about in the breeze, awaiting reincarnation (223.4–5), and later the Stoics, adapting these ideas, suggest the soul in the universe, like aether or air, which encircles the earth and sea, has attached to it the souls of the dead (Arius Didymus, fr 39.4, quoted by West, *The Orphic Poems*, p. 223).

24. Plato, *Republic*, III.386c and ff., trans. Paul Shorey, *Collected Dialogues*, ed. cit. All further references to the *Republic* are to this edition and are given in the text.

25. Plato, *Phaedrus* 245d–246a, trans. R. Hackforth, *Collected Dialogues*, ed. cit. All further references to the *Phaedrus* are to this edition and are given in the text.

26. Plato, *Timaeus*, 69c–d, trans. Benjamin Jowett, *Collected Dialogues*, ed. cit. All further references to the *Timaeus* are to this edition and are given in the text.

27. The idea of the *daimon* as a personal guide through life is also found in the *Phaedo*, 107d. This is different from the *daimones* in Homeric times that were souls of the departed, hovering around their tombs, and equally from the *daimones* to be found on the Isles of the Blest in Hesiod.

28. Aristotle, *De Anima*, trans. J.A. Smith (Oxford: Clarendon Press, 1931), 412b, 1. All further references are to this edition and are given in parentheses in the text.

29. The notable exception was Averroes, a contemporary of Aquinas, who did not believe that the soul survived death in its individual capacity.

30. For a fuller account, see Frederick Copleston, *A History of Philosophy* (New York: Image Books, 1961–65), I, ii, 130–44.

31. Plotinus, *Enneads* IV.8.6, trans. Stephen MacKenna, 3rd edn (London: Faber and Faber, 1962), p. 362. All further references are to this edition and are given in the text.

32. This is not particularly surprising, because the writings of the early Canonical Prophets (Amos, Hosea, Isaiah 1–35, Micah) are roughly contemporary with Homer. Plato was not born until Jerusalem was rebuilt following the Babylonian exile.

33. See John W. Cooper, *Body, Soul, and Life Everlasting* (Grand Rapids, MI: Williams B. Eerdmans Publishing Company, 1989), pp. 52–3. I am generally indebted to Cooper's account of the soul in Hebraic and early Christian thinking. For an older but very influential work, see also John Robinson, *The Body* (London: SCM Press, 1952).

34. Cooper, *Body, Soul, and Life Everlasting*, p. 26.

35. Ibid., p. 61.

36. 1 Samuel 28:14–15: 'An old man cometh up: and he is covered with a mantle. And Saul perceived that it was Samuel. . . . And Samuel said to Saul, Why hast thou disquieted me, to bring me up?'

37. See Acts 23:8: 'For the Sadducees say that there is no resurrection, neither angel, nor spirit: but the Pharisees confess both.'

38. See Copleston, *A History of Philosophy*, I.ii. 202–5.

39. This is the general, though not universal view. Cooper seeks to minimize the Greek influence, and argues that dualism in the New Testament was maintaining something inherently Biblical (Cooper, *Body, Soul, and Life Everlasting*, pp. 197ff).

40. *Dictionnaire de Théologie Catholique*, ed. A. Vacant, E. Mangenot et E. Amann (Paris: Letouzey et Ané, 1923–50), I, col. 985.

41. Tertullian, *De Anima*, ch. ix, *The Writings of Tertullian*, trans. Peter Holmes, Ante Nicene Library vol. XV (Edinburgh: T. & T. Clark, 1870), II, 429.

42. Copleston, *A History of Philosophy*, II,i,42.

43. 'The Hymn of the Soul', ed. A.A. Bevan, *Texts and Studies: Contributions to Biblical and Patristic Literature*, ed. J. Armitage Robinson (Cambridge: Cambridge University Press, 1897), vol. v, no. 3.

44. Ibid., 33a–34b, p. 17.

45. Ibid., 55a–57b, p. 21.

46. See Augustine, *The City of God*, Book XII, ch. xxvi, trans. John Healey, ed. R.V.G. Tasker (London: J.M. Dent, 1945, repr., 1962), i.370.

47. Ibid., Book XIV, ch. iii, ii.29.

48. Ibid., ch. xvi, ii.47.

49. St Thomas Aquinas, *Summa Theologica*, trans. the Fathers of the Dominican Province (London: R. & T. Washbourne, 1911–25), Part 1, Third Number, Question LXXXI, Third Article, p. 130.

50. Ibid., Part 2, Second Number, Question LXXIV, First Article, p. 316.

51. Ibid., Question LXXVII, Second Article, p. 359.

52. See ibid., Question LXXXI, Fifth Article, p. 410.

53. See ibid., Part 1, Third Number, Question LXXXIV, Seventh Article, p. 173; Question LXXXIX, First Article, p. 234.

Two

1. C.G. Jung, 'Two Essays on Analytical Psychology', II, 2, ii: 'Anima and Animus', *Collected Works*, ed. H. Read, M. Fordham and G. Adler (London: Routledge & Kegan Paul, 2nd edn 1966), VII, 188.

2. Jung, 'Aion', iii 'The Syzygy: Anima and Animus', *Works,* VII, 13.

3. Jung, *Works*, VII, 190.

4. Jung, *Works*, XVII, 338. Quoted by Murray Stein, *Jung's Map of the Soul* (Chicago: Open Court, 1998), p. 141.

5. Otto Rank, *Psychology and the Soul: a Study of the Origin, Conceptual Evolution, and Nature of the Soul*, trans. Gregory C. Richter and E. James Liberman (Baltimore, MD: Johns Hopkins University Press, 1998; originally published 1930), pp. 18–19.

6. Carl C. Schlam, *Cupid and Psyche, Apuleius and the Monuments* (Pennsylvania: American Philological Association, 1976), p. 4, n. 12. I am indebted to Schlam's book for much of the account of the iconographical material concerning Psyche.

7. Ibid., p. 7, n. 39.

8. Ibid., p. 5.

9. See Erich Neumann, *Amor and Psyche: The Psychic Development of the Feminine* (London: Routledge & Kegan Paul, 1956).

10. A most comprehensive survey of the various interpretations of the Psyche myth is to be found in James Gollnick's book *Love and the Soul: Psychological Interpretations of the Eros and Psyche Myth* (Waterloo, Ont.: Wilfred Laurier Press, 1992).

11. Leslie George Whitbread (trans.), *Fulgentius the Mythographer* (Columbus, OH: Ohio State University Press, 1971), pp. 89–90.

12. Mr. Lockman (trans.), *The Loves of Cupid and Psyche in Verse and Prose from the french of La Fontaine* (London, 1744), A3v.

13. Gollnick, *Love and the Soul*, p. 15.
14. Plato, *Phaedrus*, 251e–252a. See Chapter 1, p. 24.
15. Schlam, *Cupid and Psyche*, p. 26.
16. Ibid., p. 27.
17. Plotinus, *Enneads*, ed. cit., VI.9.9, p. 623.
18. Ibid.
19. Fernand Cabrol and Henri M. Leclerq, *Dictionnaire d'Archéologie Chrétienne et de Liturgie* (Paris: Letouzey et Ané, 1903–53), vol. I, pt 1, cols 1488–9.
20. Elizabeth Petroff, 'Unmasking Women: Medieval Responses to the Unknowability of the Lady', *Body and Soul: Essays on Medieval Women and Mysticism* (Oxford: Oxford University Press, 1994), pp. 25–6.
21. Hildebert of Lavardin, 'De Querimonia et Conflictu Carnis et Spiritus Seu Animae', in J.-P. Migne, *Patrologia Latina*, vol. clxxi, col. 1001.
22. Boethius, *The Consolation of Philosophy*, trans. Richard Green (Indianapolis: Bobbs-Merrill, 1962), p. 4.
23. James Howell, *The Vision: or A Dialog between the Soul and the Bodie* (London: Printed for William Hope, 1651), 'The Proem'.
24. Ibid., pp. 172–3.
25. Rank, *Psychology and the Soul*, p. 35.
26. Andreas Capellanus, *The Art of Courtly Love*, trans. John Jay Parry (New York: W.W. Norton, 1969), p. 28.
27. See *The Dream of Poliphilo*, related and interpreted by Linda Fierz-David, trans. Mary Hottinger (New York: Pantheon Books, Bollingen Series XXV, 1950), p. 20.
28. Dante Alighieri, *The Inferno*, trans. John Ciardi (New York: Mentor, 1954), II, 67–70.
29. Dante Alighieri, *La Vita Nuova*, trans. Barbara Reynolds (Harmondsworth: Penguin, 1969), II, 11–13, p. 29.
30. Ibid., II, 19–28, p. 30.
31. Ibid., XXVI, 12–13, p. 75.
32. Ibid., XXVIII, 4–8, p. 79.
33. Dante Alighieri, *The Purgatorio*, trans. John Ciardi (New York: Mentor, 1957), XXX, 36.
34. See Marianne Shapiro, *Dante and the Knot of Body and Soul* (London: Macmillan, 1998), pp. 126, 129.
35. Dante Alighieri, *The Paradiso*, trans. John Ciardi (London: Mentor, 1961), XXII, 4–5
36. Ibid., XXX, 140–1.
37. Petrarch, 'Sonnet cclxi', ll. 5–8, *Sonnets and Songs*, trans. Anna Maria Armi (New York: Grosset & Dunlap, 1968), p. 365.
38. Plato, *Phaedrus*, 250d, 251b, cited in Robert E. Norton, *The Beautiful Soul* (Ithaca and London: Cornell University Press, 1995), p. 128. I am indebted to Norton's excellent book for a large part of my account of the history of the 'beautiful soul'.
39. 'Amoretti', Sonnet 79, *Edmund Spenser's Poetry*, selected and ed. Hugh Maclean (New York: W.W. Norton, 1968), p. 433.
40. John Donne, 'Since she whome I lovd', ll. 5–6, *The Divine Poems*, ed. Helen Gardner (Oxford: Clarendon Press, 1952), p. 15.
41. Joseph Lavater, *Physiognomische Fragmente*, quoted in Norton, *The Beautiful Soul*, pp. 185–6.
42. I should point out that this view is scarcely original to my mother. John Chrysostom wrote in the fourth century: 'If you consider what is stored up inside those beautiful eyes, and that straight nose, and the mouth and cheeks, you will affirm the well-shaped body to be nothing but a whited sepulchre; the parts within are full of so much uncleanness.' Also, see Saint Augustine, *The City of God*, ed. cit., i.239: 'The meaner body may include the better soul, and the more perfect the worse.'
43. Lavater, summarized by Norton, *The Beautiful Soul*, p. 177. This is only slightly less naïve than Tertullian's notion (see p. 37) that the soul is poured into the body and takes its shape like wax in a mould.
44. Norton, *The Beautiful Soul*, p. 138.
45. Ibid., p. 65.
46. *Enneads*, I.6.5. Cited by Norton, *The Beautiful Soul*, p. 134.
47. This discussion provides only the sketchiest account of the philosophical development of the idea of the 'beautiful soul'. Readers who want a more detailed examination of the concept should read the whole of Norton's book on the subject.

48. Robert Blair, *The Grave*, illustrated by William Blake. A study with facsimile by Robert N. Essick and Morton D. Paley (London: Scolar Press, 1982), Introduction, p. 66.
49. Ibid., p. 61.
50. C.A. Meier, *Soul and Body: Essays on the Theories of C.G. Jung* (Santa Monica and San Francisco: Lapis Press, 1986), p. 100.
51. Ibid., p. 83 and Plato, *Symposium*, 189.d and 192.e.
52. Janet A. Warner, *Blake and the Language of Art* (Kingston and Montreal: McGill-Queen's University Press, 1984), p. 182. Blake also did numerous illustrations of Dante's *Divine Comedy*, a work that fascinated him although many of its ideas repelled him. The plate of 'Beatrice Addressing Dante from the Car' (an 'exquisite, glowing watercolour') 'shows the poet Dante submitting himself to the mystery of the Church, the Female Will, Blake's Vala in her fallen state as Rahab or the Whore of Babylon' (Martin Butlin, *William Blake*, catalogue of Blake Exhibition (London: Tate Gallery Publications, 1978), p. 153).
53. Dante Gabriel Rossetti, 'The Blessed Damozel', *Collected Writings*, selected and ed. Jan Marsh (London: J.M. Dent, 1999), p. 12. Rossetti, at eighteen, was barely out of his adolescence when he wrote it.
54. Christina G. Rossetti, 'Who Shall Deliver Me?', *The Complete Poems of Christina Rossetti*, ed. R.W. Crump (Baton Rouge & London: Louisiana State University Press, 1979), p. 227.
55. Norton, *The Beautiful Soul*, p. 213.
56. Quoted ibid., p. 259.
57. Dante Gabriel Rossetti, 'Hand and Soul', *Collected Writings*, pp. 47–58.
58. Ibid., p. 53.
59. Ibid., pp. 53–4.
60. Ibid., p. 55.
61. 'The Palace of Art', *Tennyson's Poetry*, selected and ed. Robert W. Hill, Jr (New York: W.W. Norton, 1971), pp. 27–34.
62. *Memoir*, I, 118–19, quoted in ibid., p. 27, fn. 6.
63. William Holman Hunt, *Pre-Raphaelitism and the Pre-Raphaelite Brotherhood* (London: Chapman & Hall, 1913) vol. II, p. 401. Quoted in Christine Paulson, 'Death and the Maiden: The Lady of Shalott and the Pre-Raphaelites', *Re-framing the Pre-Raphaelites*, ed. Ellen Harding (Aldershot, Hants: Scolar Press, 1996), pp. 177, 179.

Three

1. Sigmund Freud, 'Psycho-Analysis', *Standard Edition of the Complete Psychological Works*, ed. James Strachey (London: Hogarth Press, 1953–66), XX, 266. See also Anthony Kenny, *The Anatomy of the Soul* (Oxford: Basil Blackwell, 1973), p. 11.
2. Freud, 'New Introductory Lectures on Psycho-Analysis xxxi', *Works*, XXII, 64–5.
3. See Chapter 1, pp. 18–20.
4. All quotations are from the translation of 'Saint Bernard's Vision' by William Crashaw, published in 1622, and transcribed in Rosalie Osmond, *Mutual Accusation: Seventeenth Century Body and Soul Dialogues in Their Literary and Theological Context* (Toronto: University of Toronto Press, 1990), pp. 197–208.
5. William Crashaw, *The Complaint or Dialogue, betwixt the Soule and the Bodie of a damned man* (London, 1622).
6. See Chapter 2, pp. 60–1.
7. All the datings of the ballad dialogues are tentative. For a more detailed discussion of these ballad debates and transcriptions of two of them, see Osmond, *Mutual Accusation*, pp. 191–218.
8. See Th. Batiouchkof, 'Le Débat de l'Ame et du Corps', *Romania* XX (1891), pp. 9–10.
9. 'The Damned Soul's Address to the Body', ll. 9–11, *The Old English Soul and Body*, ed. and trans. Douglas Moffat (Wolfeboro, NH: D.S. Brewer, 1990), p. 48.
10. Saint Augustine, *City of God*, Book XIV, ch. iii, trans. John Healey, ed. R.V.G. Tasker (London: J.M. Dent, 1945, repr. 1962), ii.29.

11. Giuseppe Levi, 'Die Verurteilung der Seele und des Körpers [The Condemnation of the Soul and the Body]', *Parabeln, Legenden und Gedanken aus Thalmud und Midrasch*, trans. Ludwig Seligmann (Leipzig: Oskar Leiner, 1863), p. 354.

12. 'Als I Lay in a Winteris Nyt', printed in Thomas Wright (ed.), *The Latin Poems commonly Attributed to Walter Mapes*, Camden Society, vol. 16 (London, 1841), p. 335.

13. Dante Alighieri, *The Purgatorio*, trans. John Ciardi (New York: Mentor, 1957), XVIII, 16–75, pp. 188–90.

14. René Descartes, 'The Passions of the Soul', I.xlvii, *Philosophical Works*, trans. E.S. Haldane and G.R.T. Ross (Cambridge: Cambridge University Press, 1911), I.352–3.

15. Richard Hooker, 'Of the Laws of Ecclesiastical Polity', I.vii.6, *Works*, ed. John Keble, 7th edn (Oxford: Oxford University Press, 1888), I.223. See also Immanuel Kant, 'Popular Moral Philosophy to a Metaphysic of Morals', *The Moral Law*, 72–3, trans. H.J. Paton (London: Hutchinson's University Library, 1948), pp. 99–100. Norton comments on this passage in *The Beautiful Soul*, p. 217: 'The will thus mediates between the two realms of sensuous experience and rational thought; the will both *necessitates* (because of its association with human weakness), but also *enables* (because of its intrinsic relation to reason), our resolve to act according to laws that we prescribe to ourselves. Thanks to the possession of a free will, in other words, we are able to make up in conscious resolution what we lack in natural inclination.'

16. Hildebert of Lavardin, 'De Querimonia et Conflictu Carnis et Spiritus Seu Animae', Migne, *Patrologia Latina*, vol. clxxi, col. 998.

17. John Milton, 'Paradise Lost', IX.1127–31, *Poems*, ed. Helen Darbishire (Oxford: Oxford University Press, 1961).

18. Plotinus, *Enneads*, trans. Stephen MacKenna, 3rd edn (London: Faber and Faber, 1962), IV.4.18, p. 301.

19. Guillaume de Deguileville, *The Pilgrimage of the Life of Man*, ll. 12,287–12, 303, trans. John Lydgate, ed. F.J. Furnivall (London: Early English Text Society 1899–1901), pp. 334–5.

20. John Donne, 'Goodfriday, 1613. Riding Westward', ll. 9–10, *Divine Poems*, ed. Helen Gardner (Oxford: Clarendon Press, 1952), p. 30.

21. For a detailed discussion of the moralizations of the heavenly system by Sacrobosco, Donne and Deguileville, see Rosalie Beck, 'A Precedent for Donne's Imagery in "Goodfriday, 1613. Riding Westward"', *Review of English Studies* XIX (May 1968), pp. 166–9.

22. A.W., 'A Dialogue betweene the Soule and the Body', Francis Davison, *A Poetical Rhapsody 1602–1621*, ed. H.E. Rollins (Cambridge, MA: Harvard University Press, 1931–2), I, 197.

23. 'Un samedi par nuit', printed in Thomas Wright (ed.), *The Latin Poems commonly Attributed to Walter Mapes*, p. 328: 'Tu estoies ma dame, si me carchas la soume, | Que je ne puis soufrir, le quer me fist partir.'

24. Ibid., p. 331: 'Li engin surst de tei, y la malveise fei. | Tu le mal enginnas, e puis le me nuncias; | Tu pensas e je l' fis.'

25. Andrew Marvell, 'A Dialogue between the Soul and Body', *The Poems and Letters of Andrew Marvell*, ed. H.M. Margoliouth (Oxford: Clarendon Press, 2nd edn, 1952), I, 20–1.

26. The quantity of critical literature on the meaning of these lines is very great indeed, and it seems to serve little purpose to detail it in a book intended for the general reader. However, it should be noted that some editors give the final two lines to the soul, not the body.

27. See Batiouchkof, 'Le Débat de l'Ame et du Corps', pp. 9–10.

28. See Rudolph Willard, 'The Address of the Soul to the Body', *PMLA* L, 1935, p. 981. The address of the soul to the body predates the dialogues; the earliest dialogue is from the twelfth century.

29. W.B. Yeats, 'A Dialogue of Self and Soul', *The Poems*, ed. Daniel Albright (London: J.M. Dent, 1st edn, 1990, updated 1994), pp. 284–6.

30. Jane Roberts, 'Dialogue One', *Dialogues of the Soul and Mortal Self in Time* (Englewood Cliffs, NJ: Prentice-Hall, 1975), p. 5.

31. Amy Clampitt, 'An Anatomy of Migraine', *Collected Poems* (London: Faber and Faber, 1998), pp. 278–85.

Four

1. See Chapter 1, p. 27.

2. See Chapter 1, pp. 36–9.

3. Dante Aligheri, *The Purgatorio*, trans. John Ciardi (New York: Mentor, 1957), XXV, 20–1.

4. Marianne Shapiro, *Dante and the Knot of Body and Soul* (London: Macmillan, 1999), p. 163. I am indebted to Chapter 7 of this work for much of the discussion of classical influences on Dante's representation of the soul.

5. Aquinas, *Summa Theologica* 1.89.1–8, cited by Shapiro, *Dante*, p. 164.

6. Dante Aligheri, *The Paradiso*, trans. John Ciardi (London: Mentor, 1961), IV. 40–5.

7. John Milton, 'Paradise Lost', *Poems*, ed. Helen Darbishire (Oxford: Oxford University Press, 1961), V. 564–74.

8. '(For Earth hath this variety from Heav'n | Of pleasure situate in Hill and Dale.)', ibid., VI. 640–1.

9. 'The Castle of Perseverance', *Chief Pre-Shakespearean Dramas*, ed. Joseph Quincy Adams (London: George G. Harrap, 1925), pp. 264–87.

10. 'The Soul and Body', Gwenan Jones, *A Study of Three Welsh Religious Plays* (Bala: R. Evans, 1939), pp. 238–59.

11. 'The Soul and Body', ll. 64–6, ibid., p. 243.

12. See Chapter 6, pp. 160–1.

13. Diego Sánchez de Badajoz, 'Farsa racional del libre albedrío', *Recopilación en metro* (Seville, 1554). Modern edition ed. Frida Weber de Kurlat (Buenos Aires, 1968), pp. 309–27. This play and Calderón's 'El Pleito Matrimonial del Cuerpo y el Alma' have been translated from the Spanish for me by Cora Portillo.

14. Pedro Calderón de la Barca, 'El Pleito Matrimonial del Cuerpo y el Alma', *Autos Sacramentales*, II (Madrid: Biblioteca Castro, 1997), 473–521.

15. John T. Cull, 'Emblematic Representation in the *autos sacramentales* of Calderón', *The Calderonian Stage: Body and Soul*, ed. Manuel Delgado Morales (London: Associated University Press, 1977), p. 120.

16. Emilio de' Cavalieri, *Rappresentatione di Anima, et di Corpo* (Rome: Nicolò Mutii, 1600). The text of Scene iv between Soul and Body is from 1577 and predates the rest of the text. A modern edition edited by the Barenreiter-Verlag, Kassel/Basel/Paris/London and prepared by Bernhard Paumgartner is included with the recording directed by Charles Mackerras for Archive in 1970. Translation is from the same source.

17. Richard Tuke, *The Soul's Warfare Comically digested into scenes acted between the Soul and her Enemies* (London: Printed by S.G. for Allan Bancks at the Signe of St Peter, at the West end of St Pauls, 1672).

18. Elizabeth Marsh, *Body and Soul* (Boston, MA: Cornhill, 1920).

19. Ibid., p. 11.

20. Ibid., p. 15.

21. Ibid., p. 21.

22. Ibid., p. 87.

23. See Chapter 3, pp. 106–8.

24. Wellen Smith, Preface, *Psyche and Soma* (London: E. Grant Richards, 1906), pp. v–vi.

25. Ibid., p. 34.

26. Ibid., p. ix.

27. Jerome K. Jerome, *The Soul of Nicholas Snyders* (London: Hodder & Stoughton, 1925), p. 94.

28. Ibid., p. 31.

29. Eleanor Maud Crane, *'His Soul': A Farce in One Act* (New York: Samuel French, 1922), p. 9.

30. Ibid., p. 10.

31. Ibid. p. 22.
32. See John J. Cerullo, *The Secularization of the Soul* (Philadelphia: Institute for the Study of Human Issues, 1982), p. 23.
33. See Ruth Brandon, *The Spiritualists* (London: Weidenfeld & Nicolson, 1983), pp. 37–8.
34. N. Evréinof, *The Theatre of the Soul: A Monodrama in One Act*, trans. Marie Potapenko and Christopher St John (London: Hendersons, 1915), p. 7.
35. Ibid., p. 16.
36. The translator's justification for this crudeness in his 'preface' does not convince: 'Many critics after the first production of the play in England criticised its "crude psychology"; but Evréinof may be right in his assumption that the reflections of the soul *are* crude. Every one who thinks at all knows that the interior of a human soul has very little furniture, and that what takes place there is astonishingly simple. What a man expresses through the medium of his brain and personality is complicated . . . but the thing from which this elaboration of thought and action is evolved is, as it exists in the soul, elemental whether the soul be a philosopher's or a peasant's. For this reason it seems to me that the crudeness of *The Theatre of the Soul* is a virtue rather than a defect' (Evréinof, *Theatre of the Soul*, p. 8). All this rather begs the question as to what, exactly, Evréinof and his translator think the soul comprises.
37. J.A. Schwenk, 'The Human Soul: A Play in Three Acts', p. i. Copyright in the United States of America, 1934, by J.A. Schwenk. Copyright Registered in the Dominion of Canada 1936, by J.A. Schwenk of Kingstong, NY, USA. Typescript in the British Library, I12.20029. There is no evidence the play was ever staged.

Five

1. Johan Chydenius, *The Theory of Medieval Symbolism* (Helsingfors: Societas Scientiarum Fennica, 1960), pp. 19–20.

2. Sophocles, 'Oedipus the King', trans. David Grene, ll. 171–7, *The Complete Greek Tragedies*, ed. David Grene and Richmond Lattimore, vol. II (Chicago and London: University of Chicago Press, 1959), p. 18.
3. See Chapter 1, pp. 2, 6.
4. Following Aristotle's theory of conception (see pp. 44–5), according to which the semen of the father produced the soul of the child while the mother contributed the matter, Jesus' soul was provided exclusively by God, his father. Through association with the Word or Logos, the inseminating factor was believed to have reached Mary through her ear.
5. *Dictionnaire d'Archéologie Chrétienne et de Liturgie*, ed. Fernand Cabrol and Henri M. Leclerq (Paris: Letouzey et Ané, 1903–53), vol. I, pt 1, col. 1485.
6. Francis Quarles, 'Book 5. Emblem X', *The Anchor Anthology of Seventeenth-Century Verse*, ed. Louis L. Martz (New York: Doubleday, 1969), vol. 1, p. 233.
7. 'Lovely lordynges, ladys lyke', *Early English Miscellanies*, ed. J.O. Halliwell (London: Printed for the Warton Club, 1855), pp. 1–6.
8. Andrew Marvell, 'The Garden', *The Poems & Letters*, ed. H.M. Margoliouth (Oxford: Clarendon Press, 1952), I.49.
9. W.B. Yeats, 'Sailing to Byzantium', *The Poems*, ed. Daniel Albright (London: J.M. Dent, 1st edn, 1990, updated 1994), p. 240.
10. Yeats, 'Byzantium', ibid., p. 298.
11. See Chapter 3, p. 106.
12. See Chapter 1, p. 49.
13. Richard Onians, *The Origins of European Thought* (Cambridge: Cambridge University Press, 1951), pp. 206–7.
14. Ovid, *Metamorphoses* XV.389–90, trans. Mary Innes (London: Penguin, 1955), p. 344.
15. See the entry for 'mouse' in *Brewer's Dictionary of Phrase and Fable*, 5th edn (London: Cassell, 1959), p. 630.
16. John Donne, *Sermons*, ed. E.M. Simpson and G.R. Potter (Berkeley, CA: University of California Press, 1953–62), VIII, p. 83.
17. John Donne, 'Holy Sonnet IV', ll. 1–4, *The*

Divine Poems, ed. Helen Gardner (Oxford: Clarendon Press, 1952), p. 7.

18. Percy Bysshe Shelley, 'Asia's Song' from *Prometheus Unbound*, II.v.72–7, *Poetical Works*, ed. Thomas Hutchinson, 2nd edn by G.M. Matthews (London: Oxford University Press, 1970), p. 241.

19. Louis Janmot, 'Poème de l'âme', printed from the 1881 edition in *Louis Hanmot précurseur du symbolisme*, Études et documents réunis et présentés par Wolfgang Drost and Elisabeth Hardouin-Fugier (Heidelberg: Universitätsverlag C. Winter, 1994).

20. Dante Alighieri, *The Inferno*, trans. John Ciardi (New York: Mentor, 1954), XIII.4–6.

21. Ibid., XII.93–102.

22. Dante Alighieri, *The Paradiso*, trans. John Ciardi (London: Mentor, 1961), XIX.1–6.

23. Ibid., XXX.124–7

24. Thomas Beverley, *The Great Soul of Man* (London, Printed for William Miller at the Gilded Acorn in St Paul's Churchyard, 1677), p. 264.

25. Thomas Adams, *Workes* (London: Printed by Tho. Harper for John Grismand, 1630), p. 834.

26. John Donne, *Sermons*, VI, p. 356.

27. For an example of the latter, see Adams, *Workes*, p. 202: 'We are all housholders; our bodies are our houses; our soules our goods; our senses are the Doores and Windowes, the Lockes are *Faith* and *Prayer*.'

28. John Woolton, 'A Treatise of the Immortalitie of the Soule' (London: Printed in Paules Churchyarde at the signe of the *Brazen Serpent* by John Shepperd, 1576), fol. 52r.

29. Joseph Mede in a sermon of 1635, quoted by Geoffrey Bullough (ed.) in *Philosophical Poems of Henry More* (Manchester: Manchester University Press, 1931), p. 202.

30. John Donne, *Sermons*, III, p. 239.

31. Ibid., X, p. 112.

32. See M.L. West, *The Orphic Poems* (Oxford: Clarendon Press, 1983), p. 10.

33. Plotinus, *Enneads*, IV.3.22, trans. Stephen MacKenna, 3rd edn (London: Faber and Faber, 1962), p. 278.

34. John Donne, *Sermons*, IX, p. 50.

35. See Guillaume de Deguileville, *The Pilgrimage of the Life of Man*, trans. John Lydgate, ll. 9764–86, ed. F.J. Furnivall (London: Early English Text Society, 1899–1901), p. 269.

36. John Donne, *Sermons*, V, p. 355.

37. J. Guillemard, *The Combate betwixt Man and Death*, trans. E. Grimeston (London: Printed by Nicholas Okes, 1621), p. 120.

38. Plotinus, *Enneads*, I.4.16, p. 52.

39. See Chapter 3, p. 92.

40. 'It is when this *Herod*, and this *Pilat* (this Body, and this soule of ours) are made friends and agreed, that they may concurre to the Crucifying of Christ' (John Donne, *Sermons*, IX, p. 257).

41. See Chapter 3, pp. 96–8.

42. See Thomas Adams, *Workes*, p. 124, and Pierre Du Moulin, *The Christian Combate*, trans. John Bulteel (London, 1623), p. 56.

43. Adams, *Workes*, p. 105.

44. Du Moulin, *The Christian Combate*, pp. 3–4.

45. Adams, *Workes*, p. 431.

46. Woolton, 'A Treatise of the Immortalitie of the Soule', fol. 32r.

47. Rycharde of saynt Vyctor, *A verray deuote treatyse* (H. Pepwell, 1521), sig.A1v. Reprinted in *The Cell of Self-Knowledge: Seven Early English Mystical Treatises printed by Henry Pepwell in 1521*, ed. Edmund G. Gardner (London: Chatto & Windus, 1910), p. 3.

48. Richard Brathwait, *The Last Trumpet: or a Six-Fold Christian Dialogue*, trans. John Vicars (London, Printed by Thomas Harper, for Robert Bostocke, 1635), p. 6.

49. Ibid., p. 19.

50. John Randall, *The Description of Fleshly Lvsts* (London: William Holbrooke, 1622), pp. 12–13.

51. Jeremy Taylor, *XXV Sermons Preached at Golden-Grove Being for the winter Half-Year* (London: Printed by E. Cates for Richard Royston, 1653), p. 233.

52. Ibid., p. 240.

53. See my article, 'Body, Soul, and the Marriage Relationship: The History of an Analogy', *Journal of the History of Ideas* (April–June

1973), pp. 283–90. The play *Psyche and Soma* (pp. 128–9) might be seen as an exception. It obviously draws on sources outside the English tradition.

54. See Chapter 3, p. 100.

Six

1. St Thomas Aquinas, *Summa Contra Gentiles*, trans. Charles J. O'Neil (Notre Dame and London: University of Notre Dame Press, 1975), IV.82.2, p. 308.
2. Emily Vermeule, *Aspects of Death in Early Greek Art and Poetry* (Berkeley: University of California Press, 1979), p. 118.
3. See John Donne, 'Farewell to Love', ll. 21–30, *The Elegies and The Songs and Sonnets*, ed. Helen Gardner (Oxford: Clarendon Press, 1965), p. 82:

   Ah cannot wee,
   As well as Cocks and Lyons jocund be,
       After such pleasures? Unlesse wise
   Nature decreed (since each such Act, they say,
   Diminisheth the length of life a day)
       This; as shee would man should despise
           The sport,
   Because that other curse of being short,
   And onely for a minute, made to be
   Eager, desires to raise posterity.

4. See Vermeule, *Aspects of Death*, p. 163.
5. For much of this account of the separation of soul and body in Egypt I am indebted to Louise Dudley, *The Egyptian Elements in the Legend of Body and Soul*, Bryn Mawr Monographs VIII (Baltimore, MD: J.H. Furst, 1911).
6. Ibid., pp. 33–41.
7. Ibid., pp. 84–5.
8. See ibid., pp. 97–8.
9. See Chapter 3, pp. 88–9.
10. See Th. Batiouchkof, 'Le Débat de l'Ame et du Corps', *Romania* XX (1891), pp. 5–6.
11. Robert Atkinson, *The Passions and the*

Homilies from Leabhar Breac (Dublin: Royal Irish Academy, Todd Lecture Series, vol. II, 1887), pp. 509–10.

12. See Chapter 4, p. 116.
13. See, for example, *The Triumph of Death* by Francesco Traini, in the Camposanto, Pisa. Reproduced in Robert Hughes, *Heaven and Hell in Western Art* (London: Weidenfeld & Nicolson, 1968), p. 243 and pp. 262–3.
14. Bodleian Library, Gough Liturg. 3, fol 95v.
15. *The Rohan Master: A Book of Hours*, introduction and commentaries Millard Meiss and Marcel Thomas, trans. Katherine W. Carson (New York: George Braziller, 1973), plate 63 (Bibliothèque Nationale, Paris, MS Latin 9471, fol. 159).
16. Bodleian Library, MS Canonici Ital. 275, 18v, 19v.
17. John Donne, 'The Second Anniversary', ll. 102–4, *The Poems of John Donne*, ed. H.J.C. Grierson (London: Oxford University Press, 1912), I, 254.
18. 'Cherubs come to Take the Spirit Away', illustration from 'A View of Human Life' by Marin Le Roy de Gomberville (1600–74) engraved by Daret.
19. Gabriele Smargiassi, *The Death of Federigo da Montefeltro, Duke of Urbino*, in the Galleria d'Arte Moderna, Florence.
20. 'The Blessed Soul', ll. 130–8, 157–60, *The Old English Soul and Body*, ed. and trans. Douglas Moffat (Wolfeboro, NH: D.S. Brewer), pp. 62–4.
21. Henry Vaughan, 'Death', ll. 27–32, *Works*, ed. L.C. Martin (Oxford: Clarendon Press, 2nd edn, 1957), p. 400.
22. John Welles of Beccles, *The Soules Progresse to the Celestiall Canaan, or Heavenly Jerusalem* (London, 1639), pp. 111–16.
23. Rudolph Willard, 'The Address of the Soul to the Body', *PMLA* L (1935), p. 982.
24. 'The Good and Evil Angels Struggling for Possession of a Child', Martin Butlin, *William Blake* Catalogue (London: Tate Gallery Publications, 1978), plate 102, p. 65.
25. Robert Blair, *The Grave*, illustrated by William Blake. A study with facsimile by

Robert N. Essick and Morton D. Paley (London: Scolar Press, 1982), pp. 12, 30. (Page numbers are those of the page of text opposite. The number is repeated in script at the top of the engravings.)

26. Ibid., p. 12.
27. See Chapter 2, pp. 71–2.
28. Blair, *The Grave*, p. 16.
29. John J. Cerullo, *The Secularization of the Soul* (Philadelphia: Institute for the Study of Human Issues, 1982), p. 21. I am indebted to Cerullo's book and to Ruth Brandon's *The Spiritualists* (London: Weidenfeld & Nicolson, 1983) for much of this account.
30. Brandon, *The Spiritualists*, pp. 127–63.
31. Milbourne Christopher, *Search for the Soul* (New York: Thomas Y. Crowell, 1979), pp. 29–30.
32. Ibid., p. 31.
33. Ibid., p. 34.
34. Ibid., p. 35.
35. 'The Transference of Richard Rolle', reproduced in *The Spiritual in Art: Abstract Painting 1890–1985*, ed. Edward Weisberger (New York: Abbeville Press, and Los Angeles County Museum of Art, 1986), p. 121.
36. Luke 16:19–31.
37. This distinction between a particular judgment on an individual soul shortly after death and a final judgment on all souls was made in Pope Benedict XII's bull of 1336, 'Benedictus Deus'. Aquinas also adhered to this view. See *Summa Contra Gentiles*, IV. 91–6. The chief points that Aquinas makes in these chapters are that immediately after death the souls of men receive either punishment or reward according to their merits; that the wills of souls remain permanently fixed on good or evil after death, according to their disposition in life; and that there is also a Last Judgment when the body is assumed again.
38. Vermeule, *Aspects of Death*, p. 76; and Emile Mâle, *Religious Art in France: The Twelfth Century*, ed. Harry Bober, trans. Marthiel Matthews (Princeton: Princeton University Press, 1978), pp. 414–15.

39. Vermeule, *Aspects of Death*, p. 76.
40. Guillaume de Deguileville, *The Booke of the Pylgremage of the Sowle*, trans. from the French, ed. Katherine Isabella Cust (London: Basil Montagu Pickering, 1859).
41. Ibid., p. 36.
42. 'The Soul and Body', Gwenan Jones, *A Study of Three Welsh Religious Plays* (Bala: R.Evans, 1939), ll. 142–4, p. 251. See also Chapter 4, p. 116.
43. 'The Soul and Body', ll. 147a–d, Jones, p. 253.
44. Andrea Riccio (1470–1532), 'The Soul of the Deceased, in the form of winged infants, ferried across the River Styx'. Bronze relief. In the Louvre, Paris.
45. Quoted from the *Pahlavi Texts, Dâdistâni-I Dinik XXI*, 5–8 in Hughes, *Heaven and Hell in Western Art*, p. 164.
46. Cited from the Persian *Viraf-Nameh* in Hughes, *Heaven and Hell in Western Art*, p. 164.
47. Hughes, *Heaven and Hell in Western Art*, p. 165.
48. *The Vision of Tundale*, ed. Rodney Mearns from BL MS Cotton Caligula A II (Heidelberg: Carl Winter, 1985), pp. 96–105. See also Alice K. Turner, *The History of Hell* (London: Robert Hale, 1995), pp. 97–8.

Seven

1. See Chapter 1, p. 30.
2. Anthony Kenny, 'Body, Soul, and Intellect in Aquinas', *From Soul to Self*, ed. M. James C. Crabbe (London and New York: Routledge, 1999), p. 45. However, Aquinas also affirms the ultimate reunion of the soul with the body at the Resurrection: 'It is also clear . . . that the soul is naturally united to the body, for in its essence it is the form of the body. It is, then, contrary to the nature of the soul to be without the body. But nothing which is contrary to nature can be perpetual. Perpetually, then, the soul will not be without the body' (Aquinas, *Summa Contra Gentiles*, trans. Charles J. O'Neil (Notre

Notes

Dame and London: University of Notre Dame Press, 1975), IV.79.10, p. 299).

3. Emily Vermeule, *Aspects of Death in Early Greek Art and Poetry* (Berkeley: University of California Press, 1979), p. 121.
4. See Chapter 4, pp. 112–13.
5. See Chapter 1, pp. 37–9.
6. Thomas Hobbes, 'Leviathan', IV, 44, *The English Works*, ed. Sir William Molesworth (London: J. Bohn, 1839–45; reprinted Routledge/Thoemmes Press, 1992), III, p. 616.
7. Thomas Aquinas, *Summa Contra Gentiles*, trans. Charles J. O'Neil (Notre Dame and London: University of Notre Dame Press, 1975), Book IV, 92–4, pp. 338–42.
8. John Donne, *Sermons*, ed. E.M. Simpson and G.R. Potter (Berkeley: University of California Press, 1953–62), IV, p. 61.
9. 1 Cor. 15:52.
10. John Donne, *Sermons*, VII, p. 115.
11. Ibid., IV, p. 61.
12. 1 Cor. 15:35.
13. Aquinas, *Summa Contra Gentiles*, IV.86, pp. 325–7. Much earlier Gregory of Nyssa (*c.* 330–*c.* 395) avoided the literalism of Donne and others by arguing that the soul will shape the Resurrection body so that it will be recognizably the same body we possess at present. This does *not* necessitate that it be made of the same matter (Kallistos Ware, 'The Soul in Greek Christianity', Crabbe (ed.), *From Soul to Self*, p. 53).
14. Aquinas, *Summa Contra Gentiles*, IV.88.3, p. 329.
15. Ibid., IV.89, p. 330.
16. Meg Twycross, '"With what body shall they come?": Black and White Souls in the English Mystery Plays', *Langland, the Mystics and the Medieval English Religious Tradition: Essays in Honour of S.S. Hussey*, ed. Helen Phillips (Cambridge: D.S. Brewer, 1990), pp. 271–86
17. See Meg Twycross, 'More Black and White Souls', *Medieval English Theatre*, vol. 13 (1991), pp. 52–63.
18. Right and left, in paintings of the judgment,

always mean right and left as related to God or Christ; in relation to the viewer they are reversed. I use the terms as they relate to the position of the Judge, however, since this is the symbolic right and left used in descriptions of the Last Judgment.

19. One does not have to see the first section of this triptych as a paradise already corrupted. For a different interpretation, see Robert Hughes, *Heaven and Hell in Western Art* (London: Weidenfeld & Nicolson, 1968), pp. 85–6. Hughes points out, for example, that the owl is a symbol of wisdom as well as the bird of misfortune. The cat carrying the dead mouse can be seen as virtue triumphing over vice. Were all animals in Eden supposed to be herbivores? Similarly the fountain can be the Fountain of Life, or 'pink, tumescent, phallic'.
20. Hughes, *Heaven and Hell in Western Art*, p. 212.
21. Dante Alighieri, *The Paradiso*, trans. John Ciardi (London: Mentor, 1961), XIV.37–9.
22. Ibid., 43–5.
23. Hughes, *Heaven and Hell in Western Art*, p. 109.
24. Jules Tellier, *Abd-er-Rhaman in Paradise*, trans. Brian Rhys, illustrated Paul Nash (Waltham Saint Lawrence: Golden Cockerel Press, 1928), p. 8.
25. Ibid., p. 9.
26. Ibid., p. 11.
27. Ibid., pp. 17–18.
28. Ibid., p. 19.
29. Ibid., p. 22.
30. Ibid., p. 25.
31. Francis Bacon, 'Of the Advancement of Learning', *Works*, ed. J. Spedding, R.L. Ellis and D.D. Heath (London, 1857–74), III, p. 379.
32. Ovid, *Metamorphoses*, XV.871–9, trans. Mary Innes (London: Penguin, 1955), p. 357.
33. Mary Shelley, 'Author's Introduction to *Frankenstein*', *Three Gothic Novels*, ed. Peter Fairclough (Harmondsworth: Penguin, 1968), p. 263.

229

Eight

1. Nancey Murphy, 'Human Nature: Historical, Scientific, and Religious Issues', in *Whatever Happened to the Soul?* ed. Warren S. Brown, Nancey Murphy and H. Newton Malony (Minneapolis: Fortress Press, 1998), p. 25. This collection of essays has been generally very useful in setting out the different positions still current on the body/soul question, though, as one might assume from its publisher, it does have a particular argument to make from the stance of doctrinal Christianity.
2. Richard Swinburne, *The Evolution of the Soul* (Oxford: Clarendon Press, 1986).
3. Ibid., p. 146.
4. Ibid., p. 160.
5. Ibid., p. 310.
6. Susan Greenfield, 'Soul, Brain and Mind', *From Soul to Self*, ed. M. James C. Crabbe (London and New York: Routledge, 1999), p. 112.
7. Ibid., p. 113.
8. Roger Penrose, *The Large, the Small, and the Human Mind* (Cambridge: Cambridge University Press, 1997), p. 137.
9. Ibid., p. 133.
10. Ibid., p. 132.
11. Ibid., p. 101.
12. Ibid., p. 116.
13. See *The Sunday Times*, 'Home News' (9 March 2003), p. 15, for a report on Crick's work on consciousness.
14. Vilayanur S. Ramachandran, 'Lecture 5', Reith Lectures, 2003.
15. Ramachandran, 'Lecture 1', Reith Lectures, 2003.
16. John Donne, 'Holy Sonnet IX', ll. 1–6, *The Divine Poems*, ed. Helen Gardner (Oxford: Clarendon Press, 1952), p. 8.
17. Ken Wilbur, *The Marriage of Sense and Soul: Integrating Science and Religion* (New York: Random House, 1998), p. 34.
18. Diana Medlicott, *History of the Modern Soul: Foucault's Genealogy and the Problem of the Subject* (London: Middlesex University, 1994), p. 32.
19. An intriguing footnote to this episode of the popular television programme is contained in a small newspaper article about a man who, inspired by the story, really *did* sell his soul. Gareth Malham, 26, a hard-up artist, posted an advertisement on the eBay site. The winning bid of just $11.61 came from a man in Oklahoma who said that he had lost his own soul in a bet!
20. Alice Sebold, *The Lovely Bones* (London: Picador, 2002), p. 37.
21. Ibid., pp. 36–7.
22. Ibid., p. 120.
23. Harold Bloom, *Omens of Millennium* (London: Fourth Estate, 1996), pp. 127–36.
24. Quoted by Susanna Avery-Quash, 'The Resurrection, Cookham', *The Image of Christ*, ed. Gabriele Finaldi, catalogue of the exhibition *Seeing Salvation* (London: National Gallery, 2000), p. 204.
25. Sir Thomas Browne, 'Urne Burial', *Selected Writings*, ed. Sir Geoffrey Keynes (London: Faber and Faber, 1968), p. 142.
26. Margot Eates, *Paul Nash: The Master of the Image* (London: John Murray, 1973), p. 50.
27. Paul Nash in a letter to Hartley Ramsden, 4 June 1941, quoted in Anthony Bertram, *Paul Nash: The Portrait of an Artist* (London: Faber and Faber, 1955), p. 196.
28. Wassily Kandinsky, *Concerning the Spiritual in Art*, trans. Michael Sadlier, revised by Francis Golffing, Michael Harrison and Ferdinand Ostertag (New York: George Wittenborn, 1947), p. 75. (First published as *The Art of Spiritual Harmony*, 1914.)
29. Ibid.
30. Ibid., p. 24.
31. Ibid., p. 32.
32. Ibid., p. 27.
33. See Chapter 6, p. 170.
34. Robert P. Welsh, 'Sacred Geometry: French Symbolism and Early Abstraction', *The Spiritual in Art: Abstract Painting 1890–1985*, ed. E. Weisberger (New York: Abbeville Press, and Los Angeles County Museum of Art, 1986), p. 85.

35. Arthur Jerome Eddy, *Cubists and Post-Impressionism* (Chicago: McClurg, 1914), p. 134, quoted in Maurice Tuchman, 'Hidden Meanings in Abstract Art', *The Spiritual in Art*, p. 17.

36. Welsh, 'Sacred Geometry', *The Spiritual in Art*, p. 81.

37. Charles C. Eldredge, 'Nature Symbolized: American Painting from Ryder to Hartley', *The Spiritual in Art*, p. 122.

38. Quoted by Angela Tilby, *Science and the Soul* (London: SPCK, 1992), p. 18.

39. Czeslaw Milosz, 'The Second Space', trans. from the Polish by the author, Robert Hass and Renata Gorczynski, *The New Yorker* (4 November 2002), p. 54.

40. Wallace Stevens, 'To the One of Fictive Music', *Selected Poems* (London: Faber and Faber, 1953), p. 39.

Bibliography

Adams, Thomas. *Workes* (London: Printed by Tho. Harper for John Grismand, 1630)

Aquinas, St Thomas. *Summa Contra Gentiles*, trans. Charles J. O'Neil (Notre Dame and London: University of Notre Dame Press, 1975)

Aquinas, St Thomas. *Summa Theologica*, trans. The Fathers of the Dominican Province (London: R. & T. Washbourne, 1911–25)

Aristotle. *De Anima*, trans. J.A. Smith (Oxford: Clarendon Press, 1931)

Atkinson, Robert. *The Passions and the Homilies from Leabhar Breac* (Dublin: Royal Irish Academy, Todd Lecture Series, vol. II, 1887)

Augustine. *The City of God*, trans. John Healey, ed. R.V.G. Tasker (London: J.M. Dent, 1945, repr., 1962)

Bacon, Francis. *Works*, ed. J. Spedding, R.L. Ellis and D.D. Heath (London, 1857–74)

Barrow, Logie. *Independent Spirits: Spiritualism and English Plebeians, 1850–1910* (London: Routledge & Kegan Paul, 1986)

Batiouchkof, Th. 'Le Débat de l'Ame et du Corps', *Romania* XX (1891), pp. 1–55

Beck, Rosalie. 'A Precedent for Donne's Imagery in "Goodfriday, 1613. Riding Westward"', *Review of English Studies* XIX (May 1968), pp. 166–9

Bertram, Anthony. *Paul Nash: The Portrait of an Artist* (London: Faber and Faber, 1955)

Beverley, Thomas. *The Great Soul of Man* (London, Printed for William Miller at the Gilded Acorn in St Paul's Churchyard, 1677)

Blair, Robert. *The Grave*, illustrated by William Blake. A study with facsimile by Robert N. Essick and Morton D. Paley (London: Scolar Press, 1982)

Bloom, Harold. *Omens of Millennium* (London: Fourth Estate, 1996)

Boethius. *The Consolation of Philosophy*, trans. Richard Green (Indianapolis: Bobbs-Merrill, 1962)

Brandon, Ruth. *The Spiritualists* (London: Weidenfeld & Nicolson, 1983)

Brathwait, Richard. *The Last Trumpet: or a Six-Fold Christian Dialogue*, trans. John Vicars (London, Printed by Thomas Harper, for Robert Bostocke, 1635)

Bremmer, Jan. *The Early Greek Concept of the Soul* (Princeton: Princeton University Press, 1983)

Brown, Warren S., Murphy, Nancey and Malony, H. Newton (eds). *Whatever Happened to the Soul?* (Minneapolis: Fortress Press, 1998)

Bibliography

Browne, Thomas. *Selected Writings*, ed. Sir Geoffrey Keynes (London: Faber and Faber, 1968)

Butlin, Martin. *William Blake*, catalogue of Blake Exhibition (London: Tate Gallery Publications, 1978)

Calderón de la Barca, Pedro. 'El Pleito Matrimonial del Cuerpo y el Alma', *Autos Sacramentales*, II (Madrid: Biblioteca Castro, 1997), pp. 473–521

Capellanus, Andreas. *The Art of Courtly Love*, trans. John Jay Parry (New York: W.W. Norton, 1969)

'The Castle of Perseverance', *Chief Pre-Shakespearean Dramas*, ed. Joseph Quincy Adams (London: George G. Harrap, 1925), pp. 264–87

Cavalieri, Emilio de'. *Rappresentatione di Anima, et di Corpo* (Rome: Nicolò Mutii, 1600)

The Cell of Self-Knowledge: Seven Early English Mystical Treatises printed by Henry Pepwell in 1521, ed. Edmund G. Gardner (London: Chatto & Windus, 1910)

Cerullo, John J. *The Secularization of the Soul* (Philadelphia: Institute for the Study of Human Issues, 1982)

Christopher, Milbourne. *Search for the Soul* (New York: Thomas Y. Crowell, 1979)

Chydenius, Johan. *The Theory of Medieval Symbolism* (Helsingfors: Societas Scientiarum Fennica, 1960)

Clampitt, Amy. *Collected Poems* (London: Faber and Faber, 1998)

Clarke, Michael. *Flesh and Spirit in the Songs of Homer* (Oxford: Clarendon Press, 1999)

Claus, David B. *Toward the Soul* (New Haven: Yale University Press, 1981)

Cooper, John W. *Body, Soul, and Life Everlasting* (Grand Rapids, Michigan: Williams B. Eerdmans Publishing Company, 1989)

Copleston, Frederick. *A History of Philosophy* (New York: Image Books, 1961–5)

Crabbe, M. James C. (ed.) *From Soul to Self* (London and New York: Routledge, 1999)

Crane, Eleanor Maud. *'His Soul': A Farce in One Act* (New York: Samuel French, 1922)

Crashaw, William. *The Complaint or Dialogue, betwixt the Soule and the Bodie of a damned man* (London, 1622)

Cull, John T. 'Emblematic Representation in the *autos sacramentales* of Calderón', in *The Calderonian Stage: Body and Soul*, ed. Manuel Delgado Morales (London: Associated University Press, 1977), pp 107–32

Dante Alighieri. *The Inferno*, trans. John Ciardi (New York: Mentor, 1954)

Dante Alighieri. *The Paradiso*, trans. John Ciardi (London: Mentor, 1961)

Dante Alighieri. *The Purgatorio*, trans. John Ciardi (New York: Mentor, 1957)

Dante Alighieri. *La Vita Nuova*, trans. Barbara Reynolds (Harmondsworth: Penguin, 1969)

Davison, Francis. *A Poetical Rhapsody 1602–1621*, ed. H.E. Rollins (Cambridge, Mass.: Harvard University Press, 1931–2)

Deguileville, Guillaume de. *The Booke of the Pylgremage of the Sowle*, trans. from the French, ed. Katherine Isabella Cust (London: Basil Montagu Pickering, 1859)

Deguileville, Guillaume de. *The Pilgrimage of the Life of Man*, trans. John Lydgate, ed. F.J. Furnivall (London: Early English Text Society, 1899–1901)

Descartes, René. *Philosophical Works*, trans. E.S. Haldane and G.R.T. Ross (Cambridge: Cambridge University Press, 1911)

Dictionnaire d'Archéologie Chrétienne et de Liturgie, ed. Fernand Cabrol and Henri M. Leclerq (Paris: Letouzey et Ané, 1903–53)

Dictionnaire de Théologie Catholique, ed. A. Vacant, E. Mangenot and E. Amann (Paris: Letouzey et Ané, 1923–50)

Donne, John. *The Elegies and The Songs and Sonnets*, ed. Helen Gardner (Oxford: Clarendon Press, 1965)

Donne, John. *The Divine Poems*, ed. Helen Gardner (Oxford: Clarendon Press, 1952)

Donne, John. *The Poems*, ed. H.J.C. Grierson (London: Oxford University Press, 1912)

Donne, John. *Sermons*, ed. E.M. Simpson and G.R. Potter (Berkeley: University of California Press, 1953–62)

The Dream of Poliphilo, related and interpreted by Linda Fierz-David, trans. Mary Hottinger (New York: Pantheon Books, Bollingen Series XXV, 1950)

Dudley, Louise. *The Egyptian Elements in the Legend of Body and Soul*, Bryn Mawr Monographs VIII (Baltimore, MD: J.H. Furst, 1911)

Du Moulin, Pierre. *The Christian Combate*, trans. John Bulteel (London, 1623)

Early English Miscellanies, ed. J.O. Halliwell (London: Printed for the Warton Club, 1855)

Eates, Margot. *Paul Nash: The Master of the Image* (London: John Murray, 1973)

Edinger, Edward F. *The Living Psyche: A Jungian Analysis in Pictures* (Wilmette, IL: Chiron Publications, 1989)

Ellis, William. *The Idea of the Soul in Western Philosophy and Science* (London: George Allen & Unwin, 1940)

Evréinof, N. *The Theatre of the Soul: A Monodrama in One Act*, trans. Marie Potapenko and Christopher St John (London: Hendersons, 1915)

Finaldi, Gabriele (ed.) *The Image of Christ*, Catalogue of the exhibition *Seeing Salvation* (London: National Gallery, 2000)

Freud, Sigmund. *Standard Edition of the Complete Psychological Works*, ed. James Strachey (London: Hogarth Press, 1953–66)

Fulgentius the Mythographer, trans. Leslie George Whitbread (Columbus, OH: Ohio State University Press, 1971)

Gollnick, James. *Love and the Soul: Psychological Interpretations of the Eros and Psyche Myth* (Waterloo, Ont.: Wilfred Laurier Press, 1992)

Guillemard, J. *The Combate betwixt Man and Death*, trans. E. Grimeston (London: Printed by Nicholas Okes, 1621)

Bibliography

Hildebert of Lavardin. 'De Querimonia et Conflictu Carnis et Spiritus Seu Animae', J.-P. Migne, *Patrologia Latina*, vol. clxxi, cols 989–1004

Hobbes, Thomas. *The English Works*, ed. Sir William Molesworth (London: J. Bohn, 1839–45; reprinted Routledge/Thoemmes Press, 1992)

Homer. *Iliad*, trans. Richmond Lattimore (Chicago: University of Chicago Press, 1951)

Homer. *The Odyssey*, trans. Albert Cook (New York: W.W. Norton, 1974)

Hooker, Richard. 'Of the Laws of Ecclesiastical Polity', *Works*, ed. John Keble, 7th edn (Oxford: Oxford University Press, 1888)

Howell, James. *The Vision: or A Dialog between the Soul and the Bodie* (London: Printed for William Hope, 1651)

Hughes, Robert. *Heaven and Hell in Western Art* (London: Weidenfeld & Nicolson, 1968)

Hunt, William Holman. *Pre-Raphaelitism and the Pre-Raphaelite Brotherhood* (London: Chapman & Hall, 1913)

'The Hymn of the Soul', ed. A.A. Bevan, *Texts and Studies: Contributions to Biblical and Patristic Literature*, ed. J. Armitage Robinson (Cambridge: Cambridge University Press, 1897), vol. V, no. 3

Janmot, Louis. 'Poème de l'âme', printed from the 1881 edition in *Louis Hanmot précurseur du symbolisme*, Etudes et documents réunis et présentés par Wolfgang Drost and Elisabeth Hardouin-Fugier (Heidelberg: Universitätsverlag C. Winter, 1994)

Jerome, Jerome K. *The Soul of Nicholas Snyders* (London: Hodder & Stoughton, 1925)

Jones, Gwenan. *A Study of Three Welsh Religious Plays* (Bala: R. Evans, 1939)

Jung, C.G. *Collected Works*, ed. H. Read, M. Fordham and G. Adler (London: Routledge & Kegan Paul, 2nd edn 1966)

Kandinsky, Wassily. *Concerning the Spiritual in Art*, trans. Michael Sadleir, revised by Francis Golffing, Michael Harrison and Ferdinand Ostertag (New York: George Wittenborn, 1947) (First published as *The Art of Spiritual Harmony*, 1914)

Kenny, Anthony. *The Anatomy of the Soul* (Oxford: Basil Blackwell, 1973)

La Fontaine, Jean de. *The Loves of Cupid and Psyche in Verse and Prose from the french of La Fontaine*, trans. Mr. Lockman (London, 1744)

Levi, Giuseppe. 'Die Verurteilung der Seele und des Körpers [The Condemnation of the Soul and the Body]', *Parabeln, Legenden und Gedanken aus Thalmud und Midrasch*, trans. Ludwig Seligmann (Leipzig: Oskar Leiner, 1863)

Mâle, Emile. *Religious Art in France: The Twelfth Century*, ed. Harry Bober, trans. Marthiel Matthews (Princeton: Princeton University Press, 1978)

Marsh, Elizabeth. *Body and Soul* (Boston, Mass.: Cornhill, 1920)

Marvell, Andrew. *The Poems and Letters*, ed. H.M. Margoliouth (Oxford: Clarendon Press, 2nd edn, 1952)

Bibliography

Medlicott, Diana. *History of the Modern Soul: Foucault's Genealogy and the Problem of the Subject* (London: Middlesex University, 1994)

Meier, C.A. *Soul and Body: Essays on the Theories of C.G. Jung* (Santa Monica and San Francisco: Lapis Press, 1986)

Milosz, Czeslaw. 'The Second Space', trans. from the Polish by the author, Robert Hass and Renata Gorczynski, *New Yorker* (4 November 2002), p. 54

Milton, John. 'Paradise Lost', *Poems*, ed. Helen Darbishire (Oxford: Oxford University Press, 1961)

More, Henry. *Philosophical Poems*, ed. Geoffrey Bullough (Manchester: Manchester University Press, 1931)

Neumann, Erich. *Amor and Psyche: The Psychic Development of the Feminine* (London: Routledge & Kegan Paul, 1956)

Norton, Robert E. *The Beautiful Soul* (Ithaca and London: Cornell University Press, 1995)

The Old English Soul and Body, ed. and trans. Douglas Moffat (Wolfeboro, New Hampshire: D.S. Brewer, 1990)

Onians, Richard. *The Origins of European Thought about the Body, the Mind, the Soul, the World, Time and Fate* (Cambridge: The University Press, 1951)

Osmond, Rosalie. 'Body, Soul, and the Marriage Relationship: The History of an Analogy', *Journal of the History of Ideas* (April–June 1973), pp. 283–90

Osmond, Rosalie. *Mutual Accusation: Seventeenth-century Body and Soul Dialogues in Their Literary and Theological Context* (Toronto: University of Toronto Press, 1990)

Ovid. *Metamorphoses*, trans. Mary Innes (London: Penguin, 1955)

Paulson, Christine. 'Death and the Maiden: The Lady of Shalott and the Pre-Raphaelites', *Re-framing the Pre-Raphaelites*, ed. Ellen Harding (Aldershot, Hants: Scolar Press, 1996), pp. 173–94

Penrose, Roger. *The Large, the Small, and the Human Mind* (Cambridge: Cambridge University Press, 1997)

Petrarch. *Sonnets and Songs*, trans. Anna Maria Armi (New York: Grosset & Dunlap, 1968)

Petroff, Elizabeth. 'Unmasking Women: Medieval Responses to the Unknowability of the Lady', *Body and Soul: Essays on Medieval Women and Mysticism* (Oxford: Oxford University Press, 1994), pp. 25–50

Plato. *The Collected Dialogues*, ed. Edith Hamilton and Huntingdon Cairns (Princeton: Princeton University Press, 1961)

Plotinus. *Enneads* IV.8.6, trans. Stephen MacKenna, 3rd edn (London: Faber and Faber, 1962)

Rank, Otto. *Psychology and the Soul: a Study of the Origin, Conceptual Evolution, and Nature of the Soul*, trans. Gregory C. Richter and E. James Liberman (Baltimore, MD: Johns Hopkins University Press, 1998; originally published 1930)

Bibliography

Randall, John. *The Description of Fleshly Lvsts* (London: William Holbrooke, 1622)

Roberts, Jane. *Dialogues of the Soul and Mortal Self in Time* (Englewood Cliffs, NJ: Prentice-Hall, 1975)

Robinson, John. *The Body* (London: SCM Press, 1952)

The Rohan Master: A Book of Hours, introduction and commentaries Millard Meiss (New York: George Braziller, 1973; Bibliothèque Nationale, Paris, MS. Latin 9471)

Rohde, Erwin. *Psyche*, trans. W.B. Hillis (London: Kegan Paul, Trench, Trubner, 1925)

Rossetti, Christina G. *The Complete Poems*, ed. R.W. Crump (Baton Rouge and London: Louisiana State University Press, 1979)

Rossetti, Dante Gabriel. *Collected Writings*, selected and ed. Jan Marsh (London: J.M. Dent, 1999)

Rycharde of saynt Vyctor. *A verray deuote treatyse* (H. Pepwell, 1521)

Sánchez de Badajoz, Diego. 'Farsa racional del libre albedrío', *Recopilación en metro* (Seville, 1554). Modern edition ed. Frida Weber de Kurlat (Buenos Aires, 1968), pp. 309–27

Schlam, Carl C. *Cupid and Psyche, Apuleius and the Monuments* (Pennsylvania: American Philological Assoc., 1976)

Schwenk, J.A. 'The Human Soul: A Play in Three Acts'. Typescript in the British Library, I12.20029

Sebold, Alice. *The Lovely Bones* (London: Picador, 2002)

Shapiro, Marianne. *Dante and the Knot of Body and Soul* (London: Macmillan, 1998)

Shelley, Mary. *Frankenstein*, in *Three Gothic Novels*, ed. Peter Fairclough (Harmondsworth: Penguin, 1968), pp. 259–497

Shelley, Percy Bysshe. *Poetical Works*, ed. Thomas Hutchinson, 2nd edn by G.M. Matthews (London: Oxford University Press, 1970)

Smith, Wellen. *Psyche and Soma* (London: E. Grant Richards, 1906)

Sophocles. 'Oedipus the King', trans. David Grene, *The Complete Greek Tragedies*, ed. David Grene and Richmond Lattimore, vol. II (Chicago and London: University of Chicago Press, 1959)

Spenser, Edmund. *Poetry*, selected and ed. Hugh Maclean (New York: W. W. Norton, 1968)

Stein, Murray. *Jung's Map of the Soul* (Chicago: Open Court, 1998)

Stevens, Wallace. *Selected Poems* (London: Faber and Faber, 1953)

Swinburne, Richard. *The Evolution of the Soul* (Oxford: Clarendon Press, 1986)

Taylor, Jeremy. *XXV Sermons Preached at Golden-Grove Being for the winter Half-Year* (London: Printed by E. Cates for Richard Royston, 1653)

Tellier, Jules. *Abd-er-Rhaman in Paradise*, trans. Brian Rhys, illustrated Paul Nash (Waltham Saint Lawrence: Golden Cockerel Press, 1928)

Bibliography

Tennyson, Alfred. *Poetry*, selected and ed. Robert W. Hill, Jr (New York: W.W. Norton, 1971)

Tertullian. 'De Anima', *The Writings of Tertullian*, trans, Peter Holmes, Ante Nicene Library vol. XV (Edinburgh: T & T Clark, 1870)

Tilby, Angela. *Science and the Soul* (London: S.P.C.K., 1992)

Tuke, Richard. *The Soul's Warfare Comically digested into scenes acted between the Soul and her Enemies* (London: Printed by S.G. for Allan Bancks at the Signe of St Peter, at the West end of St Pauls, 1672)

Turner, Alice K. *The History of Hell* (London: Robert Hale, 1995)

Twycross, Meg. 'More Black and White Souls', *Medieval English Theatre*, vol. 13 (1991), pp. 52–63

Twycross, Meg. '"With what body shall they come?": Black and White Souls in the English Mystery Plays', *Langland, the Mystics and the Medieval English Religious Tradition: Essays in Honour of S.S. Hussey*, ed. Helen Phillips (Cambridge: D.S. Brewer, 1990), pp. 271–86

Vaughan, Henry. *Works*, ed. L.C. Martin (Oxford: The Clarendon Press, 2nd edn, 1957)

Vermeule, Emily. *Aspects of Death in Early Greek Art and Poetry* (Berkeley: University of California Press, 1979)

The Vision of Tundale, ed. Rodney Mearns from B.L. MS Cotton Caligula A II (Heidelberg: Carl Winter, 1985)

Warner, Janet A. *Blake and the Language of Art* (Kingston and Montreal: McGill-Queen's University Press, 1984)

Weir, Lucy Elizabeth. *The Ideas Embodied in the Religious Drama of Calderón* (Lincoln, NE: University of Nebraska Studies in Language, Literature and Criticism, no. 18, 1940)

Weisberger, E. (ed.). *The Spiritual in Art: Abstract Painting 1890–1985* (New York: Abbeville Press, and Los Angeles County Museum of Art, 1986)

Welles of Beccles, John. *The Soules Progresse to the Celestiall Canaan, or Heavenly Jervsalem* (London, 1639)

West, M.L. *The Orphic Poems* (Oxford: Clarendon Press, 1983)

Wilbur, Ken. *The Marriage of Sense and Soul: Integrating Science and Religion* (New York: Random House, 1998)

Willard, Rudolph. 'The Address of the Soul to the Body', *PMLA* L, 1935, pp. 957–83

Wolf, Fred Alan. *The Spiritual Universe: How Quantum Physics Proves the Existence of the Soul* (New York: Simon & Shuster, 1996)

Woolton, John. 'A Treatise of the Immortalitie of the Soule', (London: Printed in Paules Churchyarde at the signe of the *Brazen Serpent* by John Shepperd, 1576)

Wright, Thomas (ed.) *The Latin Poems commonly Attributed to Walter Mapes*, Camden Society, vol. 16 (London, 1841)

Yeats, W. B. *The Poems*, ed. Daniel Albright (London: J.M. Dent, 1st edn, 1990, updated 1994)

Acknowledgements

For permission to quote material, the author and publisher are grateful to the following:

Bärenreiter-Verlag: Emilio de' Cavalieri, *Rappresentatione di Anima et di Corpo.*

Boydell & Brewer: *The Old English Soul and Body*, ed. and trans. Douglas Moffatt.

Cambridge University Press: *The Philosophical Works of Descartes*, trans. E.S. Haldane and G.T.R. Ross, and 'The Hymn of the Soul', trans. Anthony Ashley Bevan.

Continuum International Publishing Group: St Thomas Aquinas, *Summa Theologia.*

J.M. Dent, The Orion Publishing Group: Dante Gabriel Rossetti, *Collected Works*, ed. Jan Marsh.

Doubleday: St Thomas Aquinas, *Summa Contra Gentiles.*

Skene Edwards, executors: John Donne, *Poems*, ed. H.J.C. Grierson.

Robert N. Essick: Robert Blair, *The Grave.*

Faber & Faber Ltd: Plotinus, *Enneads*; Amy Clampitt, *Collected Poems*; Wallace Stevens, *Selected Poems*; T.S. Eliot, *Complete Poems and Plays.*

David Higham Associates: Alice Sebold, *The Lovely Bones.*

Oxford University Press: John Donne, *Divine Poems*, ed. Helen Gardner; John Donne, *Songs and Sonnets*, ed. Helen Gardner; John Milton, *Poems*, ed. Helen Darbyshire; Henry Vaughan, *Vaughan's Works*, ed. L.C. Martin; Andrew Marvell, *Poems and Letters*, ed. Margoliouth; Shelley, *Poetical Works*, ed. Thomas Hutchinson; Aristotle, *De Anima*, trans. J.A. Smith.

Penguin UK: Ovid, *Metamorphoses*, trans. Mary M. Innes.

Princeton University Press: Plato, *The Collected Dialogues*, ed. Edith Hamilton and Huntingdon Cairns.

University of California Press. John Donne, *Sermons*, ed. Simpson and Potter.

University of Chicago Press: Sophocles, *Oedipus the King*, trans. D. Greene.

A.P. Watt Ltd: W.B. Yeats, 'Sailing to Byzantium' and 'Byzantium'.

Wylie Agency, New York: Czeslaw Milosz, 'The Second Space'.

239

Index

Index

Index

Index